Serving Life 25 – One Guard's Story
Copyright © 2017 by Neil D. MacLean

National Library of Canada Cataloguing in Publication
MacLean, Neil D.
Serving Life 25 - One Guard's Story
Includes index

Proudly written, edited, designed and printed in Canada.

Tellwell Talent
www.tellwell.ca

ISBN
978-1-77302-451-6 (Hardcover)
978-1-77302-461-5 (Paperback)
978-1-77302-452-3 (eBook)

SERVING

LIFE 25

N
E
I
L

D

M
A
C
L
E
A
N

ONE GUARD'S STORY

Chapters

Chapter 6

Out and About, the World of Prisons 107

Chapter 7

The Human Dynamic 134

Chapter 8

From Unrest to Riots, The Violence of Prison Life 159

Chapter 9

Chapter 10

Chapter 11

Dedication

Samuel Jackson once said, "What is written without effort is in general read without pleasure". You Joyce, my loving partner in the making of this book, has made "effort" a pleasure. Your willingness to listen with that critical ear, offering your objective opinion made this journey possible. You have encouraged me to tell my story, though my eyes, and to the best of my ability. You have shown extraordinary patience, and your participation has been invaluable. Thank you.

About the Author

Born in West Vancouver to Iris and Jack MacLean, Neil never went without as a child. Like most young kids, Neil was eager to spread his wings, and at the age of 19, graduated from Columbia School of Broadcasting and moved to Quesnel where he became one of the voices of Cariboo Radio. Neil would continue on his broadcasting journey to Kamloops, Vancouver, and Port Alberni.

Neil MacLean

While in Port Alberni, Neil joined the Royal Canadian Mounted Police (RCMP) as an Auxiliary Constable. From a long-haired kid, he was quick to adapt to his fledgling new position in law enforcement that would provide the foundation of what would lead to a storied career with the Correctional Service of Canada. Neil's first day at Kent was December 31, 1988 and the start of what became a privileged journey.

Introduction

For those about to join me on my journey down memory lane, I must first warn you these life stories were a form of therapy, or closure to what was a great, albeit challenging career with the Correctional Service of Canada (CSC). What started as a psychologist's homework assignment, turned from some loosely formed notes, to a manuscript, and finally a published book. Although its initial intent was therapeutic, and a way to deal with my Post Traumatic Stress Disorder, it was also a healing journey, filled with the greatest of memories.

As Correctional Officer I, Correctional Officer II, and Correctional Manager, I worked for the CSC and its many prisons throughout the Fraser Valley in British Columbia. I hope to provide a unique perspective of a dysfunctional system that seems to work despite itself. With 58 federal prisons across Canada, dozens of parole offices in each region, staff training facilities, regional and national offices and a billion-dollar budget, the CSC is tasked with the almost impossible duty to house and rehabilitate some of Canada's most notorious criminals.

Prison life is graphic, and the language may not be suitable for some readers.

Chapter 1

A Bit of Our History, Corrections in Canada [1]

F rom an unexplored frontier, Canada was fast becoming a new and exciting nation. The history of corrections goes back much further than Confederation (1867). Imprisonment as we knew it in Canada dates to the Kingston Penitentiary in 1835 when it was operated as a provincial jail. It wasn't until the British North America Act that established federal and provincial responsibilities for justice, and the management of Canada's federally incarcerated convicts that things started to change.

With the passage of the Penitentiary Act in 1868, Kingston Penitentiary was built along with Laval, Stony Mountain, and the British Columbia Penitentiary. The Provincial Penitentiary of Upper Canada at Kingston, was one of the first federal prisons blazing new paths for law and justice. During the early days our system was one of crime, and punishment. People who broke the law suffered our prison system's harshest consequences. It was repressive in nature, a system devoid of hope that included whippings, and public floggings.

Towards the end of the 19th century, new ideas unique to Canada and her specific needs were born, changing the face of corrections, and how we did business. It was in 1953, shortly after the Second World War, when a federal commission proposed sweeping changes for Canadian penitentiaries with an emphasis on crime prevention, and rehabilitation. Regulations were adopted to provide strict discipline in a humane manner. As the transformation unfolded, the revised operational guidelines focused more on programs, providing worthwhile and creative work while addressing attitudes, and patterns of inmate criminal behaviour.

In 1979 the Canadian Penitentiary Service changed its name to the Correctional Service of Canada, which brought about even more challenges. New policies and procedures, many adopted on the fly, were daunting, with more suitable ways to manage those incarcerated, and administer the sentences of roughly 15,000 men and women, in six regions across Canada. Staffing levels within the CSC have risen over the years to 17,257 including 6,500 correctional officers in 58 federal prisons across Canada.

Corrections has grown and evolved over the years, and its successes were a team effort. Many employed within the CSC who are not required to wear a uniform play an equally important role within our system. These include parole officers, program officers, psychologists, staff training officers, security intelligence officers, health care professionals, kitchen staff, Works employees, clerical staff, the clergy, nurses, doctors, the management teams at both Regional and National Headquarters to the many contract workers within each of the institutions.

The British Columbia Penitentiary [2]

As the population migrated west, the need for additional prisons became the new frontier's reality. The gold rush in northern BC, and the building of the new Canadian Pacific Railway saw an influx of unsavory characters. Prior to its construction, New Westminster was home to the province's Legislative Council until 1868, when Victoria became the new capital of British Columbia.

Construction began on the British Columbia Penitentiary (BC Pen) in the winter of 1874 at the former campsite of the BC Detachment of the Royal Engineers located two miles from the City of New Westminster. The BC Pen overlooked the fast-flowing Fraser River and was built to house 765 male and female inmates. It was the only maximum-security prison west of Stony Mountain (formally Manitoba Penitentiary).

Built in phases, the main gatehouse (now the Castle Neighbourhood Grill) held the Visits & Correspondance Department to the Administration offices for those who would pass through the threshold of the BC Pen. The original walls were of wood construction, and later replaced with 30' then 40' quarried limestone walls. The main cellblock came later in 1904.

The BC Pen adopted a strict regime of backbreaking labour during the day, with inmates restricted to their cells unless they were out on an authorized absence, or at work. The rule was silence that was strictly enforced. There was a thriving chicken farm on the BC Pen grounds supplying inmates with poultry and eggs from their 1,000 chickens.

Throughout its history, the BC Pen was the scene of unrest, which included numerous hostage-takings, and riots. It was a dangerous place.

There were 68 cells in the original construction, with basement quarters for the women, and other separate cells in the main cellblock for the men. The Dominion government paid $0.75 per day towards each inmate's food and housing. Part of the Canadian Penitentiary Service, the BC Pen was designed with the standard features of a maximum-security prison of its era, which included staff living quarters, cell blocks for inmates, a school, hospital, an industries workshop, and two chapels. There was no dining hall, thus inmates were forced to eat their three squares locked in their cells.

BC Pen with its troubled history was fraught with problems. For its time, although modern in many ways, suffered from faulty plumbing, and cramped quarters. By the time the BC Pen closed its doors, she was a shadow of her former self. Inmate uprisings had taken their toll on the once-revered prison, with complaints ranging from overcrowding, quality of food, to numerous complaints regarding living conditions. It was these seemingly endless complaints, and the unrest that would ultimately spell her end.

Looking back at the colourful, yet troubled history, I am reminded of the sad killing of Guard John Henry Joynson during the escape of Joseph SMITH (Authors note: the last name of inmates are capitalized in order to clearly identify them in reports) and Herman WILSON in October 1912.

Those who were branded trouble makers found work in the BC Pen's stone quarry. It was more about punishment than employment on the rock crushing gang. It was back breaking work, as 27 inmates were hard at work when their plan got underway. The instigators were 24-year-old Joseph SMITH who was serving 10 years for armed robbery of a Vancouver jewellery store. He was a short, fit man, filled with hate. Herman WILSON, 22 was also serving a 10-year bit for armed robbery.

BC Pen had a strict policy of no talking when both SMITH and WILSON were approached by the supervising guard Robert Craig for speaking contrary to the Penitentiary Service Regulations.

It was just after lunch, a cold and blistery autumn day, October 5th, 1912 when SMITH picked up a sledge hammer and struck Craig on the head, and taking his unloaded handgun. Craig worried about carrying a loaded gun while working around inmates, fearing it could be used against him. Now with a gun, the pair caught nearby tower guard Officer Elson by surprise, convincing him to throw down the tower keys. Not aware the gun was unloaded he complied enabling the two to escape out of the yard, one step closer to freedom. As Elson threw down the keys he managed to shoot WILSON grazing his neck.

As the felons moved quickly from the brick yard to the shop entrance they were able to disarm another officer of his loaded revolver. The desperate pair moved towards the main gate where they would come across Officer Joynson who was shot twice by SMITH while attempting to end the escape. Joynson employed at the BC Pen for only six months, was mortally wounded, and would die within the hour. He left behind a wife and children.

While the guards were able to thwart the escape, Herman WILSON who was shot, died in his cell October 30th from septic pneumonia (blood poisoning) from the bullet left behind.

Now the time of reckoning, SMITH appeared before Justice Murphy, and pled not guilty. In what was to be a brief trial, the jury would return a verdict of guilty within three hours. Judge Murphy pronounced SMITH to death by hanging, and uttered those famous words, "May God have mercy on your soul". January 31st, three months after the death of Joynson, SMITH was marched from his cell, hands bound behind his back, and led to the wooden gallows overlooking the very site of the murder. It was 8:21 am, SMITH appeared calm in the face of death as he stood on the trap door. With his head covered, SMITH fell through the spring-loaded trap door, and 13 minutes later was pronounced dead.

The unofficial reason for conducting the execution at the BC Pen was to make SMITH an example to the other inmates. His was the only execution undertaken at the BC Pen with other death sentences carried out at nearby Oakalla Prison in Burnaby.

The funeral for Joynson was held at the main gate of the BC Pen within one day of his death. His flag draped coffin was carried to his grave by his co-workers as the two-ton count bell rang out while his coffin was lowered into the cold hardened ground of the Fraser Cemetery. Joynson's wife would receive a pension of $500 per year, and a fund raiser that would help maintain her home.

Joynson was one of two officers killed during the pen's unruly days, including the tragic killing of Mary Steinhauser.

SMITH was reputed to be buried at the outskirts of the BC Pen property in an unmarked grave, forgotten.

Since the beginning of confederation, until capital punishment was abolished by Prime Minister Pierre Elliot Trudeau's Liberal government in 1967, over 1,481 people were sentenced to death, of those, 710 were executed; 13 were women.

Canada's last execution was the double hanging of Arthur LUCAS and Ronald TURPIN on December 11, 1962 at Toronto's Don Jail.

It wasn't until 1934 that the BC Pen ignited with its first riot. Inmates were complaining about poor living conditions. Riots also occurred in 1963, 1973, 1975 and 1976 in violent protests of overcrowding, and massive flooding due to poor plumbing.

As her days seemed numbered, the BC Pen prepared for the inevitable closure in May 1980. The riots, murders, and assaults would plague BC Pen up to its final year. While most hated the BC Pen, it was what they knew. Change was not welcoming and I understand many inmates were unsure, and uncertain of their move. To appease those still uncertain of what lay ahead, prison authorities organized a brief tour prior to Kent's opening. It was now or never, ready or not, the remaining inmates were transferred around the region, and across Canada. The last six inmates transferred from BC Pen to Kent included K.N. SMITH # 9865, R.K. HAY # 1258, G.T. HANDLEN # 0308, R.J. WATSON # 0110, R.A. BING # 7448, and R.A. SIMPSON # 9112.

In her final days, federal government dignitaries, prison officials, custody officers, families, and up to 45,000 visitors gathered at the closing ceremonies to say their goodbyes. Filled with anticipation and exuberance, crowds of well-wishers sent the old pen into the history books. Among them, a little five-year-old girl who hung to her mother's coat looking up at the towering walls; she remembers a darkness. Not able to grasp its meaning, this impressionable child walked through some of the most gruesome and troubling scenes of prison history. Thirty-five years later, she appreciates having experienced a piece of Canada's colourful past. Recalling the old walls filled with pockmarks, the much larger holes spoke to the violence. Struck with what she remembers, about the infamous legends in a troubled system. Were the boot impressions on the grassy hillside that of a killer? Perhaps of Billy MINER, or Andy BRUCE? The fresh air of the day was a contradiction to the stale air from the past. This little girl remembers that day as if it was yesterday. While the Pen is long gone, she can still envision the towering walls, the finality of the grand dame we called the BC Pen. Most of the buildings have since been replaced with residential housing. Only five parts of the original prison remain including the Gatehouse, the Memorial Carin, the original Gaol building, which has been converted to offices, the count bell, and the cemetery.

The remaining staff were either redeployed to various federal prisons in BC, or to other government agencies across Canada. Some accepted layoffs, others resigned, or retired. One passed away prior to reassignment.

At the onset of the demolition, Anthony (Tony) Martin, who worked at the BC Pen from 1958 until it closed in 1980 was the prison's bookkeeper, and tasked with conducting the closing audit. He saved thousands of historic pieces from the garbage. Much to his wife's chagrin, their home in Abbotsford became a haven for the many valuable artifacts.

I had the pleasure to meet Tony in 2016 at his home, and was welcomed to a most unusual, and privileged tour. Turning 84, Tony was as keen as ever, like a proud father. Each piece he showed had a story.

Tony saw the artifacts' value even if no one else did. Not able to find a home for these historic gems in New Westminster, or at CSC headquarters in Abbotsford, Tony found a permanent exhibition space in Kamloops in the dark basement of the Courthouse Museum.

The exhibited items include the Warden's desk, a portable bar oddly out of place by today's standards, a bevy of pictures, and mug shots (1133 cards) of inmates inked on glass plates.

An officer overlooks the BC Pen in this 1950s picture. The calm before the storm many would say as nearly two decades of disturbances, riots, and hostage takings would seal her fate.

Mary Steinhauser Killing [3]

The single most profound incident in the 102-year history of the British Columbia Penitentiary was the tragic death of Mary Steinhauser during a 41-hour hostage-taking on June 11, 1975. Words could hardly do justice to the memory of Mary Steinhauser, a classification officer at the BC Pen. As I sat down with Mary's younger sister Margaret Franz, I was thinking Mary would have been 75 this year (2017) and while it has been 42 years since her tragic death, her memory lives on. In an unplanned journey, Margaret would spend her life telling Mary's story. She conducted countless media interviews, collaborating with others in a theatre production, and promoting Mary's legacy through the Mary Steinhauser Memorial Bursary, benefiting Simon Fraser University's Aboriginal students in arts and social sciences.

With the pride representing the last of the Steinhauser family, Margaret was eager to share Mary's story. As a former member of the system that took her sister, I was unsure how I would be received. Was I the enemy, or a willing and impartial historian?

Mary, age 32 at the time of her death, had an exciting career unfolding. A front-line classification officer, Mary was centre stage to the dangerous drama of everyday prison life. Highly educated, Mary held a Bachelor of Arts (Honours) a double major in Psychology and Sociology, followed by a Bachelor's of Social Work in 1973. The Steinhausers, like many protective parents, never understood her desire to work in such a dangerous environment.

Within the towering walls of the BC Pen, the classification trailers where Mary worked had once housed the Sons of Freedom Doukhobors. The long rectangular building was just 150 feet from the main gate, and outside the cell blocks. The red roof building was 220 feet long, and had a four-foot narrow corridor, running the length of the building, north to south, where inmates visited to discuss their various cases.

The classification building housed several offices belonging to classification officers including the office of Mary Steinhauser. Mary's job was to determine an inmate's appropriate security classification and placement through regular monitoring of the inmate's institutional behaviour. Today's equivalent would be an Institutional Parole Officer (IPO) tasked with a wide range of responsibilities including parole recommendations, and the development of release plans.

It was Monday morning, around 7:45 am when a new correctional officer would settle into his daily routine, collecting and verifying inmate movement passes. There was only a telephone on this rookie's desk, no buzzer, or alarm system. By 8:00 am inmates having business with the Classification Department would file in, and present their passes. Andy BRUCE, a lifer with a dark and sinister past, entered the building along with Dwight LUCAS, and Claire WILSON, also serving life sentences. They had come to Mary's office under the pretense of wanting her assistance. These three were the worst of the worst, all well established in the criminal lifestyle. BRUCE, the purported ringleader, was 27 at the time.

BRUCE had a lengthy rap sheet including the cold-blooded contract killing of an exotic dancer in North Vancouver, but dates back as far as 1965 with two charges of indecent assault.

The Farris Commission, named after Justice John Farris was convened by the government of the day to delve into the details of the hostage-taking. The court heard LUCAS was feared by those who knew him. With a troubled childhood, he would later be convicted of a series of crime sprees involving the drug underworld in Winnipeg, following which he was convicted of being party to an axe murder. Claire WILSON 26, had been diagnosed early in life as antisocial, with dangerous, and poorly controlled anger issues. The three resided in the Security Control Unit (SCU), B7 or the "BC Penthouse" as it was called, just up the hill from the classification building where they had come together. Their release from the SCU was inevitable, and set in motion the slippery slope that would eventually culminate in Mary's death. Tragically, their release from the SCU allowed them open and free movement throughout the prison, and according to the Farris report, their release was deemed a mistake.

On that fateful day, escape was on their minds, to rid themselves of what they felt were the unfair chains of incarceration. As the poorly planned escape quickly unraveled, it turned into a desperate hostage taking. BRUCE was not out of place as he held the secretary position on Mary's Community Awareness Group. He used his position as an effective cover to gain entrance to the classification building. Armed with prison shanks, described as a 14" kitchen knife and a filleting knife, the three sprang into action as they herded 16 correctional staff including a correctional officer, 13 classification officers, and two social development officers into a 15' x 15' windowless vault situated at the far end of the building complex. One staff member was later released when the captures heard he was suffering a heart condition. Now joined by Claire WILSON, things reached a boiling point, the prison went into lockdown. As the standoff commenced, the reign of terror escalated in an ever-changing dynamic, growing hotter by the minute. At one point, an inmate in the vault poured Mercurochrome over the heads and in the eyes of the hostages to further inflict a stinging, and unbearable pain.

Outside the vault, BRUCE acted as the lead negotiator with Mary the principal hostage. Holding a knife to Mary's throat, BRUCE now demanded drugs and a helicopter to the airport, then transportation to an unknown country. BRUCE was heard saying during the hostage taking "either we leave, or we die". At the centre of the hostage taking was "the system" stating it was "rotten" and "if we don't get out of here now on a helicopter, we are going out on a slab".

The inmates insisted that independent negotiators be assembled, including lawyer Bryan Williams, newsman Bob Hunter, lawyer Don Sorochan, lecturer Mordecai Briemberg and popular radio personality Gary Bannerman. What the negoiators knew for certain was the Solisitor General would not let Canadian hostages be taken out of the country, a secret they withheld from the three hostage takers. Their demands included hot and cold running water for the isolation cells, and medical attention for BRUCE and LUCAS dealing with the effects from drug withdrawals. As the situation grew more desperate, the demands became ludicrous. Now demanding Demerol, a small amount at first was administered to Mary to ensure there would be no adverse effects on their captures. The acts of violence were barbaric by every account as the inmates, relentless in their threats and intimidation, called the hostages pigs, and threatened to cut their throats. It was a long two days. Things deteriorated as an "untrained tactical team" lay waiting for a chance to end this dangerous situation. Other staff deployed to the area were a fire team of six men, a demolition team of four to six men, two assault teams of six men each, and back up teams of 12 men equipped with riot gear.

At one point, BRUCE was demanding additional drugs, and was told his demand for Demerol would have to wait until 9:30 am the next morning when London Drugs opened. The hostage takers were now under the influence, and their reactions could not be predicted, so a doctor prescribed an antipsychotic sedative known as Haldol. It was hoped this drug would take the unpredictable edge off this untenable situation, and reduce their violent moods.

Not aware the situation was about to come to a crashing conclusion, the heated atmosphere prompted those inside the vault to seize their opportunity for freedom. The hostages managed to overtake WILSON, who by this time was losing his edge, and falling into a state of unconsciousness. Pandemonium exploded into a dangerous pitch. The tactical team, poised for action, heard screams for help, and saw their chance for action. The command, "attack", was immediate as correctional officers fired eight shots from their standard issue .38 revolvers. It would be one bullet that would be remembered as it spiraled down the cold steel barrel, and ripped through Mary's heart, she fell to the cold floor, lifeless. The very team trying to save her life sadly ended it. Two rounds hit BRUCE, one in his jaw, another in his stomach.

In the Farris Commission report inmate witnesses suggested that Mary had cried out "don't shoot him, don't shoot him" while others heard "don't shoot, don't shoot". The immediate aftermath, and the silence was almost as deafening. The violent standoff was over. Mary was wheeled to the waiting ambulance, and rushed to the hospital where she was pronounced dead.

In the coming months, an inquest was held, followed by the Farris Commission, in hope of making sense of those tragic events. Rumours abound, questions needed answers, including the not-so-subtle condemnation of Mary's character that fit the need to blame someone. Not favoured by the guards for her liberal beliefs on modern rehabilitation techniques, she and the guards had discord: it was no secret.

As the cleanup, or cover up began, one correctional officer, identified by Andy BRUCE, was Albert Hollinger, the officer who was believed to have wounded BRUCE and killed Mary with revolver # D643085. Later in an act that would haunt Hollinger, the Commission would learn he was a veteran officer who had collected the revolvers, making no note of which person had what revolver, emptying the cartridges, wiping tell-tale finger prints away, and rendering it impossible to determine who fired the various, and fatal shots. This action by Hollinger was looked upon as a deliberate cover up to which the Farris Commission took a hard position in its remarks about Hollinger, calling his story unbelievable. Former classification officer Terry Mallenby in a book titled, "Was Mary Steinhauser Murdered" claimed guards purposefully shot and killed her. The brazen author also inferred the Canadian government tried to cover up these persistent allegations made by BRUCE and others present at the time of the shooting. Was it a conspiracy, or a misguided cover up to protect their own? While forensics could identify which gun delivered the deadly use of force, no one would know who shot Mary. The shooting by the Emergency Response Team members was looked upon as "inept, but understandable". It was generally understood the men were not trained for the intense task at hand. Those standing at the ready were tired and lacked sleep. Most in fact had been on scene for the entire 41 hour ordeal. In one of the longest inquests in Canadian history (six weeks), a jury ruled the shooting was unintentional, and the guards, including Hollinger, acted under the belief Mary's life was in danger.

Whatever the reasons, many questions remained unanswered. I was surprised at how Margaret managed to find some semblance of peace, while never forgetting her loving sister, and Mary's lost potential.

As I reflect, and try to understand the Mary Steinhauser story, I look at the work environment of prison life. The correctional officers seemed to have an intense mistrust of non-uniformed staff. Mary was professionally driven, fearless, and compassionate about her goals. She had a dogged persistence, and an affinity for helping under-privileged people, and an endless passion for helping aboriginal inmates. This passion only fueled the mistrust.

Her sister tells of a young woman who liked to dance, was active, and enjoyed many sports including bowling. With a new boyfriend, she hoped one day to marry, she had it all. Mary wanted to affect change on prison conditions, and how inmates were treated, but her efforts were met with strong resistance from a military style of strict rules steadfastly enforced by uniformed officers. She endured workplace harassment, and experienced incidents of vandalism to her car. These were not so subtle messages that her efforts were not appreciated. There was no written evidence of any inappropriate relationship that I could uncover with any of her captors, yet urban myths abound with tales of her love affair with inmate Andy BRUCE.

As Margaret sipped her coffee, telling stories with pride, I too grew to appreciate Mary's slightly ahead-of-her time efforts. Mary was blazing trails we now often take for granted, laying the groundwork for what would become modern rehabilitation initiatives. Parole and program officers are the backbone of our rehabilitative services in today's modern penal system, and often their work is under-appreciated.

That day, the violence and tragic ending got the attention of the world press, and found its way into a Federal Commission of Inquiry, a stage play, motion picture, and a hauntingly catchy tune entitled WILSON, LUCAS & BRUCE (on You Tube) sung by folk singer Bob Mercer would be a lasting tribute to Mary Steinhauser.

The Farris Commission had concerns over lax security issues in the BC Pen, citing the physical plant as ancient, describing each building redesign and upgrade as haphazard. Many routine procedures were deemed factors in the hostage taking, including the poor classification of inmates. BRUCE, LUCAS and WILSON had demonstrated violent tendencies, and participated in several documented incidents that should have been pre-warning indicators. It was reported that between 80% and 90 % of the BC Pen inmates were extremely dangerous individuals.

The actual shooting did however crystallize several debates over the running of our prisons.

In the aftermath of this incident, prison guard Albert Hollinger would not be charged despite the efforts of BRUCE who identified Hollinger as the shooter of both him and Mary Steinhauser. BC Chief Justice John Farris strongly rejected Hollinger's explanation for mixing up the guns, calling it an "insult to the intelligence of the three-man inquiry". Hollinger was not liked by many staff yet lacking any proof to his intentions they would not bring charges. Hollinger was transferred to Regional Headquarters as a security maintenance officer (SMO) until he eventually retired. Suffering from PTSD some staff said Albert was tense, unhappy and bitter, leading to his death in 2015 at the age of 82.

Mary lives on in the memories of those who knew her, and for those who didn't, they are reminded when they visit the provincial monument for fallen Canadian police and peace officers standing proudly on the grounds of the BC Legislature. Further tribute to Mary and other police and peace officers can be found at the federal monument on Parliament Hill in Ottawa.

Forty years after that fateful day, BRUCE now living in downtown Vancouver, lived for the most part an uneventful life. If it weren't for his last alleged indiscretion in 2016, the once-famous BRUCE might have been forgotten. BRUCE, the central figure in the killing of Mary Steinhauser has remained charge free for over 40 years. In 2004 BRUCE received day parole, and full parole in 2010. Though he admitted to a breach of parole conditions (alcohol and drugs) no charges were ever filed.

Aging, and now retired, BRUCE is touching this side of 70, and was recently picked up on an allegation of performing an indecent act while in the bushes next to a Vancouver bus stop. It is an allegation that he vehemently denies. It was during the alleged act that BRUCE supposedly pointed a can of bear spray at a man who confronted him. While he never sprayed the man, police received a call that he had a knife. In the ensuing take down Vancouver Police broke three of BRUCE's ribs, where he was hospitalized for five days. BRUCE now found himself back at Mountain awaiting further legal hearings.

BRUCE's lawyer speaks of an old man having extensive cardiac conditions that prompted the placement of a pacemaker. Has time played a part in his rehabilitation, or like many has he just become tired of playing the game?

Classification Officer, Nurse and inmate advocate, Mary Steinhauser, was killed by an Emergency Response Team Member.

Boot Hill, the BC Pen Cemetery [4]

While the staff have long since departed, Boot Hill, hidden deep within the former penitentiary grounds is one of just a few historic reminders of the existence of the once proud BC Pen.

The cemetery, lined with broken fences cordons off a green space many think is just a dog park. While it was poorly maintained, I am happy to say the City of New Westminster and their Cemetery Task Force has undertaken a revitalization plan to clean up the once forgotten cemetery. The Task Force recognizes the historical significance of the site, and the historical value it holds as part of the monumental piece of the history of the City of New Westminster.

Prior to 2017 many residents in the upscale neighbourhood of Glenbrook Ravine Park were unaware of its existence. The cemetery can be located via GPS: latitude 49.21688, longitude-12289903, within the Victoria Hill development, just behind the towering condominiums on Francis Street.

The New Westminster Heritage Preservation Society in 2007 named the BC Pen cemetery one of its top 10 most endangered heritage sites in New Westminster.

Between 1913 and 1968, 47 men are believed to be laid to rest in Boot Hill. Those who lived, and died at the BC Pen were collected either by their next of kin, or given an unceremonious burial on the grounds. Headstones contained no dedication, memorial, or dates, not even a name: simply a poured concrete slab inscribed with a prisoner number is all that would tell their story. The prisoners interred in the cemetery came from a variety of backgrounds, and were incarcerated for a wide range of crimes, including murder, rape, drug abuse, trafficking to theft. One inmate was convicted of the theft of socks, valued at $15.00.

There were two sections in the turn-of-the-century graveyard, one for Roman Catholics, and another for Protestants. Strangely enough, many of the Doukhobor graves were marked as Buddhists. The earliest recorded occupant was Gin O. Kim #1948, believed buried in an unknown grave. The dark soul Joseph SMITH #1433, who killed correctional officer John Henry Joynson during an escape in 1912, was hanged only steps away from the spot where he killed Officer Joynson, is buried somewhere on the sprawling BC Pen grounds also in an unmarked grave.

Herman WILSON #1629 was shot while attempting to escape the high walls of the Fraser River fortress and is believed buried in an unmarked grave on the property. The last inmate buried in Boot Hill was Harold Gordon MCMASTER #3237 on February 20, 1968, who had been convicted of Break and Entering, and Theft. MCMASTER was sent to Oakalla Prison, and later to Riverview Hospital to recover from his mental illness.

He later died in provincial custody at Riverview Hospital, and buried within Boot Hill.

The New BC Penthouse, Kent [5]

As the transition between the old and the new began, the building of Kent commenced in 1977 at a cost of 17.8 million dollars, and was ready for occupancy in 1979. Kent was designed to house 192 inmates, completed in time to receive a select few inmates from BC Pen.

Corrections officials had to re-think the corrections model, and Kent was the result. This new modernized way of thinking would blaze a trail, or so officials thought, to a hopeful future on how we would carry on the business of corrections in Canada. Resting on 17 acres of reclaimed farmland, this hidden little gem of a prison lay smack in the middle of the District of Kent in the historic farming community of Agassiz, known as the "corn capital of BC".

As the visitor drives up the access road, Kent looks like any other government building. Unassuming at first, the barbed wire once gleamed in the sun of earlier days, now tired and rusted as it looks up to the looming guard towers. The visitor's perception quickly turns into the harsh reality we call prison. As the mobile patrols creep around the perimeter, they watch your every move, reinforcing this realization.

Kent was first labeled as luxurious when compared to the living conditions of other BC prisons. Politicians were quick to coin the phrase, "The Vanguard of Change". Gone were cramped cells and the green paint, replaced by more modern colours. It contained smaller modern units, food serveries, and common areas that allowed inmates to meet and mingle during the non-work times. Corcan furniture built by inmates adorned the units with a comfortable and welcoming feel.

Inmates were no longer required to eat alone in their cells, but could consume their meals in the dining hall. Detractors of corrections, those who preferred the harsh deterrent of punishment, were slow in coming around to the new ways. There were many who claimed the inmates in H-unit, and later Segregation, were virtually buried alive in concrete tombs for periods of up to 23 hours each day, with little space to exercise. A coat of new paint could not silence the protests from some critics who still hung onto the belief Segregation was considered cruel and unusual punishment.

Punishment was no longer dished out; rather incarceration was the extent of the punishment allowed. The cellblock concept was replaced with living units, bulls or guards were referred to as living unit officers (LUs), or correctional officers. Their turn-of-the-century thinking was now focusing on programs, and rehabilitation. Over the century, convicts were called inmates, offenders, clients, and residents. The new LUs were not required to wear uniforms, all part of the dynamic way of thinking that allowed inmates to view LUs as less of an authority figure: it was a way to encourage better communication. Many of these LUs were the old guard, and some struggled with the change from the old punishment mentality, to the new gentler style of corrections. The LUs would wear jeans and t-shirts, looking more like inmates than the new, modern correctional officers. One day, as I was sitting in the E/F control post envisioning what was next in my day, when an LU with his stringy long hair approached the bubble in preparation for a range walk and count. He wielded a baseball bat, going up on the tier, he threatened to knock anyone out of the park if they did not lock up. He brought a unique style to the job that was effective to say the least! He managed to strike fear into our hearts, and for the most part got co-operation from both inmates, and staff.

Kent's new courtyard.

Mission Statement [6]

Introduced in 1989, our Mission Statement had grown from a few simple words, a list of core values, to one that now included respect for democracy, people, integrity, stewardship, and excellence. Its purpose was to give clear direction to those who worked within the CSC, a light leading staff in a new, and better direction. The Mission offers practical guidance for today, and inspiration for meeting the challenges of tomorrow.

The early architects of our Mission Statement met in Banff Alberta in November 1988. They included such notables as the late Commissioner, Ole Instrip along with former Deputy Commissioner, the late Pieter de Vink who would meet to update, and modernize the original document in hopes of giving it a much-needed face life.

Warehousing of inmates was no longer the standard, and the Correctional Service of Canada had to change, or they would suffer the costly ineffective policies of yesteryear, a tired system that no longer worked.

Our Mission Statement

The Correctional Service of Canada as part of the criminal justice system, and respecting the rule of law contributes to public safety by actively encouraging inmates to become law abiding citizens, while exercising reasonable, safe secure and humane control.

Chapter 2

My Journey Begins

Correctional Officer Recruit Training [7]

I was only 34, getting bored as an armoured car driver in Vancouver when I decided to apply for a government job that I hoped would provide security, and comfort in my old age. While my original application was intended for Canada Border Services (Customs), as fate would have it, my resume ended up with the Correctional Service of Canada.

"Not even the most imaginative Hollywood screenwriter could conjure up a job description where the so-called clients would slit your throat, given the opportunity". (Neil MacLean Reader's Digest, ("A Week in a Max", 2007).

Our job description:

> *Correctional Officer / Manager Working Conditions, in part reads:*
>
> *The work is performed in a federal correctional institution with frequent interaction with inmates where there is risk of verbal, and physical assault.*
>
> *There is risk of fatigue, stress and post traumatic effect, and working within a high-risk environment.*

Fresh from Correctional Officer Recruit Program (CORP), I undertook three months of training that was a mix of classroom lectures, legal studies, basic arrest and control procedures, revolver, rifle, and shotgun training.

Some classmates that made a strong impression on me included "Outstanding Recruit" Stan Beacon, as well as Mark Noon-Ward, Don Scisson, Brenda Brown, Eric Chen, Dawn Halliday, Cheryl McWilliams, Linda Fehr, Doug Lawrence, Neil McPhail, Pat Castro, Barrie Coates, Virginia Dearden, Roland Turgoen, Ray Patenaude, Margaret Smith, John Wallace, and Dale Culpepper. The innocence of CORP, sharing the unknown seemed to bring us closer together during a challenging time, a time of building confidences, all while discovering new insecurities. I was a good student who loved to study, and thrived in this environment, organizing everything from after-school study sessions, to the many social events at the Lone Star Pub in Sumas Washington. I was proud to have been voted "Mr. Congeniality" of CORP 264, but even prouder to now be part of an organization steeped in history. Feeling unsure, but optimistic about the future, reality had not yet set in.

This young man from West Vancouver, used to the fast-paced life of the big city was somewhat shocked to be thrown into what I viewed as the nowhere cow town of Agassiz British Columbia. It took a few years to appreciate Agassiz's history, and its gracious people.

It was an exciting time for me, the door leading to a dark, secretive world was about to open: a membership into the private world of law enforcement. I considered public service an honour, and my starting wage of $23,873.00 was like winning the lottery. Finally, job security was mine.

Kent had been built to replace the aging BC Pen, the Pacific Region's only maximum-security prison. Opening its doors in 1979 to 65 inmates, it would later house up to 250 of BC's most incorrigible male inmates this province had to offer.

Kent's First Murder [8]

Turning back the clock, prior to my arrival in 1980, Kent experienced its first murder, which fell on the heels of its grand opening. RCMP were called to investigate the stabbing death of a 25-year-old inmate, Dean Thomas LANGFORD 25, in the gymnasium washroom. LANGFORD had been convicted in 1979 of the high profile killing of two Aboriginal sisters, residents of Sooke BC, who were hitchhiking through the up-island town of Courtney when they were killed. LANGFORD was just starting his life sentence when he was viciously attacked. He had been placed in General Population (GP); however due to the "Con-Code" that forbids the killing of young girls I believe placement on the Protective Custody (PC) side would have been more appropriate. Due to poor visibility, staff were unable to keep track of the ongoing dynamics in that part of the gym. This flaw in design allowed inmates to stage many assaults and murders over the years. Inmates were quick to find the vulnerable locations around the prison to carry out their twisted sense of justice. Inmates Robert MOHR, William Frank SMOKE and Adam NORRIS were charged jointly in LANGFORD's murder.

Kent's First Riot

Following in the footsteps of Kent's first murder, Kent experienced its first riot. 1979 was fast becoming a banner year for unrest, and an embarrassment to the "architects of change" as inmates rioted, setting fires, and damaging 39 cells.

June of 1981 Kent experienced its second riot, lasting only two hours, but saw 100 inmates partake in one of the institutions most troubling riots. Two inmates were stabbed, and several inmates injured when guards fired warning shots hitting several with shotgun pellets. The riot occurring on a Sunday evening around 6:20pm in the gym spreading to what was called the west wing over disciplinary action taken against two inmates. The inmates ended up cooling their heels in the sports field over night until they were marched back to their cells, one-by-one. Most of the riots in Kent's early years were over the inmates' perception of overcrowding, and the quality of the food being served. During these violent incidents staff were often placed in harm's way.

One such day on the GP side, a C-Unit staff member was struggling to restrain an angry inmate. These types of situations can go sour very quickly, and turn deadly. With no concern for his own safety, Correctional Officer Sammy Thuraisamy intervened to deflect attention away from his partner. Sammy was stabbed. For his actions, he was later awarded the Commissioner's Citation for Bravery. Sammy was an experienced, old-school correctional officer, and offered sage advice to this inexperienced rookie. Although he was kind to a fault, Sammy's mantra was, "Fuck 'em, lock 'em up and feed 'em rice".

Down the Lonely Cemetery Road

From the hilarious to the tragic, Kent had it all. Traveling from Mission as a recruit, I enjoyed the drive through the picturesque Fraser Valley, passing by the sprawling fields of the farm-rich communities along the way. Driving those country backroads was a time of peace, as I would prepare myself for whatever the day might bring. Who would suspect at the end of Cemetery Road was the dark and sinister world of prison life, where countless souls took their last breath?

I started as a part-time employee working two days a week, with other shifts coming available to round up my hours to full-time. We were part of the same guards' union, but some of the more vocal, so-called brothers resented the part-timers taking "their" overtime, and made their hate-filled opinions known. Eventually the ill-fated part timers' program would disappear. Surprisingly, I was not aware to the extent of the deep divide between the living unit officers (non-uniformed) and the uniformed security officers. There was deep-seated mistrust between the different factions, which took shape in a ritual called "ratting". Ratting was common, growing up as a child in school, and carried over to the workplace. These old ways were carried on in the "Old Boys Club" which sadly exists today.

I would have expected my life experiences would have better prepared me for what was to come, however nothing could have been farther from the truth. Like many recruits, we weren't prepared for, or too immature to handle this foreign environment. No amount of training could ready us for the high-jinx, and danger awaiting. Our instructors warned us to expect more trouble from staff than from inmates. How could this be? Were we not part of a brotherhood? This drama ranged from the spreading of malicious rumours of who was sleeping with whom, petty jealousy over the job competition process, to behaving badly, and rarely, illegal activity both on, and off the job. I soon discovered correctional officers could demonstrate a wide range of personalities that were sometimes disappointing.

During my 25 years with the CSC, I worked at Kent, Matsqui, Mountain, and Mission Institutions as well as a brief stint at Regional Headquarters. I have worked as a correctional officer I, working static, sedentary positions on both the GP and PC sides of the prison including mobile patrol, gun walks, and guard towers. I worked as a correctional officer II, acting correctional supervisor and correctional manager.

The armed control post A/B, was a caverness dingy fish bowl where I overlooked two units. The floor to ceiling windows were void of any expectation of privacy from the inmate's prying eyes. It had the stale odour of many previous smokers, which had turned the walls a putrid yellow. Control post officers were afforded a bird's eye view of each tier, and were the safety link to unit officers on their hourly range walks. "Open the doors", "close the doors", the jailbirds would chirp. Inmates were rude, impatient and dangerous if they didn't get their way, right away. I often thought I was nothing more than a glorified doorman! Not being allowed to read in these control posts (bubbles) the ever so resourceful correctional officer could conjure up creative ways to pass the time. Whether it was begging coffee from the unit staff, or studying my ground school homework and various flying maneuvers, helped pass the time, much to the surprise of the noisy inmates.

My First Day at Kent, the CHARTRAND Murder [9]

December 31, 1988 was a cold, typically Canadian December morning, my first day working for the CSC. Filled with nervous anticipation, I reported to the correctional supervisor's office. My shoes polished, I felt overdressed wearing a tie and forge cap when those around me were not. Sticking out like the rookie I was, the leers did not deter me. As I walked by the different posts inmates would yell out, "new meat", or "I smell fresh fish". I was filled with adrenalin at the realization I was in the "Big House", a maximum-security prison. I remember thinking it doesn't get much "badder than that".

Paired up with a training partner, we made our rounds to the various posts. A few minutes into my new career, a Saturday evening shift, the portable radio screamed out, "staff assistance to the gym". Startled but without hesitating, we responded, thundering into the gym. Arriving at the washroom, we stopped short of the ghastly sight. Hanging, his face red, strangle marks around his neck, toilet paper stuffed down his throat inmate CHARTRAND was dead. An autopsy later showed that he was hot capped and killed. The smell of death hung in the air. A sea of crimson red blanketed the concrete floor. Only moments before, inmate Ray CHARTRAND was alive. In the hours leading up to his death, nothing seemed out of place for his young inmate, nothing to give rise to our suspicion that his life was about to come to an abrupt, and violent end.

Correctional Officers arrived at the scene as the correctional supervisor started barking orders to lock the joint down. With reality setting in, I quickly concluded my first day on the job had become a crime scene. As expected with any murder, managers were recalled from their time away, many enjoying the holiday season. Police arrived, along with the Coroner and a forensic team to start their investigation into his untimely demise. Staff were quickly brought together as we conducted a count of inmates in the gym, looking for any tell-tale signs of criminal involvement, including bloody shirts, bruised knuckles, (knuckle check) or any evidence offering the slightest clue that would lead us to a suspect. It didn't take long for one of the officers to discover a blood-soaked t-shirt stashed in a storm drain just outside of the gym.

Any death in custody was tragic, but I had to laugh years later when I came across a newspaper article with the headline, "Police Suspect Foul Play". My first day on the job left me to wonder what the second day would bring.

My Second Day, Not Much Better, as I Met the Headhunter[10]

Ringing in the New Year, my second day was not shaping up any better than the first. Working in the G/H control post, one of five-unit bubbles, an inmate, naked, with his manhood well in hand came to the bubble requesting his cell door be closed.

I pondered for just a moment, was he the welcoming party, or just a truly bent human being. I turned my head in disbelief? At the time, I was not aware of this inmate's notoriety, but later learned he was John Melvin RITCEY. RITCEY was dirty and unkept, he reeked of BO, wearing green issued pajamas most times. He got his nick name, the "Headhunter" from his non-stop quests for oral sex.

Prior to joining the CSC, I toured the popular Vancouver Police Museum hidden in the dark alley of Vancouver's most dangerous part of town when I came across his shocking life story on public display. Little did I know our paths would one-day cross.

Working as a garbage man for the City of Vancouver during the summer of 1969, he lured two young men back to his run-down three-story apartment in Vancouver's west end. Killing Kenneth Black, the second man was held hostage in RITCEYs apartment for over two months. RITCEY went so far as to tie him to Blacks body only releasing his bonds to fulfill his sexual desires. RITCEY would strangle Kenneth Black before dismembering his body and stuffing him into an old steamer trunk which he buried in a lime-filled grave just a few miles outside of Hope British Columbia.

Steve Thorlakson was just 19 when he left his employment in New Westminster looking for new opportunities. Thorlakson was on his way to Peace River Alberta to start a new job with Avco Finance. It was on this road trip the kind hearted and somewhat naïve Thorlakson picked up RITCEY and his companion north of Prince George unaware of RITCEYS' dark and sinister past. He said of RITCEY, he seemed normal but would brag about his early life of crime starting with an armed assault at 13. It was early in the conversation when the bridge over troubled water led to an innocent comparison of RITCEY to a member of a popular US singing duo. It was this comment that RITCEY became paranoid holding a Colt pistol on Thorlakson for the entire 30-hour ride snaking their way through northern BC. Short on funds, RITCEY would rob his capture of $86.00. RITCEYs companion, sleeping most times in the back seat was able to escape his grasp and notified police. Police issued an APB but their task was made all the more difficult not having an accurate vehicle description.

Their dragnet expanded eventually throughout BC into Saskatchewan. Tholakson would tap out SOS with his brake pedal in hopes someone would notice. By chance an observant police officer now following the pair noticed the cryptic call for help, and radioed ahead. A road block near Summit Lake in the southeastern part of BC ended RITCEYs reign of terror without incident.

Thorlakson would count himself lucky that he escaped the killing hands of John RITCEY who he later learned was a predatory sexual psychopath. Tholakson described him in more unflattering terms by simply calling him a monster.

Now in police custody RITCEY would try to commit suicide as is evident by the bandaged neck in the mugshot. His picture made headlines as he would be marched across the tarmac of the Prince George airport secured in body restraints, including handcuffs and leg irons, and bound in a strait jacket for his return to Vancouver to face charges of Capital Murder in the death of Kenneth Black and the kidnapping of Thorlakson.

Spending most of his adult life behind bars, RITCEY was incarcerated in the BC Pen, Kent and Mission Institutions. He was an aggressive homosexual, terrorizing his cell mates spending in an inordinate amount of time in Segregation. Despite his dangerous and troubling institutional adjustment, the Parole Board saw fit to parole this deviant killer in 2007. In his declining years he suffered from various maladies including congenital heart failure to which he would succumb in 2010 at the age of 68.

The Parole Board would telephone Steve letting him know "it was over". What struck me as odd when he told of the Parole Boards diligent notification I concluded they could never understand, for the victim, "it would never be over".

Steve Tholakson served as the Mayor of Fort St. John proudly for 15 years. Married, father of four children he was a fixer of problems. It was only when he found forgiveness, that he could heal. Life goes on he would say.

Often I would ponder their crimes, wondering how people could take a life without so much as a second thought. I quickly concluded that if the public were to read their criminal profiles, rather than watching the 30-second media clips most saw on TV, they, like myself, would believe in the return of capital punishment. The more notable inmates, like the Headhunter and the Abbotsford Killer had me mesmerized.

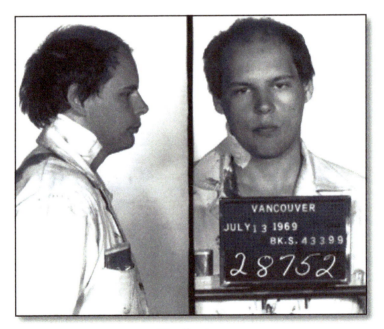

Headhunter.

The Segregation Unit by Any Other Name, the Hole

Prior to 1986, the operation of the Segregation unit at Kent remained unchanged from the days of the BC Pen. Although the physical appearance looked the same as other living units, it could be identified from the outside by a small exercise yard located on the east side of the living unit.

The Segregation unit was officially known as H-Unit, but was simply called the hole by those who worked there.

With the move of inmates from BC Pen to Kent, the practices, routines and operations remained mostly unchanged. While other living units operated with two correctional officers on the day shift, Segregation operated with up to six.

The operational routine was based on historical practices to ensure inmates housed in Segregation were under constant supervision. Inmates were divided into two categories—administrative and disciplinary—they were treated mostly the same. The administrative inmates were allowed a few, but significant privileges that punitive inmates were denied. Segregation was not so much about a place, rather a status whereby in extreme situations we could segregate an inmate anywhere within the prison should the need arise.

The administrative Segregation inmate was a person who had to be removed from normal population for various reasons, that is, some were too dangerous to be in contact with other inmates. Some bullied, while others were victimized so badly that they had to be segregated.

Punitive segregation was a common penalty given to inmates found guilty in what we called "Warden's Court" for offences against the Penitentiary Act. These offences ranged from being caught with drugs, or other offences against the good order of the Institution. With the new Corrections and Conditional Release Act (CCRA), punitive punishment would no longer be tolerated in Canadian prisons.

Six years into my career, I took the bold step to a correctional officer II position in the units, and later a rotation through Segregation, Main Communications Control Post (MCCP) and Central Control at Kent. When most got tired of the prison politics, we were fortunate to be able to find respite in MCCP-Central Control that overlooked the entire prison. While just another control post, MCCP in the pecking order was the pinnacle of responsibility. This nerve centre monitored everything within the fence lines, from alarms, issuing weapons in an emergency, to tallying the daily count. MCCP-Central served up different pressures which included both staff and public safety. We monitored cameras and the comings and goings of both staff, and inmates. In the event the correctional managers went down, that is taken hostage, the correctional officer at Central Control would be delegated as officer-in-charge.

MCCP was located in the central part of the prison, which made a convenient stop for staff on their way to their next post to drop by for a fresh cup of coffee, and share the latest gossip. There was no shortage of tall-tales and belly-laughs.

It was a two-year stint, and for action junkies, Segregation was the place to be. Being accepted by my peers, and securing a work assignment in Segregation was a rite of passage. It was truly a city within a city, and had its own special hierarchy. We were the police, the jailers, and first responders to an ungrateful, and angry population. Being a "Digger Pig", a nickname for those working in Segregation was a badge of honour, and came with its own sense of pride.

It was a cool place to work if you enjoyed the rush that came from fighting. Feedings, legal calls, showers and yard, along with the hourly range walks were just a few of duties performed in our day's routine. Intakes, and inmate movement times, meant we had to be hyper-vigilant. More often than not, inmates were not happy to be in Segregation, and acted out in creatively violent ways. Lighting fires, throwing feces, and yelling like babies was a daily occurrence. All inmates who entered the inner sanctum were stripped searched as we looked for contraband, which included drugs and weapons. Occasionally we received intelligence information of drug smuggling as inmates wanting to pass drugs into Segregation would gain entrance under the guise of inmate committee business, or some other fabricated reason. This was followed on occasion by placing the inmate in a dry cell: no running water, and two lucky officers watching his every move, or movement. Sifting through the inmate's waste was not glamorous as you can imagine, often assigned to innocent rookies. On occasion we were lucky to find packaged drugs dangling shamefully from an inmate's rectum.

The Preventative Security Officers (IPSO) were often the unappreciated members of our team. Fondly referred to as the "Secret Squirrels", these dedicated, and often mistrusted individuals worked in the shadows. Acting as the Institution's detectives, we relied on their intelligence gathering to expose those involved in the drug trade, or others looking to escape, or cause harm to staff or inmates.

Segregation was where the action was, and you needed to be on your game—a heightened sense of security was necessary as anything could happen. A simple range walk could turn dangerous in a flash. It wasn't just the daily threats; I've lost count of how many distressed inmates we have come across while on a shift. Some wanting out would be found dangling from a bed sheet; we called them "hangers". Others more commonly would slash their arms as they made one last cry for help. We became acutely aware of those who wanted to commit suicide, and those who were simply looking for attention. Inmates who truly wanted out knew the process of bypassing the veins making a vertical cut deep inside the wrist where the arteries lay waiting.

As we ventured down the tier on our hourly range walks, always on the lookout for our next tragedy, inmates would throw feces and urine through the cell door food slot as we walked by.

CHARALAMBOUS, Call Me Doctor [11]

There were many inmates posing different management problems while in Segregation, some famous, others infamous, most troublemakers, all dangerous.

The devil came in many shapes and sizes, and one inmate, a social outcast, for a brief time after his arrival was known as "Doctor Death", Dr. Joseph (Josephakis) CHARALAMBOUS.

The Surrey MD captured headlines when he hired a contract killer to snuff out the young life of 19-year-old Sian (pronounced Shawn) Simmonds.

Convicted of First Degree Murder, CHARALAMBOUS like all inmates convicted of heinous crimes (murder) would start their time at a maximum-security prison. Prior to his arrival at Kent we had been briefed that he possessed a black belt in karate further adding a heightened level of concern towards staff safety. When the shorter than-average unassuming doctor arrived, I was taken aback at his unremarkable demeanor. Dr. CHARALAMBOUS, or Mr. CHARALAMBOUS as I would later call him, was married, and had graduated from the University of British Columbia in 1981. His unhealthy attraction to young women was evident in his early relationship with a 15-year-old girl by the name of Shelley Joel, who would later become his wife. He was 43 when they first met.

By all accounts, Dr. CHARALAMBOUS had a successful medical practice. Cyprian-born, he along with his mother, father and siblings immigrated to Canada, settling in Vancouver to start a new life, better than the one in Cyprus. CHARALAMBOUS, while maintaining a busy practice, enjoyed risky behaviours such as a lunchtime passion for prostitutes, and gambling. A scandalous case, the public was riveted to the steamy details that dominated the media. Undertones of sex, drugs, and high-stakes gambling would be this man's downfall as he lived life in the very fast lane. What should have been a perfect life was anything but, as his sexual bent crossed over into his work life.

A young and trusting patient, Sian was reported to have been sexually assaulted while in his care, triggering a complaint to the College of Physicians and Surgeons. She would claim that CHARALAMBOUS had inappropriately touched both her and her sister during a medical examination. Now worried the sister's complaints to the College would end his successful medical practice, the doctor panicked. He was desperate, and would go to extraordinary measures to silence her for the last time. Two months before the disciplinary hearing was to commence, the ever-so-resourceful doctor managed to seek out the services of a hit man to kill Simmonds on Jan. 27, 1993—one day before her 20th birthday. Sian was slain in the basement of her Surrey home; two shots were effective in ending both her complaint, and her young life. David SCHENDLER, a cocaine-addicted killer later admitted to the tragic deed, outlining the $1,900 cash he was to receive, and a $5,500 drug debt that was to be forgiven.

CHARALAMBOUS came to Kent to start his 25-year sentence as I was beginning my time in Segregation. As an inmate food server brimming with confidence, CHARALAMBOUS and I worked side-by-side. I dished up the food, he would deliver the meals to each GP cell. It was during our work time we would share small talk about the latest medical advances. I found great pleasure poking the now shamed doctor at every opportunity but despite the daily digs, commenting on his annual income being reduced to a mere $6.90 a day he showed great composure never letting his contempt show.

Two years after the cold heartless murder, CHARALAMBOUS was unceremoniously stripped of his medical standing. In 1998,

CHARALAMBOUS was transferred to Mission where he appealed his conviction. The basis of which, he claimed, was his now-estranged wife was embroiled in an affair with the very Mountie investigating his case. CHARALAMBOUS, in his appeal would claim the court findings, and his conviction were now an injustice. He would assert these findings now the fruit from the poisonous tree. It came as no surprise, his appeal, along with his marriage, ended. His once prosperous medical practice destroyed, he now faced 25 years in prison.

It's What We Do

Correctional Officers are a vital link in the chain of protection of Canadian society, and the fulfillment of our Mission Statement. Every hour of every day, correctional officers staff the most dangerous posts in Canadian prisons. They do their utmost, and in most cases defy the odds of success ensuring the nation's penitentiaries are safe, and inmates are treated in a humane manner.

More than two hundred correctional officers and valued staff face off each day at Kent. I was too young, or naïve to realize the chance I was given was a valuable learning opportunity. Any day we came home alive was a blessing.

Any rookie officer, or visitor to Kent would tell you the passage through the green steel barrier, metal on metal slamming behind, was daunting. We made our way down the short Programs Corridor, but the journey seemed to take forever. We were taught to take a wide berth around each door opening, and be aware of our dangerous surroundings. Not a very positive environment to start my career.

The Programs Corridor held the Chapel, Library, National Parole Boardroom, Psychology offices, Admissions & Discharge and washrooms. It was often the scene of staff thundering down to the gym, Segregation or units, possibly responding to an emergency, which was a daily occurrence. With its freshly-waxed floor, was the Programs Corridor, the leading path to the main courtyard and cellblocks.

As you enter the courtyard, you are flanked by eight cellblocks, or living units. Each unit was compact, and self-contained, with a pool room, cooking area (servery) and 24 cells able to house 48 double-bunked inmates. A through H, split down the middle, A-B-C-D were general population units, and on the "opposing side" were the protective custody inmates, E-F-G-H.

You can't help but notice the brick walls riddled with bullet holes, each chip in the bricks façade was a telling story of a previous riot, and a reminder of Kent's violent past. Her resilience was testament to her strength and determination. Kent seemed to withstand the relentless attacks on her complex concrete, brick and steel construction.

The courtyard was the hub, the divide if you will, between east and west units. Four populations had to remain separate from each other. Venturing through the courtyard, it was not uncommon to hear the bellowing voices of the K-10 movement control officer supervising inmate movement (south end, Industries) with an iron fist, and partner, K-13, handling inmate movement from (north end, hospital control, visits to agency visits in V&C). Black or white, no grey areas. No pass, no movement.

The Importance of Having a Witty Comeback

Having a witty comeback was important for both staff, and inmates if one was going to survive a workplace hazing second to none. While crossing the courtyard during the lunchtime meal line I glanced over to a group of inmates eyeing my every move. I was just about to exit the courtyard when one inmate piped up, and shouted, "hey piggy, where's your tail"? Fearing the worst, and needing to respond to save face, my voice cracked,

I said, "waiting for me at home". A small insignificant event maybe, but to me it was everything. My sigh of relief, I am sure, could have been heard throughout the courtyard as I slinked to safety. Walking through the courtyard during movement times was stressful in my early days as we were outnumbered 100 to just a few, and like me, many of the newer officers were equally unnerved. Making the noon-hour trek to the lunchroom for the so-called "free lunch" was a questionable journey. Most days I would bring my own lunch until I became acclimatized to the short walk through the daunting inmate gauntlet.

Another witty comeback I used for a while when people would ask what I did for a living I would say, "I was someone's girlfriend in a hostage taking". In the beginning, I thought this was a funny thing to say; however, early in my career, being trapped in C-Unit, unable to escape the inmates and their death threats, was anything but funny.

A Correctional Officer's Lot Can Be Boring

The first thing I hope the reader will understand is a correctional officer is disconnected from the real world: inside those high walls, barbed wire fences, or solid iron gates. They are isolated from the public, their families, and sometimes from their co-workers.

Working as a correctional officer can be a fundamentally boring job, creating many opportunities for self-doubt, self-criticism, and self-destruction.

We relished the moments of peace on the job; however, there were few, often interrupted with sheer pandemonium. It wasn't a matter of if there would be a fight, or murder; it was a matter of when. I spent those early years on edge, waiting for the deafening radio call for help. There were two radio calls we would listen for, PPA, (Personal Protection Alarm) which was a small pager-like device worn on the officer's belt that could summon staff in an emergency. All too often these PPA alarms, designed to save a life, were false. A staff assistance call on the other hand, was an actual officer witnessing a problem, and calling for staff assistance. Correctional Officers filled with adrenaline never faltered, and responded like the professionals they were. I never witnessed a moment's hesitation.

The need for good communication was paramount as the job became more complex. Yelling at an inmate "go to your room" was a phrase I once used, and regretted. Choosing one's words carefully, not unlike a marriage, was critical to our survival. If one was well educated, the old guard, often threatened by the new breed of correctional officers, would make our lives a living hell. Only a few of the dinosaurs clung to the misguided belief a degree had no value when compared to on the job experience.

Loneliness on the job for those who did not fit in (me included) meant we would find ourselves harassed, and teased just like the not-so-good old school days. Harassment was rampant in the correctional environment, and no amount of respectful workplace seminars brought about change. That is just the way it was. As a recruit, I was told to sit down, and shut up, and heard, "opinions, bud, are like assholes, and everyone has one".

Control posts were mind numbingly boring, and we would rely on the unit CO-II for coffee along with other forms of entertainment of chatting on the telephone, or reading the newspaper wrapped in post orders. We sat in a giant fish bowl with the peering eyes glaring upon us, never offering a moment's piece from the endless demands. "Hey boss, crack 2", "lights on in 3", or "close 4 when I get in". Inmates demanded things right away, and were devoid of patience.

Mobiles (armed security vehicles) were as equally boring as unit bubbles. Rounds in the mobiles could whisk us away from the dangers of prison life, albeit short-lived. A break from the prying eyes of management, mobiles at least allowed us to get some fresh air; however it too, was challenging, as our four-hour patrol would land us back exactly where our journey began. The mobiles were the last defence against escape; fence and motion alarms broke up the monotonous routine of driving at such a slow speed, around, and around. For the most part these alarms could be triggered by a strong wind, or intruding wildlife, and were often false. Real or false we took great pleasure responding to fence or motion alarms as we would race our engines, and smoke our tires and speed to the activated alarm location. Other late-night entertainment for a bored motor patrol officer was the possibility of witnessing a visiting family of raccoons as they invaded our prison looking for an easy meal from various cell windows. You could almost set your watch to their arrival as mother, father, and babies would climb the fence, and carefully maneuver their way through the maze of sharp wire with ease. Each year brought a new generation of offspring.

In fairness, the environment, the system, and what it does to you, causes many guards, including me, to become jaded. Unfair treatment from management, harassment from staff, or getting in the way of others' personal agendas was the reality. An old guard once said, "We eat our own". It was simply not a nurturing environment, and did nothing to encourage personal growth.

Can you imagine a place where the entire population of those in residence were the worst ilk society could conjure up? To understand our prison system is to know we are the police of a small city. Inmates came to jail with colourful yet troubling background stories, growing up in abusive homes, with parents lashing out because of their own issues. Drug addiction, poverty, and in many cases a violent street life was often to blame. Now they realized their liberty, once enjoyed, was gone. The stigma of doing time, the family shame, and the monotonous daily routine of prison life was now their reality. Killers, drug dealers and sex offenders were my typical day at the office. The horrendous nature of their crimes, the entitlements many held as a right, was not for everyone. I often said I didn't really care what someone was in for, baby killers to murderers were all treated the same. Their crimes were horrendous, and unthinkable to any rational human. To even attempt to understand, or show compassion would usually end up compromising the officer, or being labeled a con-lover.

Kent was designed to be a self-contained facility, complete with hospital, school, and recreation (gym, weight pit, and tennis courts and sports field). For work, the inmates had in-unit jobs including unit cleaner and the ever-challenging shower cleaning position. There were the more coveted jobs in the kitchen that came with the privilege of extra food, to working in Industries, or taking programs.

When asked "how did work go today", my answers were filled with human tragedy, drugs, broken lives, and daily violence. To me, work at the prison was more about ridding society of its unwanted, as opposed to the rehabilitation of those cast off by society. Prison was not a place to get better, rather a trial of survival at best. I found the corrections model, with few exceptions neither protected the public, nor did it rehabilitate inmates. As with most, inmates upon completion of their sentence had become hardened, and wiser to prison life and criminal ways.

What little peace we had, or hoped to have, could suddenly be interrupted by total mayhem, or sheer terror. Many of the newer officers would dread the call for staff assistance not always because of the danger, rather because of the critique from peers, as they conducted a post-mortem on our every move. Managers were no better as we gathered around the boardroom table for the ever-condemning managers' briefing.

The Motorola Slap, a Defining Moment [12]

I was working the afternoon shift and my radio call sign was K-9; my partner was another correctional officer with the radio call sign of K-10.

The positions were referred to as Movement Control. Working with MCCP, it fell upon us to ensure neither the GP and PC populations mixed during movement times. Carrying only a radio, and stationed in the grass-and-concrete covered courtyard we were, for a brief four hours, the eyes and ears of the Institution. Our job was to oversee the clearing of inmates, and in the event of an emergency, be the first on scene.

My career was off to an awkward start, as I never seemed to fit in, not being one of the cool kids, some questioned my abilities. It was that afternoon when my true sense of self-worth would be put to the test. Standing in the courtyard I had overheard on the radio a CO-II, one of the B-unit officers now located in the phone room was terminating an inmate's telephone call due to inappropriate language with his girlfriend. Angry, the inmate stormed back to the unit and quickly became my problem. Witnessing his rather animated rant, I updated the staff member in the unit through his office window on the inmate's aggressive, and threatening disposition. As I walked toward the unit door, thinking I would sit in, suddenly the earth-shaking voice from MCCP emanated from my radio, "PPA Bravo-Unit". This was the real thing I thought, as I rushed to the unit, franticly pulling on the door. The doors echo reverberated loudly, alerting the bubble officer to my presence. I braced myself for what was waiting only steps away.

As I arrived at the unit office, unsure of what I was about to see, a ghastly sight of the inmate straddling the CO-II's almost lifeless body. The inmate frothing like a mad dog, was hitting the officer's temple with his closed fist. With the other he was striking devastating blows to the officer's left ribs. Hit after hit, seeing the blood-soaked officer, I realized I had only a second to act. The battering attack, still in progress, required desperate actions. What to do?

Not being an experienced fighter, it had to count. Armed only with my faithful Motorola radio, I withdrew it from its worn leather holster, and in one fluid motion struck the inmate with all the strength I could muster. This improvised smack down seemed effective as I heard the loud thump as my radio found the right side of his temple. He went down, and for a moment, lay stunned and lifeless on the cramped office floor. The momentary stillness was my chance to take control, the opportunity to once again improvise an arrest and control technique that would become known as "pure Neil MacLean". I launched my entire weight on the now-dazed inmate whose resistance seemed futile. I placed my two fingers up his nose, threatening as loud as I could, "Move mother fucker, and I'll rip your face off". Covered in blood, both of us struggled on the floor as the troops, my best friends of the moment, stormed the room to take control. My unorthodox take down technique later became known as the "Motorola slap", and had won the day.

There it was, the first knock-down-drag-out fight of my career. Though a tragic, and troubling assault, it was a proud moment for me, as I was able, in my small way to help. As we were cleaning up, one of the most respected correctional supervisors, Doug Cassin, handed me, as only Doug could do, a hastily penciled letter of commendation. Doug was a man's man, a wrestler in his off time, and a no-nonsense manager. He was liked, respected, and feared by those who played the fool. Though I managed to work through the horrific circumstances, it became the first of what seemed to be a career of endless fights, riots, and bloody murders. Those out-of-control days, the fights, and tragic deaths were the troubling foundation of PTSD, which quietly grew as the years went by.

Chapter 3

My Journey Continues

We've Been Called a Lot: Early Names, and Jailhouse Slang

Many expressions used in modern prisons came from the early days of jolly old England. Our laws are based on English Common Law, so it seems only fitting we would adopt a few of these quaint terms along the way. We have been called "turnkeys", "screws", "pigs", "bulls", "coppers", "boss", and "the man". "Keeper" was old school to mean keeper of the jail, and is still used to this day, albeit informally. A "gaol" (the British spelling of jail) dates to 1225, or a more modern name for a jail is "joint". Other slang included a "jail", "pokey", "slammer", "clink" or "cooler". To "jug up" was requesting a drink. Known as a "kite", often a small piece of paper that would detail a cryptic warning of a pending crime. "Ratting", or "dropping a dime" was telling on someone. "Rat" notes often were used as a redirection of an officer's attention, or to mislead staff. "Gassing" was throwing human feces or urine upon another. A "shank" or "shiv" was a knife, and a "rig" was used to inject drugs. The term "screw", originating from the French used by the English, referred to a turn-of-the-century work project requiring inmates to turn a water wheel by hand. When the officers wanted to inflict their own measure of justice, they would tighten the screw, making the water wheel rotation more difficult. A "window warrior" was either an officer who put on a false show of bravado towards inmates from within the safe confines of the control post, or an inmate who would beak off from behind his cell door. "Brew" was alcohol made from anything including ketchup, fruit juice, or bread.

Nicknames for sex offenders included "skinner", "diddler", "hound" "snapper", "cheese eater "or "Chester the Molester". These inmates were classified as Protective Custody inmates. A "fish" or "new meat" meant either a new inmate, or officer. When an inmate was in trouble with other inmates because of his crime, debts owed, or other conflict, he would often have to walk across the courtyard in a walk of shame to check in, or "go PC". To segregate an inmate, you would "scoop" or "box" them. To insert drugs or contraband into one's rectum was called "suit casing" a common practice for visitors coming to see loved ones.

Urban myth, or prison folk lore, but the rule never to be broken was whistling inside the prison walls. It seemed that when the jailer would march the condemned to his execution they would whistle a happy tune. The ban on whistling came more from the early pages of the "Con-Code" an understanding with the guards that any indiscriminate whistling would invoke a backlash from the inmates, including acts of violence.

Calling an inmate, a "goof" could be a death sentence as it implied one was a child molester, or sex offender. Taken from our English heritage to mean simpleton, it was transformed into a prison vernacular used for the most part in Canadian prisons.

My favourite was the importance we placed on two simple words: "no duff". This meant that an officer was telling the truth. One would only have to hear this disclaimer to instantly believe the storyteller.

If one inmate was up to no good he would enlist a tier mate or buddy to "stand 6" acting as the lookout while his buddy participated in an illegal activity such as tattooing, having sex or "tuning up" (beating) another. Catching a tattoo artist was the easiest because of the noise emanating from the tattoo gun. Those who stood "6" at the entrance to a living unit tier was a dead giveaway to trouble brewing down range.

Most times inmates would find a quiet place off the unit, in the gym, or at the back of a classroom to conduct their business. Usually the control post officer would advise us, allowing us to respond, hopefully catching them in the act, which was not always the smartest thing to do. Rookies would pounce upon the scene and could find themselves in something more sinister than simple tattooing. A "tune up" or "shanking" was a completely different matter, and always placed officers in a precarious, and dangerous position. It became a game of cat and mouse, and was fun when you caught the mouse. The smarter inmates were more discrete and difficult to catch, as they were aware of our hourly range walks. Some staff, not wanting the hassle, made it clear when they did their range walks, and never varied from their recognized pattern.

Later in my career, I noticed staff adopted the term "6 up" from inmates to warn staff as the correctional manager did rounds. The mad clicking of the radio transmitter button was another way to warn, or wake up an officer in a post about to be visited by the correctional manager.

Staff were to be referred to as correctional officers, so came the edict from the Assistant Commissioner of the day. Those with any measurable time in referred to "experienced officers" as guards: which to many was a badge of honour. I understood the need to be recognized as professionals, and the term of correctional officer was just another transition into the modern world of corrections, and the respect we so deserved. Correctional

Officer was a term or job title the media never understood, always referring to us as Guards.

Defining Who You Are, Classifications in Jail

The big tough GP inmates were the meanest, or so they thought, and hated the PC inmates who had raped women, children, killed or ratted. The robbers and murderers versus the sex offenders and rats was a real hate-hate relationship. Moving these very different inmates around the institution required the utmost of care. Each step was carefully choreographed via radio communication, as mixing the two populations was a recipe for disaster, and could prove deadly. One such occurrence was an incident between G/H units where opposing populations mixed. Funny when it happened to someone else, not so much if it happened to you.

I gravitated to the drama of daily prison life as I read inmate files (Author's note: no confidential or protected documents not released through Freedom of Information or already in the public domain were referenced). The depths to which they had fallen was beyond my comprehension. The higher the profile, the more horrific a crime, the more intriguing the read. The best crime novelist could not compete with these real-life crime stories.

I concluded over my years on the job that dysfunctional upbringings, drugs, and desperation led to poor life choices, and were usually at the centre of each inmate's tragic tale. Most inmates came from poor or abusive family backgrounds, but there were memorable ones who came from good homes, and wealthy parents. They ranged from the well-educated to those who were illiterate. It seemed there was no clear formula for success or failure, and parents with the best of intentions raised children who ended up in jail.

To define who they were, whether inmates or staff members, many used tattoos as a means of expression. Tattoos have long been associated with criminality, as gangs used this poor man's so-called art to show membership in various criminal organizations. Originally synonymous with the higher classes of society, tattoos had been the indelible marks of royalty, religious devotion, or pledges of one's love.

Among criminals, tattoos could record one's personal history. A teardrop under the eye could mean a variety of things including that the wearer had killed someone, spent time in prison, or the loss of a family, or fellow gang member. Sometimes only the person wearing the teardrop tattoo would know its true meaning.

The unexpected value of gang tattoos often warned others to stay clear, or marked their territory. The recording of gang-specific tattoos allowed authorities to place the inmate in an appropriate prison, unit or block. It identified the inmate's affiliations that often sprung from many Aboriginal gangs such as the Posse (prison gang formed in Stoney Mountain), the 712 and Indian Outlaws within BCs interior. Gangs across Canada include the Manitoba Warriors, Saskatchewan Warriors, the Native Syndicate and the Manitoba Bloodz. Police estimate up to 120 different gangs operate in British Columbia, mostly in the greater Vancouver area, and include the United Nations (UN), Independent Soldiers, Hells Angles, Chinese Triads to the Red Scorpions, all sporting their gang specific tattoos.

Most gangs have their claim to fame in the distribution of drugs, prostitution or money laundering, but also claim certain geographic areas (turf) as their own. Wearing colours on the outside is another way to identify one's gang loyalty. These organized crime syndicates also operate within the prison walls, and were an extension of the street gangs with each faction staking out their territory. Prisons were ripe for recruiting new members and selling drugs within the prison.

The tall prison walls and wired fences did not deter the gang's influence and reach to members on the inside who would be called upon to seek revenge against incarcerated gang members.

As another example of the CSC's ability to window dress, we no longer called them gangs; rather "security threat risk groups". Putting lipstick on a pig didn't take away from the fact it was still a pig.

A tattoo artist working within a gang was worth his weight in gold as this art form was the latest prison currency, and used by inmates as payment for drugs, gambling, or sex. In some cases, those in need of a tattoo would invite an inmate to their unit, or request an inter-unit transfer to be closer to the tattoo work location. Discovering the latest tattoo artist was also a game. We would see who was sporting a new "tat" during gym, or when they were shirtless in their cell. Prison tattoos were rather pedestrian in nature, and often became inflamed and infected.

During one afternoon shift on B-Unit, a young inmate from the GP side walked into my office beaming with pride over his new self-inked tattoo. The tattoo would spell certain death should his secret be uncovered. Two letters: "H A", seemed harmless enough to him. Nearly falling off my chair at the sight, I was quick to dash his hopes by explaining that unless he was a Hells Angels member, he couldn't walk around sporting another gang's brand. Membership after all, had its privileges. This inmate, childlike in many ways, made me wonder how he could survive in the GP population. His attention-seeking methods included coming into the unit office eating his own feces. I had seen many disturbing sights in my time, but this seemed to cap my tolerance level. A grown man eating his own feces was enough to turn any man's stomach.

With many forms of entertainment for inmates within the prison walls, inmates drinking prison hooch posed the most dangers to our staff. As a popular stress release for prisoners, a powerful jailhouse juice could be deadly in the wrong hands. "Brew master" was a term referring to an experienced maker of jailhouse elixir, and it took a certain level of skill to get it just right. Pruno, another slang for alcohol, could be made from apples, oranges, fruit cocktail, candy, ketchup, sugar, milk, and any type of bread that contained the much-needed yeast. The yeast in bread was used to shorten brew time. Some described the finished product as bile favoured wine cooler. The more sugar added, the greater the potential for a higher alcohol content. Prison hooch had to be brewed and consumed quickly to avoid detection. Whether it was brew made from catsup or various fruit cocktails, you would need a strong stomach to digest some of the more creative libations. Inmates needed clever hiding places for their concoctions, and were limited only by their imagination. Brew bags could be stashed in the old-style toilet tanks, mop rooms, common areas, and air vents to name a few. Staff took brew parties seriously, as many inmates became violent when they consumed alcohol. Taking a page from the BC Pen, and an experienced officer known as Bob, I would punch holes in the garbage bags in hopes of stifling the production of brew.

A look into an empty mop room was followed by a whiff in hopes of smelling the ever so pungent aroma. Fruit was closely monitored, however it was hard to deny fruit provided in a healthy diet. The search for brew, as with weapons or drugs, was a never-ending battle. In an effort to put the brakes on its production, we looked at ways of banning the distribution of fruit, or restricting its consumption to the dining hall. Despite these attempts to restrict fruit from leaving the dining hall, inmates managed to smuggle it out. Regular cell searches were an important part of the strategy against the war on drugs that also included the making of prison brew.

The "Con-Code"

The "Con-Code" can be traced back to the beginnings of prison life, and was established as a set of values with guidelines outlining a series of behavioural norms. Its tentative existence started to show its cracks as early as the 80s as the inmate population makeup started its gradual decline. Each classification of prisoner had its own "Con-Code" however, over the years, these jail-imposed rules seemed to become less and less important. The code of silence was the foundation of the "Con-Code" used with gangs in the community as well as prison populations. At Kent, we noticed an ever-changing profile of GP inmates that included a younger style of punk inmate, if you will. Crimes were becoming more violent, and just doing your own time was in jeopardy as gang violence, and drug dealers infiltrated the prison ranks.

Other "Con-Code" beliefs included: do not mess with others, refrain from arguments with fellow prisoners, do not exploit inmates, do not show weakness, and do not give the guards, or the world they represent any respect. Over time, many new rules were added to the "code" as were taken away. Honour among thieves, and "thou shalt not steal" were included as was the killing of a woman, or any offence against a child was forbidden. Any violations of these inmate principles could put you on the run, or worse, get you killed. Those who could not stand up to the lofty GP standards would end up going PC. Those with rival gang affiliations, pedophiles, and those needing protection due to the heinous nature of their crimes would often seek protection across the courtyard. High profile inmates like Terry DRIVER known as the Abbotsford Killer,[13] or Willy PICKTON automatically went PC as the sheer nature of their crimes would not be tolerated within the GP ranks. Ratting, or being a cell thief would also cause you a world of hurt.

As a correctional manager, I was tasked with avoiding the placement of an inmate in Segregation, or going PC. Alternatives included inmate committee mediation, or perhaps trying to work out a debt repayment plan. Once you take that plunge, you can never go back. We had many special needs, or needy inmates on the PC side who formed an unofficial PC within PC. They called themselves Super PC which I found ironic as they were the lowest, most pathetic high maintenance inmates one would have to deal with.

The GP inmates seemed to cling to the label of being stand up cons, yet many had buried secrets deep within their criminal profiles. One of the more memorable inmates I came across had killed his mother, father and siblings in a high-profile case in hopes of inheriting the family home. How he managed to stay GP to this day puzzles me.

Another GP inmate on my caseload killed his mother, and raped her dead body four days after her passing. One day while on a range walk, and listening to his fat gob harassing me with each step I took, I had had enough. I asked this stand-up con how his mother was doing. Fearing his secret would be exposed to his GP friends, he slunk back to his drum (cell), and never gave me another moment's trouble. I'll never forget the look on my partner's face, thinking we were going to be killed. She said later about me that I always kept it interesting.

Sticks and Stones, the Story Behind the Word "Goof"

I am reminded of the word "goof", and what it meant in the prison environment. To the average member of the public, it was silly, and only a little insulting, but in prison it could get you killed. Goof in prison means child molester, sex offender, bottom feeder, or lowest of the low. This one simple word caused a chain reaction never seen before in my time at Kent. An officer, no longer with us, made an off-the-cuff comment that had far-reaching ramifications when he told a GP inmate to "stop acting like a goof". Whether you call someone in prison a goof, or tell them to stop acting like one, makes little difference.

The Con-Code dictated that an inmate, embarrassed in front of his peers, would need to seek his twisted sense of revenge. Lashing out, he would beat the officer with a crudely fashioned aboriginal wooden paddle.

The inmate, now placed in Segregation, was quick to realize the consequences of his actions, and he himself, a victim of the officers "blue code".

As emotions turned to rage, another seasoned and respected officer not involved in the original situation, paid a late-night visit to Segregation for his own vigilante sense of justice. It was said he convinced the control post officer to open the cell door. The inmate now exposed, the officer offered our own so-called tune up, a vindication for the heinous assault against one of our own. This well-meaning, but foolish officer coerced others to buy into this scenario of revenge, and used the "blue-code" to convince others to keep quiet, dummy up, or deny any involvement. An assault of this magnitude would be expected to ignite a major investigation, and not long after, the stories being concocted, unraveled. The only access to the Segregation cells was either through a remote switch from within the J/K control post, or by special Folger Adams key also kept securely within the control post. Clearly, this was a conspiracy. At day's end, the officer in question after a long-distinguished career was terminated, and later allowed to retire. All for the blue-code. This well-respected officer and occasional acting correctional supervisor turned an honourable career into his shameful undoing.

As the spokesperson for the new union, I had stated correctional officers were tired of their working conditions, and this high-profile assault illustrated yet again the dangers of working in a prison. This assault added yet another to the 31 officers who had been assaulted in the preceding year at Kent. The union would call for the routine issue of pepper spray and handcuffs. Our victory was not forthcoming, nor was it a generous gesture from the system that claimed our safety as their concern. Lengthy battles, and an adjudication would force the CSC into compliance.

Death in the Private Family Visit Trailer—the Patricia Williams Story [14]

Few things ravage a family more than a period of incarceration, and every inmate, whether you like them, hate them, or are repulsed by their crime, realizes their families can be affected by the separation that incarceration brings, and its contribution to the families' breakup. This sad tale and the jailhouse drama provided allegations of drug use, and murder. She was 45, he 31, and by all intents was true love, or was it?

Patricia Scott was the proprietor of a successful antiques shop in Blackheath England, just south of London. This millionairess had been consumed by her thriving business, leaving her lonely. She answered a seemingly harmless pen pal ad from Canada – sharing her deepest desires for just over a year with Greg WILLIAMS an inmate at Kent. Eventually, Patricia, against the wishes of her family, specifically her brother Tom Scott, pulled up stakes, and ventured to Canada to marry the incarcerated man of her dreams. Madly in love, this unsuspecting wife would become his next victim. On Saturday, November 12, 1994 this 72-hour conjugal visit had been arranged.

The object of the Private Family Visit (PFV) program is to assist in maintaining relations between both the incarcerated inmate, and their family. As such, the program was open to everyone irrespective of any family ties: spouses, common-law, married, children, parents, foster parents, siblings, grandparents, or anyone the Institutional Head (Warden) felt had a clearly-established relationship with the inmate.

The PFV program consisted of a small cluster of mobile home style trailers on each penitentiary reserve, and dedicated exclusively for use by inmates and their family's private visits. The three PFV shacks located just feet away from the main entrance at Kent are surrounded by two exterior fences, just out of reach of freedom. These two-bedroom mobile homes were also called "sugar shacks" for obvious reasons, and were designed to replicate a typical apartment. These mobile homes may not have been the Hilton, but to most inmates they were valued escapes from the daily perils of prison life. Anything was better than the 9 x 12 cement cells, often unwillingly shared with another. While the program expanded in the 1970s, it really was not until the 1980s that the PFV program became a desired escape. A single occupancy PFV was called "Quiet Time". Each was mandated to offer PFVs with measures designed to promote and encourage behavioural changes of those incarcerated. There had to be a close familial bond to qualify, but it did not take much to meet the program's standard. After establishing a pattern of visits, following a correctional plan, demonstrating good behaviour (charge free), the inmate could apply for, and reserve a Private Family Visit. Many inmates would marry in prison, and honeymoon in the PFV.

Patricia Williams had arrived, filled with the hopes and dreams of any new bride, consumed with love, and the thought of seeing her new husband as she entered the gauntlet of security procedures. Her husband was known and described as a charmer, easy going and low key. One could see how an insecure female looking for love in all the wrong places could fall for the likes of him. A honeymoon of sorts, a 72-hour PFV with a sinister twist that would end tragically.

There was no doubt in anyone's mind Patricia was truly in love, but staff, unaware of the pending doom would approve their application. Her scheming new husband had orchestrated her demise with an overdose, a hot cap of heroin in hopes of inheriting her estimated 1.5-million-pound estate. Testimony at the BC Coroner's Court heard that a well-known drug dealer from within the walls was to supply heroin to kill WILLIAMS' wife.

Following this horrible event, the court heard the fabricated testimony as he described the death of his wife to be part of a mutual suicide pact. He would thank officials, and credited staff for prompt medical attention resulting in his survival. RCMP reports stated quite a different bone-chilling story of WILLIAMS taking just enough heroin to render himself unconscious, while administering the fatal dose to his new bride. Video evidence showed what was described as an angel, dressed in her pink pajamas, dead, lying next to her unconscious husband. In a plea-agreement WILLIAMS pled to the lesser charge of manslaughter, and received a 12-year concurrent sentence.

WILLIAMS was no stranger to the violent, criminal lifestyle he had willingly embraced. For his original crime of killing a 24-year-old mother of three, the courts now added another murder charge for Patricia's death, netting the psychopath a 25-year life sentence.

A few years later, he convinced his case management team that his behaviour warranted a transfer, and found his way over to Mountain. Looking older, but none the wiser, this killer's salt and pepper hair did nothing to hide the demon lurking just below the surface. I was working as the correctional manager responsible for Living Unit 2. This devil in human form was trying to plead his innocence to a prison charge in minor court which some called "Kangaroo Court". Sitting in a chair on the other side of my desk I said, "I remember you". This normally in control, middle-aged man was not in the driver's seat anymore. Try as he might, he could not remember me, which derailed his troubled train of thought as he stammered through his presentation.

Within a year of Patricia's passing, Reform Member of Parliament Randy White, the Official Opposition's Justice Critic, brought before Parliament 14 recommendations from the Coroner in Patricia Williams' tragic death. Being reactionary in nature, the Correctional Service of Canada adapted new polices hoping to avert tragic events like Patricia's death from ever reoccurring. A CSC Board of Investigation (BOI) found that the correctional officers were "sloppy in their supervision" and "slipshod in monitoring the couple's activities". Staff were reported to have "failed to take appropriate action" when they telephoned the PFV, and no one answered, it was reported that they did nothing.

Inmates, when booking their PFV package many had specifically requested not to book PFV #1; known as the death house as some said they felt Patricia's presence overlooking the PFV compound. Some inmates returning from their PFV, unaware of its gruesome history, spoke of an unsettling presence.

Due to the tragic death of Patricia, the program came under intense scrutiny resulting in new changes to polices which affected their use, and how they would be administered. The PFV Program became an earned privilege with stringent applicant screening guidelines. In addition, a big change would be "stand to counts" and random "wellness checks" for those participating in the PFV Program. During these checks, two officers would show up at the PFV with the intention to complete a walk-through inspection. We would try to keep it quick, and casual, looking for any signs of discord. Those convicted of sexually related, or family violence crimes were to be tracked, and those family members, or girlfriends wishing to participate in a PFV were made aware of the true nature of their loved one's crime.

This program is open to all inmates incarcerated in our federal prison system except for those in Segregation or the Special Handling Unit in

Quebec. It is during these visits inmates can cook up their own sense of normalcy, and pursue the physical, and emotional intimacy not possible in the regular visiting areas.

Some inmates were not eligible to participate in the program due to a demonstrated risk of family violence. Other exclusions resulted from an inmate found guilty of a disciplinary offense, or his behaviour threatened the safety of staff, or the institution (posed an escape risk). Inmates who have been convicted of drug smuggling, or participating actively in the drug sub-culture could also find themselves being excluded access to this coveted program.

Inmate Greg WILLIAMS lures his new bride into the Private Family Visit. He was later convicted in her death.

The Courtyard Killing of Gary ALLEN [15]

It was a Tuesday in February 1994, shortly after the noon feeding. Enjoying my lunchtime in the confines of my PC unit office, I was relaxing, feet up, taking in the peace that was soon to come to a crashing end. The courtyard was the usual buzz of activity, but today Hugh MCDONALD was about to be released from Segregation back into the open GP population of Kent. An ongoing feud between Gary ALLEN, and Hugh MCDONALD would bring these two foes together for one last time. Now in the courtyard, with a 25-centimetre shank taped to his arm, MCDONALD was ready to strike, and without hesitation came running up to ALLEN seeking his revenge. MCDONALD plunged the makeshift shank deep into ALLEN's stomach. Over and over he stabbed him, until ALLEN lay helpless on the grassy courtyard.

Nothing lasts forever, I thought, as a blood-curdling scream cut through the air, bringing my startled body to my feet. Looking through my barred office window, only a few feet away I was horrified to see Gary ALLEN lying in his own blood. Paying little notice of the dozens of cheering inmates in the courtyard, staff came to the aid of the fatally wounded ALLEN. One officer, a CORP mate, was quick of mind to kick to safety what would later be identified as the murder weapon. As staff removed his lifeless body you could see a trail of ALLEN's blood across the courtyard marking his final journey. Rushed to Kent's Health Care nursing staff tried to shore up the massive bleed. The once white floor tiles of Health Care now soaked up the bright red blood. ALLEN was transported to Chilliwack General Hospital, and later to Vancouver General Hospital where he succumbed to his injuries six days later.

MCDONALD, 11 years ALLEN's senior, was a slight man. Wiry and disheveled is how I remember him. His presence unassuming. Despite a two-page memo from a veteran Security Prevention Officer recommending

MCDONALD remain in Segregation, he was reintroduced back into the GP population.

MCDONALD had received information that ALLEN was looking to even the score, and would seek his revenge.

Gary ALLEN had an imposing stature, intimidating to most. Incarcerated at Kent and housed on the GP side, I did not much care for his bullying ways. His story, and violent criminal past dated back to 1974, mainly property offences; however, one charge of manslaughter.

MCDONALD was reported to be a killer doing time from back east for manslaughter when their paths would cross. MCDONALD had a deeply troubling criminal history. He was 36, working in the kitchen of Collins Bay when early one Sunday morning in the fall of 1978 MCDONALD stabbed correctional officer, and union Vice-President Francis Eustace outside the kitchen office. Eustace was in the process of talking inmate MACDONALD down after the initial incident when the inmate snapped, and fatally stabbed Officer Eustace.

Also killed was Food Services Officer Paul Maurice who was stabbed to death by MACDONALD in the kitchen area of the institution. Assistant Food Services Supervisor Frank Davall immediately rushed to the aid of Mr. Maurice and was stabbed in the attempt, but survived.

MCDONALD's actions that day earned him his elevated status as a "guard killer" within the "Con-Code" of the inmate population, and received another life sentence, 25 years without parole.

All violent inmates too dangerous to remain in open population are involuntarily transferred to the Special Handling Unit (SHU) in the Regional Reception Centre located in Sainte-Anne-des-Plaines, Quebec. Inmates transferred to the SHU through what we call a SHU package remain under close watch, and the tightest of security. As with all inmates within our service, a correctional plan is carefully developed to recommend programs specific to each inmate's criminogenic factors.

Transfer of an inmate to the SHU is an exceptional last recourse. The SHU, built in 1984 accommodated nearly 90 inmates divided into five wings, with two ranges on each wing.

Before an inmate can cascade down, (transfer, or return to a maximum-security environment) his file is closely tied to recommendations issued by a National Advisory Committee chaired by the CSC Commissioner.

Eventually MCDONALD's behaviour was deemed manageable, and after an extensive review by a Transfer Coordinator, he was transferred to Alberta's Edmonton Institution (Edmonton Max). MCDONALD and ALLEN had conflicting interests while incarcerated at Edmonton Institution competing in the institutional drug trade that would find them in a dangerous tug-of-war. In a fight over the control of the distribution of drugs within Edmonton Max, MACDONALD would confront ALLEN, stabbing him in 1984.

ALLEN was known as a strong-arm bully, and was feared by most. He had control of the flow of drugs using intimidation on those who fell from favour. During their time at Edmonton Max, the two had numerous violent confrontations resulting in their transfer to Kent.

In his defence, MCDONALD described a situation of "kill or be killed". The facts were indisputable, MCDONALD killed ALLEN. MCDONALD's legal pleading in part stated that a prisoner who defends himself by using deadly force where he believes, on reasonable grounds that he is facing a threat of death or serious bodily harm, is acting within his legal right.

Management, now faced with a public relations disaster, went into spin mode. To say they did not have an "inkling" as to MCDONALD's guard killing past was laughable. It was not plausible that a guard killer of MCDONALD's magnitude transferred into an institution would go unnoticed by staff and without their knowledge of his killing ways. It just didn't happen. Transfers are reviewed multiple times where high-profile inmates like MCDONALD had red flags, figuratively attached to their files. The sending Institution, Edmonton, would complete a report for the Warden's review. It would be further reviewed by the receiving institution's (Kent's) Warden.

MCDONALD was acquitted.

Looking back, I shudder at the blood-soaked crime scene in the idyllic courtyard of Kent, but I am filled with pride for the heroic staff who intervened without consideration for their personal safety. ALLEN's common-law spouse filed a civil suit against the Correctional Service of Canada. Named in the suit were several senior managers who claimed they should have reviewed the memo penned by the Security Intelligence Officer, and if so would have acted accordingly. The coroner's inquest held October 4, 1996 said that if they had paid credence to the report, the outcome that day might have been different.

A Novel Idea, An Author's Book Release [16]

I never paid much attention to the goings on in the Programs Department, thinking the only true rehabilitation was the six-cent solution (a bullet). Programs, I thought were for con lovers, the liberal thinkers, and the "take a skinner to dinner" types who were seen in an unflattering light by many in uniform. If I had had the insight to see past the anger and hate towards inmates I might have been surprised at their creative side, observing the normally repressive nature of prison that could not stifled.

The Simon Fraser University Writing Program encouraged inmates to channel their energy into this innovative writing program. Bruce CHESTER, Rod SCHNOB, and the more famous writings of Stephan

REID, married to well-known author Susan Musgrave were part of this program. Kent was a strange backdrop for a book launch of this nature, and became the first federal prison in Canadian history to hold such an event.

Kent's first author, REID penned Jackrabbit Parole which chronicled the life and times of a bank robber and escape artist. It was 1986 when the formation of the Stopwatch Gang was just getting underway. Ringleader Michael "Paddy" MITCHELL, Stephen REID, and Lionel WRIGHT organized what would become a whirlwind of crime sprees ending in a cross-border manhunt. The Stopwatch Gang was nicknamed for their use of a stopwatch worn by Stephen REID during their precision robberies of 100 banks in the United States and Canada, netting over 15 million dollars before being added to the Federal Bureau of Investigation's (FBI) most wanted list. Law enforcement officials called the gang's largest haul the "dream score" when they stole over 700 thousand dollars in gold bars from a Brinks armoured car at the Ottawa International airport in 1974.

MITCHELL had a long criminal history, and was captured during a solo bank robbery. MITCHELL would receive a 65-year sentence, and soon after was diagnosed with lung cancer. He would die in 2006, alone in a US prison.

REID who was eventually captured in an FBI raid in Arizona, was returned to Canada in 1980 and called Kent home for the next several years. REID was released on parole one year after my arrival at Kent, and lived with his new wife in Victoria until 1999. Struggling with a heroin addiction the court heard REID was strung out, and looking to score. He entered a bank in a homemade police uniform carrying a loaded shotgun, and made off with $93,000.00 cash. REID was convicted of a hostage-taking and attempted murder. Reflecting on his life lost, REID said there was nothing nostalgic about his first days holed up in a Vancouver Island jail in the fetal position as he battled withdrawal from his addiction. REID was sentenced to 18 years.

CHESTER, not one of my favourite inmates, presented as an angry man of Metis descent. He achieved the rank of published author with his book of poems entitled "Paper Radio". CHESTER described his motivation to write was born from boredom as he sat listening to the same old songs on the radio. Paper Radio provided insight into his prison experiences, and was a compilation of love poems with Aboriginal and prison themes. He gave a reading from his book outlining his high old times drinking homemade blueberry wine in his cell. Another Kent inmate who would follow the cerebral path of those before him was inmate Rod SCHNOB and his contribution, "A Thought before I Sleep".

Reader's Digest Comes to Kent [17]

Our chance as correctional officers to tell our story about real life inside a federal penitentiary came in 2006. It was in direct contrast to the usually closed, and secretive management policy of "no news was good news". Our 15 minutes of fame offered a surprising, if not shocking, insightful look into the Canadian prison system. "If it bleeds, it leads" was the theme in these true stories from Reader's Digest. Crime writer Jim Hutchison came to Kent in hopes of exposing the underbelly of a maximum-security prison. I had to admire the writer as he sat with us in control posts, drove in mobiles, and sat in many of the unit offices talking with both staff, and inmates. I have never witnessed such unprecedented access to our officers, their stories, and the risk it presented. The title page was "A Week Inside a Max". "There is no other job where every day you work with people who hate you, and given the opportunity, would slit your throat", so says Neil MacLean, Acting Correctional Supervisor. I will give this reporter credit for staying the course over several weeks, listening to our stories, risking his own life to feel the pulse, and tell the unadulterated story. As you pass through the green barrier, you may take notice of the red line running across the waxed and shiny tiled floor of the Programs Corridor. Although it was never written, inmates understood the consequences of crossing the red line: one risked being shot by an officer through the gun port at Central Control.

He starts his story with shocking statistics from the year where 48 staff assaults occurred during a very trying year at Kent. Wanting to experience prison life at its roots, the ever-curious reporter had himself locked in a typical concrete cell. He notes a rather cold and impersonal cell (or drum as they are called) with dirty toilet, wash basin, single bed and small worn desk with plastic chair. Staff tell Hutchison the stomach-churning stories of Kent, pointing out the now-faded bloodstains throughout the prison that illustrate their own horrific stories.

Hutchison wrote of the black day, June 16, 2003, when inmates in Alpha, Bravo and Charlie units stormed the offices to attack and kill staff. Some were wearing balaclavas and carrying makeshift weapons such as sharpened broomsticks. Personal Protection Alarms (PPAs) were activated, and rang out in MCCP calling staff into action. The inmates set the cellblocks on fire.

Staff were lined up in the courtyard side by each armed with shot-guns and pepper spray watching in horror as our beloved prison was brutally attacked from within. As the night dragged on, 30 heavily armed Emergency Response Team members were summoned from the community. By the early morning hours, Kent was contained, and the riot was finally over. Although there have been numerous riots, and hundreds of incidents over the years, never in our history had I seen such destruction. I was proud to be one of the many staff interviewed, spinning many a story from my 19 years at Kent.

Chapter 4

Life on the Unit

The units, big or small, had much in common; they housed inmates, staff watched them, and bad things happened. The job of a COII, or living unit officer had a unique set of challenges, different than the static job of a CO-I I was accustomed to.

A regular unit with an assigned partner could be a blessing, or curse, depending if you got along. I was honoured to have worked with exceptional officers the likes of Al, Mark, Shawn, and a cast of remarkable characters left me with lasting memories. After six years, I had made the transition to CO-II in Charlie Unit (C). At the time, C-Unit was possibly one of the toughest GP units, but provided the greatest learning opportunities. Sensing my inexperience, a few inmates were relentless in their daily efforts to intimidate. It was black and white. No blurred boundaries with me, I just followed the rules. As most inmates wanted more, I found myself at loggerheads trying as they might to wear me down.

After the morning briefing we would march off to our assigned units and start the day with the morning count. Some inmates who were employed as kitchen workers went off to work early, so we had to be mindful of their absence so as not to telephone the count board with the wrong numbers.

There was a pressure to get it right, a responsibility lost on a select few. Some correctional officers did what we called a "board count", too lazy to go up on the tier they would call in whatever the board indicated. Board counts most times did not reflect the correct numbers, causing annoying delays. Once the count was correct, our day would begin. "Release the hounds" we would say, as inmates would rush to breakfast. We would then report to either the meal line, or courtyard duties.

Getting "courtyard duty" was a chance to give the smokers a much-needed smoke break (later ironically called a "health break"), which left the lone officer in the unit to perform range walks, and answer a volley of inmate questions. To understand the mentality of the inmate, one had to realize they were not unlike children. The difference being, their demands were backed with the risk of extreme violence. Policy dictated the use of written request forms, however many inmates would try to circumvent the system by asking the officer to phone in their ever-so-important demand. Patience was not an inmate's strong suit, and good communication between staff would identify "guard shoppers". This meant asking different staff the same request in hopes of eventually snagging someone to expedite their request.

I enjoyed working the units; they were compact and the population smaller in numbers. To "crack to the man" (jailhouse slang for talk to a guard) was for the most part unheard of on the GP side so for me, most times, it was a quiet shift. The reversal was true on the PC side as we couldn't keep them away from the office. PC inmates were needy, taking every opportunity to strike up conversations with officers, or share a joke.

Picking up supplies, making booked phone calls, doing range walks, and arguing with inmates was our daily grind. Most officers had their own routines, or special quirks; mine was cleaning, and neatly rewriting the unit count board. Maybe it was boredom, or perhaps Obsessive-Compulsive

Disorder (OCD) as I enjoyed mopping my office and washroom floors, and making coffee. Before computers, our Incident Observation Reports and Casework Records were hand-written, and picked up daily for input by the unit clerks. Our first computer, known as an Intel 8036 microprocessor, introduced in the mid-80s, provided an exciting new way to pass the time, and my first introduction to these high tech marvels.

Inmate behavioral reports known as Casework Records were an important aspect of our duties providing IPOs with vital information. I would interview each inmate on my caseload throughout the month noting the behavioral changes of inmates. These reports could be invaluable, understanding the inmate's daily progress against their identified objectives.

Inmates had many shortcomings, including lack of anger control, drug abuse, and a myriad of mental health issues.

Inmates fell short on many personal care and social fronts, resulting in their cells becoming cluttered and dirty. Many lived liked pigs, yet when it came time for visits they would be washed up for mommy, daddy, or their girlfriend as part of their ongoing charade. Cell searches were an important part of our duties. Some inmates would booby trap their cells with hidden razor blades, or some would spread feces, or other bodily fluids about their cell awaiting the unsuspecting correctional officer.

Even though communication was important to safety and efficiency, only specific movement control officers, mobiles, or control post officers had two-way radios. Working in the units, we used hand signals while communicating on the range, or listened in on the intercom of each tier. Sometimes the calm was rudely interrupted by the storm when our control post officer would scream "PPA" (Personal Portable Alarm), calling us to action. The PPA was acquired by hard-fought battles between union and management. An article taken from the Kent Peeper, a newsletter for staff, colourfully articulated their importance, which read, "Without warning,

Joe enters the unit office where he starts demanding a legal phone call NOW! Officer Chesneski (a fictional officer featured in the Kent Peeper) attempts to calm Joe down, but the task was impossible as Joe became irate, finally taking a swing at the officer. A quick move of his right hand, Chesneski activates his silent partner, the PPA. A few seconds later, the announcement is made "PPA in Echo unit". Suddenly, the welcome troops arrive. Two, five, 10 staff arrive, willing, and ready to assist. In addition, what of Joe? Thirty days punitive dissociation. Chesneski was shook up, but unharmed. The Health & Safety Committee, comprised of staff, and management wrote articles like this in attempts to simulate a real-life emergency, and show the value of the PPA. All too often these life savers of technology would be activated in the most embarrassing situations including those in the washroom with their pants down, or when staff were sitting with their feet up taking advantage of a well-deserved break.

Responding to emergencies throughout my career I am not surprised at the beating my knees took with all the running on the unforgiving concrete.

Working the unit, I would first set up for the day, making coffee then joining my partner on our first range walk and count, hoping we wouldn't discover a hanger (suicide). I have seen many things through the cell door window, many peculiar, and horrible things I could not unsee.

Prior to the riot in 2003 one of our jobs was meal line duties. Imagine if you will, a small dining hall with the absolute worst in human beings, all with table knives in hand, a recipe for disaster. Two officers would stand in the dining hall, with an armed correctional officer overlooking from the gun walk with two or three officers stationed at the entrance to the dining hall. Our job was to maintain the peace, and ensure the GP kitchen workers would not taunt the PCs who were eating. Inmates were given 30 minutes to eat, with an additional 30 minutes to clear the dining hall and courtyard before reporting to work, school, or their units for lock up. Often the inmate kitchen workers would yell "skinner" and other comments through the meal tray slide trying to provoke a response in the ongoing battle of nit-wits.

One morning, like any other, groggy inmates sat down for breakfast. Our food service officers (FSOs) prepared generous meals consisting of a healthy portion of eggs, bacon, cereal, milk and coffee and juice.

Clearing the dining hall was always a chore as inmates were disrespectful towards authority, and pushed back at every opportunity. One inmate not finished his morning porridge was having nothing to do with my directions. As I approached this stubbornly rude inmate, I gave him a direct order. Refusing to budge, the inmate responded with, "I'm not finished yet, you fat fuck, take a hike". Angered at the disrespect, but not wanting to be shown up by an inmate, I took my gloved hand, and placed my thumb in his "just right" porridge stating "I guess you're finished now"?

Once inmates returned from the courtyard, we conducted a "shop count". Unless an inmate was employed in one of the unit based jobs such as unit cleaner, shower cleaner or another make-work "McJob", the inmates were locked up until the next mealtime. Many stubborn inmates who refused to be locked up would be met with a direct order, or charge, often ending in name-calling, daily threats, or a PPA.

As the day progressed, inmates were scheduled for a multitude of meetings, appointments or work. Every movement needed a written pass authorizing the inmate for specific appointments in Health Care, Chapel, or to see their IPO. Inmates were relentless in their efforts to forge passes, or convince staff to allow an authorized pass to be issued.

When things got boring, I saw the value of working the different units. From GP to PC, Segregation to MCCP, I never allowed the dust to settle. I took advantage of new positions, promotions, and learning opportunities that would later serve me well. When others were engrossed in what would later become "email gate", I was researching Commissioner's Directives putting together study packages for upcoming competitions.

Starting out at Kent was a blessing. Just over 19 ½ years at a maximum-security prison provided me with a strong foundation in security work, and a chance to build my character, or brand as an officer. Like proud milestones, each day challenged my innermost fears. Passive by nature, I had to reinvent myself, or die trying.

One of my early performance evaluations from 1991 drew a smile as I reflected on the early days, and how I was received.

> *"Mr. MacLean is a conscientious officer who, if anything, tries too hard, things seem to go too slow for him. He must try to settle down, and let the rest of the world catch up with him then he will see things as everyone else does".*

At the time, outraged at the impersonal, and uncaring evaluation, 25 years later I concluded my supervisors' remarks were in fact spot on.

Working in a maximum-security environment meant I experienced just about every human emotion and tragedy. When I say, I have seen it all, I mean, I've seen it all. Murders, suicides, assaults, and drug overdoses, all were a part of our day at the office. In such a tough place, most made it out alive, but some did not. I understand that 1 in 20 correctional officers (2017) and staff suffer from the effects of Post-Traumatic Stress Disorder (PTSD). The compounding effect was sometimes more than a fragile human spirit could take. I was not specifically aware of the stress, as it was subtle, raising its ugly head in the form of personality quirks, including short tempers, poor coping skills, to an aversion to loud noises. Many professions from the police, paramedics, firefighters, nurses, the

911 Operators who deal with the stress as they dispatch those troubling calls, to my personal heroes in Canada's Armed Forces. PTSD would wreak havoc on many levels, and a wide variety of professions, leaving the unsuspecting worker stressed out, burnt out, unable to cope with the workplace horrors.

Drugs in prison, as on the street, was a growing problem. Heroin was cheap, and easily accessible to the desperate drug addict. To address the growing number of inmates addicted to drugs coming to prison, the medical community developed the Methadone Maintenance Program designed to assist inmates to either kick their habit, or reduce their dependence on various narcotics. Each morning like clockwork the place would come alive as inmates leaped from bunks racing to the medi-line to down their morning elixir.

To combat the war on drugs, we established brew searches randomly selecting, or profiling specific inmates known to dabble in the drug trade, or those known as brew masters. Prison brew was deadly in the wrong hands, and finding it was an important part of our search strategies.

On a Sunday morning range walk we would take extra time to perform a weekly "bar bang". Taking our sledgehammer, we would check for loose or hollow cell window bars to ensure no one was planning an escape. Authorities later banned dental floss from the inmate canteen, as inmates would coat the string-like material with toothpaste to assist them in cutting through the bars. Little did they know just how ineffective this escape method was, yet we were vigilant in our morning routine, along with our daily cell searches.

On a nice day, courtyard duty was a chance to get out of the stale unit, and take in the fresh air. Officers stood watch on the opposite side of the courtyard while the inmates enjoyed Mother Nature. When the word came down via the public-address system to "clear the courtyard, return to your unit", we would slowly converge on the inmates, herding them like cattle, back into the units, ever so slowly. Most times inmates would only move as we approached, wanting to make every moment count, or simply show defiance towards "the man".

One day while working C-unit, a rather obnoxious GP biker type inmate came into the office and attempted to intimidate me as he tried each working day. He asked if it were true, "You ride a Jap bike"? he asked. Owning a Harley was the standard of the criminal elite and the thought of riding anything else was beneath him. My response was "yes", but at least my bike wasn't wrapped in plastic for 10 years.

Throughout my career I worked the bubbles to the units, unlike some I enjoyed the change. Recognizing it was time for a move, I was offered an opportunity to act in the correctional supervisors' office in 2004. It was a wild ride lasting my remaining 10 years of my career.

Chapter 5

Brazen Escapes

Those in the business of corrections understand that as long as there are inmates, there would be escapes. No surprise that the CSC Pacific Region has had its share. In our relatively short history, correctional officers have adapted, and stepped up when needed, responding to the occasional escape attempt. Most inmates have nothing but time on their hands, thus providing ample opportunities to plan their getaways. To staff's credit, they have thwarted more escape plans than not.

Shaughnessy Hospital, the Escapes of Inmate LAVOIE [18]

Within months of the grand opening of Kent, the paint barely dry, Gilbert LAVOIE escaped lawful custody while in Vancouver's Shaughnessy Hospital. In for elective hand surgery, LAVOIE somehow acquired a gun, and held it on the guard, demanding his hands and legs be unshackled. Fearing for his life, the guard on duty, Daniel Cowie complied.

LAVOIE was serving just over eight years for armed robbery, and possession of a restricted weapon when the escape occurred. Cowie was quickly arrested for what authorities thought was his involvement in the escape, and later charged with three counts of aiding in an escape from custody. The judge heard of this daring escape during Cowie's court testimony.

On the lam, LAVOIE was recaptured at a house party in Vancouver and later he refused to give evidence against the veteran officer stating he wanted to remain neutral. Cowie, innocent until proven guilty, was suspended without pay until a "stay" of proceedings was announced. Police officials stated Cowie was a "damn fine officer". He would later be acquitted on all charges.

Later on July 22, 1980, LAVOIE was once again at Shaughnessy Hospital and during a pre-surgery shower, LAVOIE produced a zip gun (prison made handgun) and locked the unsuspecting guards in a shower stall. He escaped wearing a flimsy hospital gown, only to be recaptured a short time later.

Hospital escort duty was great for getting away from the drama that befell prison life, but it came with its own set of risks for officers, and the community. We were always on high alert, and I assume, the reason nurses cringed when we arrived on their hospital doorstep. I remember one supervisor directed me to empty the rounds of my revolver before we would enter the hospital. This was an outrageous direction as any gun is always assumed to be loaded. Not wanting to be disciplined, or the drama, I went into the washroom on a pretense of cooperation, returning minutes later satisfying my partner, thinking I had emptied the revolver's cylinder.

BUTLER-MARTIN Box Escape [19]

In May 1982, Inmates BUTLER and MARTIN from F-Block were working in Kent's cabinet shop, one of the more coveted jobs due to the pay, and a chance of overtime. Going unnoticed by staff, the pair managed to fashion a hiding place out of an equestrian jumping box that was constructed as part of the government's Corcan furniture contract. Later, riding within the transport truck departed Kent undetected, the two felons with the driver unaware of the unauthorized and desperate hitchhikers. Only when stopped at the Rosedale railway crossing did the driver notice two inmates jump from the confines of his vehicle. Shocked at what he had witnessed, he called the RCMP, and the two escapees were recaptured a few hours later. Although many historians believe the STEWART box escape was Kent's first box escape, it was in fact 1982 the BUTLER-MARTIN box escape that held that dubious honour.

Mad Dash to Freedom [20]

Early one morning, the weather conditions were perfect for an impromptu departure from the maximum-security facility of Kent, as low-lying fog shrouded the fence line. Each morning inmates would be marched behind the units to their various work locations. With the day's work underway inmates Stuart STONECHILD (guard killer) and Willy BLAKE managed to crawl out the school window and cut a hole in the perimeter fence just behind G/H units. The mobile patrol officer driving the perimeter noticed the cut fence, and radioed his shocking discovery. The two inmates, now fugitives, made the rough trek with each foot step sinking into the freshly tilled farmers' fields surrounding Kent, and across Number 7 Highway.

By now the morning count was "not correct", two were confirmed missing, and staff would sound the alarm. With all escapes there is a level of organized confusion as officers follow escape protocols. Several were dispatched into the community in hopes of maintaining an impenetrable perimeter. One officer told his version, laughing at the confusion. Spotting the two inmates near a pile of freshly cut lumber, he radioed Mount Woodside as his position. Only yards off the road in plain sight the inmates refused to give up. Correctional Officer Matt Brown, was ordered to observe and report while he waited patiently for the nearest RCMP dog team to arrive on scene.

As the Surrey Mounties arrived, it didn't take long for the pair to realize the hopelessness of their predicament, and surrendered without incident. Both had taken their medicine bundles along, which were later seized by police. The police would claim the medicine bundles were devices to disguise human scent in case tracker dogs were used.

Medicine bundles represented an important aspect of their spiritual beliefs, and dumping the contents to the floor outraged inmates giving purpose to an impromptu protest decrying the outrageous police actions with a hunger strike. Lasting 34 days, the protest spread throughout BC involving other prisons across Canada. The Correctional Service of Canada would eventually recognize the spiritual significance of the medicine bundles while keeping them tightly controlled. Medicine bundles to the Aboriginal people were no different than the rosary, or the cross in regard to the spiritual significance held by most Christians. Many of the cloth bundles were kept in their cells with tags identifying them as such. During a search, we would request an Elder to attend, or in their absence, a native officer would be called to observe the search.

LANDRY Box Escape[21]

In the spring of 1985, yet another inmate unhappy with his lot in life tried to escape the forbidding double fences of Kent. Working in the warehouse, inmate LANDRY managed to hollow out a stack of corrugated cardboard boxes used to ship completed Corcan orders. Knowing the pickup and delivery schedule, he lay in wait. Because the count was not correct, staff in each department were desperately searching every possible hiding place. Hoping to evade detection, LANDRY lay still for what must have seemed an eternity. A few hours later, warehouse employees discovered his hiding place.

Canada's First Helicopter Escape [22]

As the morning of June 18, 1990 progressed, the sun was not quite ready to shine, dew still on the morning grass as I arrived home from my graveyard shift. The events that would launch us onto the international stage were about to commence. Poised and ready for my daily infusion of caffeine, I was joined by my correctional officer friend and carpool buddy, the late Ellen Daniels. Our mundane conversation was suddenly interrupted. The phone rang; it was an officer from Kent. The voice at the other end sounded stressed, "Can you come in, there's been an incident"? His final words as the receiver went crashing onto the phone's cradle were "No duff". I knew there was trouble. "No duff" was military slang indicating this was not a drill. We grabbed our jackets as I explained to Ellen what had transpired, we made our way, still in uniform, to her car. Not knowing what to expect, and filled with adrenaline, we raced as fast as her used import would take us. When we arrived at Kent, the parking lot was awash with cars. We reported to the correctional supervisor's office where we were quickly directed to the staff briefing room. A sea of uniforms, all looking equally curious, as Correctional Officer Gary Bennett, who by chance was working in the mobile patrol (Kent Patrol 2), now relieved was entertaining his audience. On the edge of my chair and eager to find out more, I learned the shocking news: Kent was the scene of a horrific helicopter escape, leaving one officer seriously injured.

Gary's animated arm gestures had his peers in a state of disbelief. Taking aim, Gary motioned to the crowd showing his two-handed grip as he pretended to shoot at the underside of the helicopter hovering above. My thoughts raced, who stands directly under a helicopter and tries to shoot it down? I asked myself what had Gary done? How was the union going to defend his actions? My mind conjured up different scenarios. Was he in real trouble, or the hero he later became?

It all started just after 7:00 am, Fred Fandrich, owner of Valley Helicopter was busy going about his daily duties planning a flying tour for a local realtor when a masked man wearing green coveralls, work boots, and rubber gas mask stormed into his hangar.

Fred, who founded a new helicopter business in 1985, was working at the Hope Airport, three hours east of Vancouver. As the need for flying services increased, so had the demand on Fred's new business. Flying is what Fred loved, and as he built his business, he went where the money was. Valley Helicopter steadfastly growing when Fred saw a great opportunity and capitalized on the building of the new and exciting Coquihalla Highway just in time for an expected flow of eager tourists as they made their way to Expo 86. This well-educated 50-year-old business man understood the mechanics of running a business, but also knew what made his birds fly. He had been in the aviation business most of his adult life, from the fixed wing adventures of a fly-by-the-seat bush pilot, to obtaining his helicopter endorsement in 1968.

Fred found himself at the wrong end of a Ruger mini 14 semi-automatic rifle when the gunman forced Fred to ready the helicopter for the unexpected flight. He was kidnapped, and forced to fly his Bell Jet Ranger 206 helicopter to a small abandoned airstrip just outside of Hope.

Setting down, hidden from prying eyes, the pair would wait until just the right moment before descending into the Upper Fraser Valley's only maximum-security prison.

Kent would soon go down in the annals of Canadian history. The gunman had come equipped to kill the police would later say, as they noted he carried a semi-automatic rifle, wore a bulletproof vest, and carried on his belt what appeared to be grenades.

At 7:30 am the unknown gunman jabbed his rifle in a threatening manner towards Fred, demanding he remove the helicopter's radio headset. "From now on, all you do is take orders from me". Fred described how every minute was marked by his beating heart: it grew louder and louder. He forced himself to keep his cool and stay in control of his emotions. Failure to do so would mean certain death.

As Fred approached Kent, he swooped in low, 50 feet above the ground, by Tower 2 at the south end of the prison behind the Industries Department. Normally the prison was a buzz of routine activity, but today was going to be different.

As correctional officers and other staff were briefed, management was arriving for the day, preparing for the Warden's Lockdown Briefing. Works staff were in place and getting ready for a busy Monday. On a regular workday most departments had inmate workers, however during a surprise lockdown staff completed assigned work duties on their own while officers searched the units. The Works Department, in the bowels of the prison at the southernmost point, would be the centre of attention in the minutes to come. The Industries area included the school, Supply and Services (SIS) and Corcan (furniture fabrications). At the back of Industries was an outside break area where inmates and staff could enjoy a smoke.

On the inside, at the entrance to a long, cold tunnel leading to Works was the galvanized "egg slicer" (turnstile) as some staff called it. Working for the Chief of Works, a clerk was busy in her windowless office reviewing data entries on the computer when they heard the faint whop, whop, whop of a helicopter emanating from the rear of the building. Their curiosity got the better of them as they decided to leave the safety of their office to investigate. The noise became unbearably loud when it dawned on them that it would be highly unusual for any helicopter to be found flying around the prison. The pair proceeded cautiously down the corridor leading to the exterior of the building, carefully opening the door. They heard the unmistakable sound of gunfire. The pop, pop, pop seemed relentless, like firecrackers. The clerk, a former correctional officer, knew intuitively it was gunfire. As fast as the door opened, it slammed shut. The two retreated to the safety of their office when moments later they could hear the pounding footsteps of the responding correctional officers, their boots hitting the hard-concrete floor in unison as they raced to the scene.

The gunman's original plan was to swoop down behind Industries, pick up two inmates, one a Kitchen worker and the other a Works inmate, and make their escape. According to court documents, with the surprise lockdown and the relocation of inmates to the sports field a new plan had to be devised. With no ability to telephone his community accomplice with the change in pick up location, a new plan unfolded on the fly. Inmate Robert Lee FORD normally employed in Works to empty the garbage bins from behind the kitchen was unaware of the surprise search that would prove to be a daunting change in his plans. A well-known drug dealer, FORD had a history of escape, including one from Wilkinson Road Provincial Prison just outside of Victoria where he was awaiting trial for the murder of Gary Hardy on January 18, 1988. After his conviction he had been transferred to Kent. FORD was now in "my house", and served his time until June 18, 1990 when his back-page story became an international front-page headline.

Known as the mastermind behind the helicopter escape, FORD collaborated with another inmate, known to the "in crowd" but never officially charged. Due to his foreboding stature, he was unable to climb the internal fence, and was left behind in the sports field. Inmate Dave Ross THOMAS, also in the sports field, took FORD's last-minute invitation on a lark, and joined FORD in what later became known as the Run, Climb, and Fly escape.

With all these unexpected changes, FORD and THOMAS decided to make a swift run across the sports field, and circumnavigate the inmates scattered about. They climbed two interior fences, and ran through the Native Sweat Lodge. Overlooking the sports field were two-armed guards in each of the two towers, and two armed officers in each of the two security mobiles that patrolled the perimeter road along the prison fence line.

As Fred approached the prison the masked gunman barked orders to land at the rear of the yard to snatch up the two inmates. Fred managed to dodge the officer's bullets as they cut through the summer's air, managing to maneuver between the many obstacles in the prison yard. Other obstacles that would challenge even the most seasoned veteran included the over-powering, in-your-face, two-storey metal tower, a fence line topped with barbed wire, and an assortment of lawn maintenance equipment that lay strewn throughout the makeshift landing zone. The pickup spot would prove a worthy adversary for even this experienced helicopter pilot. There was no dress rehearsal, just swoop in and out, with only seconds to complete the task hoping not to be blown out of the sky. The slightest slip of the flight stick could prove deadly.

This type of daring escape was not in our training manual. Fred was under incredible stress, not knowing whether he would be shot, shot down, or die in a fiery crash. Was the pilot a hostage, or a willing participant? These were questions racing through everyone's mind, and with no time to think, they just reacted to the best of their abilities! Fred later told of his treatment by the RCMP. They believed him initially to be a suspect, and grilled him like a common criminal.

As the helicopter approached the landing zone, Fred's sweat-covered hand guided the helicopter in. The gunman screamed at Fred, "Keep going lower". Just moments before the fence alarm sounded, Correctional Officer Rip Kirby, who had been patrolling the staff parking lot saw the chopper approaching Tower 2, and notified the prison's communication centre. As the helicopter approached the exterior fence, it hovered above the ground, and the gunman let loose with what seemed like a never-ending explosion of rifle fire, almost bursting Fred's eardrums. The wash from the helicopter's rotor blades stirred up a dust storm setting off the motion-sensitive fence alarms, and alerted the other mobile patrol officer to the real-life intrusion. It became clear, very quickly this was not a routine fence alarm like so many before. The officers who were patrolling the perimeter were at the ready, and both responded. Gary Bennett responded to the getaway point outside the fence line and just under Tower 2.

At 8:43 am, the unknown gunman in the chopper opened fire on Rip, who was now pinned down. Rip was seriously injured but surprisingly, managed a combat roll out of Kent Patrol 1 to find cover behind the oversized propane tank in the flat bed of his green Dodge pickup. Rip lay bleeding, his knee torn apart and bloody he was still able to return fire. Multiple motion and fence alarms sounded with screeching radio chatter, as Rip would yell out "helicopter escape, "I've been hit, I've been hit, I need an ambulance"!

It was like a war zone, as a volley of gunfire was exchanged between Correctional Officers Rip Kirby, Gary Bennett and the attacking chopper.

The escaping inmates scrambled onto the waiting helicopter as the masked gunman would scream out "GO, GO, GO"! Fred recounted that he could hear the pings from four bullets as they skimmed across the rotor grip and pierced the helicopter's thin aluminum skin while the officers attempted to blast him out of the sky.

Racing to the scene, Gary Bennett drove into the direct line of fire attempting to draw attention away from Rip. Bennett, also a rookie tried unsuccessfully to remove his automatic rifle, an AR-15, from its locking bracket as the sling had become entangled. Not giving up, he improvised, jumping from the protection of his patrol vehicle, drew his side arm, an old-style Smith and Wesson six-shot revolver and fired all six rounds in the direction of the helicopter. Gary, now at Rip's side, remembers screaming out "KP2 to 839" into his radio. "KP1 has been shot and he needs an ambulance".

Neighbours to the prison, Ken Roos and his wife Lori, who lived only a few metres from Tower 2, woke up that Monday morning, and while relaxing in their living room gazed through the window. They could see the compound, and Ken heard what he described as a bang, bang, bang but was unaware it was gunfire from what would become Canada's first helicopter escape. Ken recounted every detail, and the feelings of disbelief on the phone to the RCMP. At first the constable at the Agassiz Detachment was polite, not yet convinced the caller was legit, until Ken overheard the all too familiar radio tone, followed by a police radio announcement, "Attention all members. There has been a helicopter escape from Kent, number of those escaped unknown". The constable, now a believer pumped Ken for further details. "They flew just around our property", he said, "flying in the direction of Harrison Hot Springs". After the call was completed, he made yet another call, this time to the local radio station where his news tip won him $40.00 as "News Maker of the Year" (1990).

It had been 137 seconds of sheer terror. With the skills of a pro, Fred maneuvered his helicopter over the fences, and just above the tree line of the surrounding farmer's fields, gone as fast as his unexpected arrival. Staff, still reeling in shock, had protocols to follow. An acting correctional supervisor (CS) was quick to establish an Emergency Command Centre in the CS office amid the ensuing frenzy. Shortly after, Warden Scissions took over the role of Crisis Manager. The Crisis Management team was now sequestered in the Warden's office. An armed guard was posted at the door of the Crisis Command Centre to ensure staff had limited access to the Crisis Manager and his team during a declared emergency. A Regional Command Centre in Abbotsford and a National Command Centre in Ottawa were set up to work in unison, and to keep stakeholders in the loop to ensure necessary support up and down the chain of command.

The closest tower officer to the escape zone, for several real, or imagined reasons failed to take a shot and his excuses were flying as fast as the bullets raining down on Rip and Gary. A CSC Board of Investigation (BOI) report (#1410-2-158) revealed the officer claimed the tower windows were stuck, and despite having 40 seconds to act, he was unable to intervene. Since elapsed time of the helicopter from its initial sighting to departure was two minutes and 17 seconds, the tower officer should have been able to move to the exterior catwalk, but did not.

The rookie officer's reputation was now being questioned. Sadly, staff were no better in their cruel taunts as nicknames followed this young officer. Many staff thought he should have done something, anything, however the CSC had no policy on the shooting of a helicopter during an escape, or policy on firing a warning shot. It's easy to second guess someone's actions, or inactions, we are famous for that, but who really knew what they would do? To second guess this officer was so-typical. The BOI concluded that it was tempted to criticize the officer's inactions, and failure to fire, but there may have been circumstances that mitigated against the officer opening fire, notwithstanding the reasons he supplied to the Board. The officer in Tower 4 at the north end of the field had been too far away to have taken an effective shot. Our weapons instruction did not train us for such a scenario, nor give us the marksmanship skills needed to effectively intervene. Taking into consideration the distance, firing was not practical. I understand CO-I Pam Ludwar in Tower 4 remained calm throughout, reporting the escaping helicopter's direction as it flew over the rooftops of neighbouring farms, stirring up the dust from the farmers' fields below.

During the mad exodus, FORD had engaged Fred in idle chat, asking how much he earned in a typical day. "$4,500.00", Fred replied. FORD would offer Fred $7,500.00, which he promised to send in the mail. A hollow offer to say the least.

Confusion was immediate as two correctional supervisors and a correctional officer drew firearms from the armory, and responded to Rip's aid. Luckily a visiting physician who was seeing inmates in the "Doctor's Parade" responded, telling Rip, now laying in the blood-soaked gravel, with the hardened bedside manner of a seasoned physician, "You're not going to die, but your knee sure is fucked". The steel-jacketed bullet, designed for use in modern day warfare, shattered Rip's fibula (bone in the lower leg), splattering what was left of his knee throughout the vehicle's cab.

As two correctional supervisors tried to bring some semblance of order to this chaotic scene, a couple of additional staff were later ordered to the gym gun walk on the other side of the prison to identify those inmates who remained in the sports field. In a show of solidarity, inmates zipped up their parkas, covering their faces to conceal their identities. The group of otherwise passive inmates were heard cheering as the helicopter lifted off with two of their own on board.

Three sharp shooters took positions on the roof, with an additional six members from the Institutional Emergency Response Team (IERT) to deal with the inmates in the sports field each carrying a shotgun. The four-person BOI looked upon as arm-chair quarterbacks would later conclude the show of force by the IERT was excessive, when the inmates who earlier presented as disruptive, were now offering no resistance.

As with emergencies of this type, other resources like the RCMP, or the military would inject their expertise into the situation. As it happened, an escort team from Mountain was driving to Hope Hospital with an inmate on a routine medical appointment. Upon their return, they pulled over to assist the RCMP who by this time had set up a roadblock on the outskirts of town. In an act that was a highly-questioned departure from police policy, the local guards were given shotguns, and asked to assist. Only after the Crisis Command Centre was operational, those at National Headquarters learned of the two Mountain officers and their unauthorized involvement as the drama unfolded live on CNN (Cable News Network).

Not knowing the Mountain staff were already involved, RCMP at Kent emphatically declined any assistance. Throughout the day as events unfolded, management held several briefings to groups of very angry staff. Most were in a volatile mood, and wanted to retaliate against those inmates in the sports field. These discussions were animated and hostile, as some staff were calling out to kick their asses. It was reported that staff needed a win in the midst of such a violent attack against one of their own. Frustrated that the lead negotiator, "the man with a thousand ties" seemed unable to convince the inmates to return to their units.

Staff in the briefing room yelled out their displeasure that the inmates should not be allowed to negotiate a "direct order" to clear the yard. Inmates wanted assurances there would be no lengthy lockdown. At 14:08 inmates finally agreed to return to their cells for lock up. As the teams converged, inmates were escorted back, five at a time without incident.

In the meantime, Fred, only 30 miles away was ordered to land in a clearing near Harrison Lake. Fearing his usefulness was coming to its conclusion, he worried he would be shot. In a compassionate moment, they spared his life. Fred was tied to a helicopter skid, and watched the felons' attempt a getaway in a stolen Mercury sedan. The battery of the getaway vehicle now dead, left the inmates no choice but to again enlist Fred's assistance in removing the helicopter's battery for a jump-start. After FORD and THOMAS left the area, Fred managed to free himself, and flag down a passing logging truck, and subsequently call police. It was alleged that Alan JUPP had stolen a car from a Chilliwack dealership to haul his canoe and supplies. Observant police noticed the rut marks left by the canoe's keel on the shore of Harrison Lake leaving telltale bread crumbs; ultimately giving up their clandestine location on Echo Island. The pair huddled around a campfire with no thought to the summers campfire ban, giving their not so secret location away.

Now closing in, the RCMP's five-member Emergency Response Team raced across the frigid waters of Harrison Lake, the waves pounding against their Zodiac inflatable as they had their sites on the pair.

Realizing the RCMP were fast approaching, and knowing their brief taste of freedom was coming to an end, the felons frantically started tossing any incriminating evidence into the campfire. Reportedly the police fired a single shot, tearing through THOMAS' loose-fitting clothing.

A police K-9 search team found a 12-gauge shot gun buried on Echo Island along with 53 live rounds of ammunition. An RCMP dive team found two additional rifles in the shallow waters just off shore. Search as they might, there was no trace of the third man. The only evidence that would identify JUPP being involved was the single finger print left on a receipt in a back pack at the campsite. Although there was no concrete evidence linking JUPP to the crime, Fandrich was certain he was the man.

JUPP was living in Rosedale, just miles from the prison when a month later, Alan JUPP, who was thought to be the suspect gunman and long time, loyal friend of FORD, was arrested and finally in custody. It was a time of reckoning for JUPP. A year after the famed escape he would appear before the BC Supreme Court.

After only a few days of freedom both inmates were soon returned to Kent's Segregation Unit and continued with their incarceration.

Now before the courts, JUPP faced a slew of charges including Wounding, Possession of a Weapon, Kidnapping, Robbery, and Escape. The case became difficult for Crown Attorney Don Wilson, as most of the evidence was circumstantial at best. Lawyers for the Crown said they may never know the identity of the masked gunman. Canadian law said a person suffers the same penalties, whether he planned it, or whether he participated. JUPP, now in court claimed he had married his young bride two days prior to the escape, and was honeymooning in Nelson BC at the time. JUPP received nine years for his part, and was sent to Kent.

The legal requirement for placing someone in Segregation was to complete a Segregation Placement report. The following paragraph was taken in part from their case file stemming from the helicopter escape.

> *"You have been identified as participating in a violent escape from Kent by helicopter with the assistance of person(s) unknown in the community on 1990-06-18 in which an officer was shot. You have made statements indicating your willingness to repeat this incident at any opportunity. Therefore, you are an extreme risk to the safety, security, and good order of this Institution, and will remain in Administrative Segregation until transferred to a more secure facility such as a High Maximum security Unit. (Segregation report was provided by author and lawyer Michael Jackson found in the pages of Justice Beyond the Walls)."*

THOMAS, during an on-the-fly interview with members of the hovering press camped outside the Chilliwack courthouse, was heard saying, "It was a blast, and I would do it again".

Tried separately, it was FORD's turn to face the music before the BC Provincial Court in Surrey. Security was tight as throngs of on lookers jammed the courtroom. FORD had a history of prison breeches that found him behind a ceiling-high wall of bulletproof glass. FORD received an additional 14 years added to his life sentence. The news media labeled FORD a small-time punk whose Hollywood-style prison escape ended in a laughable anticlimax only two days later.

Canada's first helicopter escape made the front page of the National Enquirer, and was ablaze with depictions of graphic, and shocking details. Fred told a reporter from the National Enquirer, "I flew into the jaws of hell".

There have been a small number of helicopter escapes since then, but none more notorious than Kent's. Recently I found myself reminiscing with the owner of a small, quaint family eatery as he told how the media from all corners of the globe converged on the town of Agassiz, setting up a media scrum in this tiny, unassuming bistro. Business was never better, the owner would say, as members of the media looked for a local slant on this international story.

Understandably shaken, Fred had spoken to the media shortly after the court proceedings about his PTSD, and how he suffered because of the helicopter escape. Fred got on with his life. Now in his 70s, and retired, he is somewhat guarded about his feelings. During my time with Fred, he struggled to remember the harrowing experience. He presented as a kind man, reluctant to trust, however as the minutes turned to an hour, Fred opened up albeit still worried of saying the wrong thing.

Brought together over the last 27 years, new friends Rip and Fred shared an occasional lunch on the anniversary of the escape, and talked about the events that day.

Shrouded in secrecy, the damage to Fred's helicopter was in excess of $40,000.00, yet out of the blue one day, a cheque arrived from the federal government in the amount $25,000.00. I was surprised to learn the old bird, a Bell Ranger 206 based out of Merritt BC, still flies today.

A 74-page internal investigation penned by the Correctional Service of Canada obtained through an Access to Information and Privacy Program (ATIP) request stated that Kent remains vulnerable to helicopter escapes. As the blame game heated up, as with all major incidents, the CSC denied that any clear warning was received, yet an RCMP Constable said he warned officials FORD would most likely break out using a chopper several months before it occurred. The officer cited a network of local informants telling of FORD's plan. An intelligence picture was developing, indicating there was a reasonable probability that FORD was planning an escape, and the police were satisfied he had the knowledge, the resources, and the ability to put his plan into action. While management suspected something, official or not, they directed staff to submit tracking reports. Management would later say they couldn't segregate an inmate on pure speculation, that they needed proof before acting. While staff watched FORD around the Institution, they were helpless to do much else.

A few years later, I remembered an informal chat with JUPP. Sweeping cigarette butts, from the courtyard of Kent, he casually provided a rare insight into his background. JUPP was a highly trained Rocky Mountain Ranger, a part of a primary reserve regiment of the Canadian Armed Forces. JUPP would also tell his IPO he aspired to become a Mercenary in Guatemala.

Fast forward one year, Rip pens an open letter published in the Kent Peeper.

"June 18th, 1990 is not a day many of us will forget. I know I won't. The first anniversary has now passed, and has given myself a chance to reflect on just what happened. There was more than a little irony and justice to the fact the man accused of wounding me, and breaking our jail was found guilty, exactly one year to the day of the original incident".

Rip received a plaque from staff that inspired him to write the following note:

"I would like to say my family appreciates the efforts of the officers and staff of Kent. You've made me feel like a part of a larger family".

As for Rip, 27 years later, after more than 12 surgeries, an artificial knee, and lifelong pain he is reminded of that day with each step he takes. Rip later received the Commissioner's Citation for Bravery.

Rip Kirby's courage that day will never be forgotten. His brave actions were the measure by which we define today's professional correctional officer. The events to some may be a faded memory. To those involved, those 137 seconds will be forever etched in our memories.

In the end, the Correctional Service of Canada would determine that anti-helicopter devices would prove ineffective in a helicopter escape citing reports from the US Federal Bureau of Prisons.

Correctional Officer Rip Kirby.

Helicopter pilot Fred Fandrich.

The master mind behind
Canada's first helicopter escape.

David Ross THOMAS was a
last-minute substitution who
just went along for the ride.

Popular t-shirt I sold to commemorate Canada's first helicopter escape.

Shaughnessy Hospital, Parking Lot Justice

For many correctional officers, the hospital escort was an opportunity to escape the confines of both prison life, and its drama. One such escort to Vancouver's Shaughnessy Hospital on November 28, 1990 would turn our worlds upside down, or at least "backwards".

Unsuspecting officers, Correctional Officer I Jim LeBlanc, and the late Correctional Officer II Tom (the Beast) Beeson, made the 2 ½ hour journey to Vancouver's Shaughnessy Hospital. It would provide Beeson an opportunity to grab a few winks along the way before Paul David LAMBERT, (a 22-year-old inmate from Kent) was scheduled to see an ear, nose, and throat specialist. Sitting in the back seat of the Dodge van, LAMBERT patiently waited for his opportunity. Noticing the guard now sound asleep, he managed to slip out of his leg irons and handcuffs in preparation for his chance at freedom. As they readied for the shackled walk to the hospital, the officer slowly opened the van door. LAMBERT, seeing his chance, bolted, knocking one startled correctional officer to the ground. While the struggle was brief, LAMBERT managed to break free, and dash across an almost empty parking lot. A nearby witness, Surrey resident Bert van Den Ham, heard footsteps, and remembered the officer commanding the man to stop.

Taking aim, Leblanc, his breath held as he carefully aimed, letting off a single blast from his 38-special, stopping the felon almost dead in his tracks. As he lay seriously wounded, bleeding profusely, he was rushed to the trauma unit of the Vancouver General Hospital for surgery. In a follow-up surgery, both a fellow officer and I had the gruesome task to watch both the surgical prep, and initial cutting. Dressed in surgical scrubs and packing a gun on one hip with two radios, the attending physician remarked saying that I looked like "Doctor Death". It must have been quite the sight! LAMBERT lying on the cold operating table, now under general anesthetic, enough mistakes had already occurred, we weren't risking a break out from the community so we shackled him securely to the operating table.

Upon our return to the institution, management's message to the union and its members was to reposition the escort van's passenger seat facing to the rear, thus placing the officer in direct line of sight to the inmate. Seen by some as a punishment, after the typical union outcry, the change in policy ended quickly, as the correctional officers were complaining that riding backwards made them nauseous.

STEWART Box Escape[23]

The 90s was turning out to be a decade of lessons for Kent. There was unrest within the inmate population, culminating in murders, escapes, and a riot.

There was Kent's world-renowned helicopter escape, and now the "con-in a-box escape" in 1995 which the media, and its front-page headlines dubbed the most embarrassing. A calamity of errors to say the least, with most of our policies being completely ignored.

On the evening of June 1, 1995 an elaborate plan was underway. Kevin Walter STEWART, 44 also known as Kenneth Joseph BRONICKI was a stocky inmate when he first arrived at Kent. He was placed in a PC unit, on the dark side of the prison.

STEWART had been known as a "master of disguise", able to change his appearance at will. Court documents describe STEWART as a notorious inmate with a record of multiple escapes. His criminal career was estimated by Crown Counsel to reach back as far as 1968 with five Robberies, and a Rape charge in 1981. Convicted in Edmonton of several other offences including Break and Enter, Forcible Confinement, Arson, Assault, Use of a Firearm, and Aggravated Assault, some 80 criminal charges in total. He was a determined escape artist with three escapes from Saskatoon, and subsequently Drumheller Institution in 1992. When he arrived at Kent that same year, staff, during a routine strip search found him in possession of a handcuff key, and mini blow torch like device suit cased (inserted) in his rectum.

He was overweight, but this so-called master of disguise would shed enough pounds that would aid him in yet another escape. Was it a simple diet, or part of his master plan? STEWART was having quite enough of prison life, and not looking forward to completing the remainder of his lengthy sentence. He wanted out! Difficult to work with, he challenged authority, and in my experience was arrogant. Motivated to go, he had been planning his escape from the Fraser Valley's only maximum-security prison. Another PC inmate, Victor ALEXANDER, 28 was scheduled to be paroled on June 2nd and alleged that he allowed STEWART to pack himself in a box meant for Alexander's personal effects. The box, made of sturdy cardboard, was kept in STEWART's cell under the guise the box would be used to ship out his next order of carvings. STEWART was an internationally renowned native carver, "carver to the stars" he was called, who sold two carvings to Frank Sinatra, and gifted the likes of US President Ronald Reagan with one of his creations.

In the interim, staff allowed it to be used as a TV stand in STEWART's cell. When he was ready, it was available, reinforced with wood and strong rope handles. It was a long shot but his hatred of prison fueled his dogged determination to leave that life behind.

STEWART found the right moment on the quieter evening shift and carefully placed himself in the specially constructed box that would be portrayed as containing personal effects of ALEXANDER. The circus like contortionist inserted himself into his tiny overnight home. The odds were against him! An attempt of this magnitude was unthinkable, or perhaps just crazy enough to work. So intricate the plan, STEWART had even taken medication to mitigate the pain of spending a night cramped in a small box.

Reports show staff locked the box in the F-Unit side office at 7:00 pm. Nothing was left to chance, including the music playing in the nearby common room left on in hopes of masking any telltale sounds that might alert correctional officers on the graveyard shift. STEWART remained in the box throughout the night, while breathing through carefully placed air holes.

Staff working the units on the graveyard shift were required to walk four units in this case E, F, G and H, using the Diester wand (the Rat) to record their foot patrols. With each cell check, staff were required to determine if an inmate was alive and breathing. Oftentimes as inmates lay still, it was difficult to see any signs of movement, let alone a live and breathing body. Our flashlights would only serve to exacerbate an already difficult situation by waking other inmates resulting in a tirade of verbal abuse. It was a delicate balance, and totally understandable that staff mistook the paper mâché dummy tucked carefully under the covers of STEWART's upper bunk, thinking they had in fact a live and breathing person. It seemed, as luck would have it, the cards were falling into place. The unit staff on dayshift were settling into their routine, making coffee, and preparing for the morning count. Seeing the box in the secondary office from the night before, day staff must have concluded that staff from the preceding evening shift had processed ALEXANDER's belongings, and safely tucked the box away awaiting delivery to Admission & Discharge (A&D). Compounding the problem, regular staff in A&D had booked off sick, leaving the duties of processing the inmate's personal effects to the urinalysis officer, a young, enthusiastic new officer. As ALEXANDER readied for release, he wheeled a red canvas laundry cart across the courtyard, and down the programs corridor to A&D. Arriving at the door, ALEXANDER would ring the bell to summon staff. He looked sheepishly down towards the floor, avoiding eye contact as the officer peered through the tiny window. He saw ALEXANDER, but was unaware of the dark secret ALEXANDER was hiding. He was unfamiliar with search protocols of inmates exiting the institution and like others assumed the neatly taped box had been searched. As the work day commenced, there seemed nothing unusual, just like any other Friday. Suddenly, however, calm turned to chaos as a correctional supervisor realized the release certificate, and money for ALEXANDER was unavailable. The taxi was turned away at 7:00 am and told to return for 8:00 am in hopes the administration staff, soon to arrive, would complete the process, and send ALEXANDER on his way. Staff were under the gun, as it was now a race against the clock. The correctional supervisor, impatient at the best of times, was moaning "hurry up, hurry up, you hemorrhoid, the taxi is waiting".

The attorneys would later claim the process was now more about expediency than a duty of care. The CO-I seeing the box neatly taped and secure, must have assumed unit staff had checked it, an assumption STEWART was counting on. After a brief time in A&D, ALEXANDER received his street clothes, possessions, money and his lawful release certificate, or "spring order". The next, and pivotal stage was the front gate. Bypassing any physical inspection, ALEXANDER, STEWART and the box got out of jail, free!

STEWART was nicely tucked away in his box to freedom, while ALEXANDER and the unsuspecting cabbie, Dave Leccher, loaded the abnormally heavy box of what everyone thought were personal effects into the trunk of the waiting taxi for their journey to the nearby City of Chilliwack. As dayshift staff began their morning count, staff noted the large cardboard box normally used as a TV stand in STEWART's cell was missing. The significance of this was not truly appreciated until they realized the count was incorrect. Staff reported their observation, and noted STEWART's whereabouts could not be ascertained. A recount announcement was ordered on the institutions paging system. It wasn't until an emergency count at 11:10 am staff concluded the missing box, normally in STEWART's cell, was likely related to the recent release of

ALEXANDER. Fearing the worst, an escape, Deputy Warden (DW) Jessie Sexsmith ordered his Executive Assistant to open, and set up the Emergency Command Centre, and notify police. A lockdown of the prison was called at 11:30 am. Assuming this was a joke, his Executive Assistant ignored his direction, and went about her normal duties until minutes later the DW questioned the lack of action. At 11:45 am, STEWART was declared officially missing. Warden Bob Lusk, now on site, assumed the position of Crisis Manager, and ordered staff to initiate escape protocols. Correctional Officers were dispatched to Agassiz's nearby McCaffrey Elementary School in hopes of assuring residents that their children were safe.

Once unloaded from the taxi, now free, the next leg of STEWART's dangerous adventure was a local music shop, JC Sound on Yale Road in Chilliwack where STEWART had arranged to sell a number of his wood carvings on consignment. Stewart's carvings were popular works of art, yet these masks somehow failed to sell, much to his dismay. The money was needed to fund his new freedom, and lacking funds, STEWART faced some desperate choices.

Now wanted by the police, STEWART started to make his way to Vancouver while continuing his criminal rampage. Now desperate, he decided to rob the Libonati's Gun Shop and Sporting Goods store in Burnaby. Denzil Libonati proprietor of the landmark business on Kingsway, was on duty. Brutally beaten, and later hospitalized. Libonati would swear in his legal pleading that he lost the enjoyments of life, and sued the CSC for undisclosed damages. STEWART continued his crime wave of robberies, now brandishing his stolen shotgun, he robbed a teller at a Vancouver Bank of Nova Scotia. It was during a routine street check, on June 16, 1995, immediately after the armed robbery police questioned STEWART. Unaware of the villain in their midst, it was not until a search of STEWART's pockets they discovered a newspaper clipping outlining the story of his escape, and revealing their suspect's true identity. Fearing the jig was up, STEWART made a dash for freedom, through nearby bushes, when he was caught with the aid of a Vancouver K-9 Unit. Now returned to Kent, bruised and bitten, STEWART was securely tucked away in Segregation, cooling his heels awaiting yet another trial. ALEXANDER had his parole revoked, and returned to Kent to await his trial as a suspected accomplice. Unbelievably the courts determined ALEXANDER was not a willing participant, yet he received an additional two months. STEWART on the other hand, received an additional seven years for his violent escape from custody.

Working for the CSC for as many years as I had, I found our system to be reactionary in nature. Always putting out fires, too busy going from one investigation to another, we just didn't think outside of the box, so to speak. Being proactive was difficult as we were tasked to do more, with less. There was always the pressure of performance, and time lines in most cases, came with deadlines of yesterday. The BOI team was sent in, and asked many pressing questions. What happened to the 10:30 pm count from the preceding night, and why had staff failed to notice during the hourly range walks a live and breathing body? The BOI said warning signs were either minimized, or ignored, pointing to STEWART's abysmal escape record, and poor institutional adjustment. Fifteen telephone calls to JC Sound over a 28-day period, their relevance never connected. Staff later admitted range walks were completed too quickly. A comedy of errors that in the end, took a personal toll on the urinalysis officer. These tragic mistakes were magnified by STEWART's headline-grabbing escape, and the embarrassment it caused. The events of those few days of freedom brought about a multitude of new procedures including "Stand to for Count" requiring inmates to stand by their bed for the late-night count. All boxes leaving the institution with a paroled or transferred inmate would now be checked against the inmate's personal property, and then scanned by the front gate officer before anything left through that final front door.

In the prison environment, time, or the lack of it, was the enemy to good corrections. Rushing to get the job done was the root cause of most incidents equaled only by a rush to assign blame. Many mistakes from the cheap seats of blame concluded it didn't fall on just one officer, but a flurry of bad decisions, and lack of communications.

If there were words of wisdom relevant to this situation, they would be "what we learn from history is that we learn nothing from history".

Mr. Libonati a popular gun shop owner was savagely clubbed on the head, and about the body with a big wooden mallet, knees smashed almost beyond repair. If inflicting unbearable pain was not enough, STEWART stole his wallet, and standard shotgun. Mr. Libonati later required knee replacement surgery, destroying his independence, and sense of confidence. With PTSD and Vertigo, he now was physically no longer able to run his 25-year-old family business.

Before he passed, Denzil Libonati, businessperson, husband, and father claimed he could no longer drive, nor enjoy the simple pleasures of fishing and swimming.

Donald Renaud, a skilled, and personable Burnaby trial lawyer, represented Mr. Libonati seeking damages in a lawsuit against the federal government, the Correctional Service of Canada, and the many staff involved. In documents dated September 16, 1997, the statement of claim from Mr. Libonati sought compensation for STEWART's debilitating, and brutal attack. Using a shotgun approach, his lawyers painstakingly built their case requesting all documents on the actions, or inactions, of staff. What were staff doing, playing chess, or sleeping? I knew what the lawyers were trying to achieve, asking these questions, but staff according to court documents maintained that "blue wall of silence", acknowledging nothing.

In the end, the wide-sweeping broom would reap financial rewards. The legal pleading stated the Correctional Service of Canada failed to follow their own procedures to keep a violent inmate behind bars. There was no duty of care, or responsibility the CSC would claim, once the inmate was no longer incarcerated, and under their control. Recognizing confidentially agreements in place, Renaud was handcuffed by the disclosure agreements, and unable to discuss the financial outcome for his client.

A difficult case to begin with, the lawyer for the CSC would state they were not responsible for the actions of STEWART. Their responsibility was an arm's length responsibility, they would say. We do know the plaintiff's recourse was limited to loss of enjoyment of life, loss of income, and pain and suffering. Mr. Libonati's business interests at the time of the attack were winding down causing him to seek part-time employment as a truck driver. In the end, so typical at the eleventh hour, it was not a mediation, but rather a take it or leave it settlement.

Mr. Libonati, Denzil to his friends and family, never got over the physical, or mental pain, leaving him bitter, and broken. Now passed, his family remembers the struggles of their father as they tried to move on.

The newspapers glorified Inmate STEWART as a "master of disguise", "a master mind" who was shrewd and cunning. To me, he was a heartless thug, a psychopath who did not deserve the star-studded attention the media afforded him. It was a dangerous escape, inflicting devastating life-debilitating injuries on a valued member of society. Not a time for snickers, or witty headlines, it was a time to reflect on the serious nature of our profession.

Like many stories, staff are hard on each other. The concept of family is often lost with each opportunity to mock, tease and harass those more vulnerable than themselves. The press was no less kind as they waded into the carnival style media feeding frenzy, willing to take jabs at the events surrounding the box escape, providing a tongue-in-cheek "con in a box" headline complete with mocking cartoons. From my perspective, and reviewing court documents, it was not one person's fault, rather a group of professional correctional officers, caught on a bad day of misfortune. No staff member was disciplined for their inactions.

The many faces of inmate STEWART.

Chapter 6

Out and About, the World of Prisons

Washington State Penitentiary, Forever Walla Walla[26]

E arly into my career, 1992, I became somewhat restless looking for new adventures when I organized prison tours down the west coast of the United States. I chose to tour maximum security prisons for an apple to apple comparison.

Washington State Penitentiary (Walla Walla) was the first in a string of memorable prison tours that our group of 20 undertook.

I was careful to incorporate pre-tour briefings that included the expectation of appropriate dress and deportment. My tours were educational in nature, but included group dinners to the late-night hijinks that the bars and honky tonks provided. The off-hour get togethers provided the evening's entertainment, and a chance to unwind with co-workers, discovering some juicy untold stories.

Some of us, feeling the effects of the night before, lined up at Walla Walla's front gate, and processed through security. We were herded into our pre-tour briefing, filled with the thrill of the unknown.

Sitting around a large boardroom table a young-looking man, Lieutenant Gleeson stood before us to address this eager group of Canadians. His uniform represented his pride in service, with the razor-sharp creases in his "class A" uniform. There was a sacred trust as he spoke of the various security features of the prison, and provided an overview of each department, and their daily operation.

Prior to the tour, we were required to sign a standard "no negotiation for hostage" agreement, and informed that in the event of trouble, or an alarm sounding we were to get out of the way. As the tour leader, I piped up with beaming pride, "Sir, we're Canadians; we don't get out of the way". It was that willingness to pitch in during an emergency I think helped foster a life time relationship.

Walla Walla Prison was edgy, and known to the locals by a variety of names including Concrete Mama, (after a bestselling prison book of the 70s) Walla Walla, or simply WSP.

At the time, Walla Walla was a multi-level facility, housing 2,116 state, and federal inmates. It was home to the likes of Kenneth Bianchi, the notorious Hillside Strangler, and Gary Ridgeway, the Green River Killer. At first glance, the 20-foot high stone, and brick walls that surrounded the complex were topped off with guard towers overlooking various parts of the prison. This turn of the century walled prison was constructed in 1886 and designed to house 1,988 prisoners. Situated in the southeast corner of Washington State, Walla Walla, the city was home to Walla Walla sweet onions, award winning wineries, the birth place of Adam West, TVs Batman, and a prison filled with the states most infamous inmates.

A history that spanned 130 years, Walla Walla had undergone a myriad of changes. The Hollywood style striped prison garb saw its demise in 1908 making way for the more economical and fashionable street clothing.

From the 30s to the 70s Walla Walla was the scene of two sensational tunnel escapes, one in 1957 when two men managed to dig a 42-foot tunnel, but caught just 10 feet short of freedom, to the last tunnel escape in 1978 when two inmates managed their get-away only to be shot just outside the walls by an attentive tower guard. These types of stories are so typical of the violent unrest that befalls so many prison environments.

Another sad story was the death of Sergeant William Cross who had observed a native gang member holding a knife just outside the kitchen. When he confronted the inmate, sadly he was stabbed five times. It was June 15th, 1979 while in an area known as the "People's Park", at the south entrance to the kitchen where a predominantly displayed plaque was a grim reminder of the violence.

Walla Walla was the state's only prison tasked with carrying out court-ordered executions, until the newly elected Governor Jay Inslee placed all executions into a state of abeyance during his term in office. Prior to his election, inmates on death row had a choice of either the gallows, or later, death by lethal injection.

More than 50 inmates were executed under the state's death penalty provision with the last execution in 1963. Captain Dick Morgan kept us on edge as he regaled the group with his ghastly stories from the gallows.

He was a proud partner in the prison's history, and went to great lengths to explain the science of knot tying, and how hanging had evolved into an art form at the time. It prevailed as the most popular means by which to carry out the death sentence.

Scientifically known as the standard drop, this calculated procedure took into consideration the inmate's height and weight. Having the right amount of slack on the ligature would ensure the spinal cord would not become disconnected (neck broken) but not so slack as to allow decapitation. Hanging was described as barbaric, and eventually gave way to the implementation of lethal injection.

If ever there was a shining example, or model of the free enterprise system, Walla Walla was it. Running a prison of its size, came with a multi-million-dollar operating budget that required all departments to fall in line to a very lean bottom line. The Industries Department found itself challenged to compete with the private sector for various business contracts.

The Farm Program boasted an award-winning dairy herd providing inmates, and the community with both milk, and milk by-products, including a generous supply to local schools, and local veteran's associations.

Walla Walla offered a variety of certified vocational programs including a full-service auto body shop, engine repair, and auto mechanic certification training. A tailor shop was responsible for producing law enforcement jackets, while the Design, and Graphics Department produced the state's green travel, and mileage signs seen along the various interstate highways.

At every turn, these out-of-the-box thinkers looked for creative ways to reduce operating expenditures. Since 1923 Walla Walla has been pumping out state license plates as part of their lucrative manufacturing venture. The program proudly employs 30 inmates and four paid staff as they churned out 2,684,762 sets of plates in 2015.

There were many unique security features and leading-edge programs of note; but to me, it was the people who left an indelible mark. In all, Walla Walla staff were proud of their correctional system, and shared their achievements in the field of incarceration, and rehabilitation.

It had been 27 years since our tour, and I have learned Lt. Gleeson has since retired. Captain Dick Morgan has moved on in his career, now the Assistant Secretary of Washington State Corrections. As if he wasn't busy enough, Dick also holds the elected position of Councillor in Walla Walla.

He was coaxed out of so-called retirement in hopes of fixing the States ailing prison systems, and despite his busy schedule, managed to find time to share fleeting memories, and enjoy a laugh with this old guard.

Tour Dynamics That Worked

I always found time when I was not hosting unofficial prison tours to venture out on my own, or with Joyce, visiting prisons across Canada, and around the world.

First stop on my cross-county tour was Kent's sister institution, Edmonton Institution[27] in Alberta. Edmonton Max as she was fondly referred, was designed, and laid out in the mirror image of Kent. Built a year prior to Kent, 1978, Edmonton was built on the Sharps farm and informally called the Farm. Like most prisons, Edmonton Max had their share of infamous inmate alumni including Ormar KADAR the child terrorist, returned to Canada and placed at Millhaven then Edmonton when he was threatened by inmates. There were only two successful escapes both perpetrated by one inmate known as Harvey ANDRES when he fooled guards with a dummy in his drum, and then using a garbage truck to make good his escape. He was captured two weeks later in 1981 after a shootout with police.

In 1982, ANDRES and three other inmates managed to cut the perimeter fence during a famous Prairie snow storm. While the others were recaptured, ANDRES was the only one that got away clean only to be captured in a strip mall in Saskatoon.

As I journeyed east, no stop would be complete without a visit to Kingston Penitentiary[28]. KP as she was called, held an important place in Canada's penal history as one of our country's earliest prisons. A provincial jail at first, it was originally built in 1835 to serve the provincial needs of Upper Canada. Kingston and its surrounding municipalities were quick to become known for its dark association with crime and punishment. While Kingston may be the areas third largest employer in the region it is known as Limestone City for its many historic buildings made of limestone. It is a cultural mecca with a thriving arts centre and home to many creative arts and entertainment celebrities including the birth place of Bryan Adams and childhood home of Dan Ackroyd. The former capital of the Province of Canada, 1841 Kingston, and Canada's military played a proud role in defending Canada's borders.

Like all prisons, KP had experienced their share of violent outbreaks and riots. The complaints always seem to be the same, including overcrowding, and general living conditions, food, pay, and access to programs.

In her 178-year history, KP played host to many infamous inmates including disgraced former Colonel Russel WILLIAMS, Paul BERNARO, Clifford Robert OLSON (Beast of British Columbia), and Wayne BODEN (Canadian Vampire Rapist). Celebrity guest visitors have included Charles Dickens, who in 1842 praised Kingston to be an "admirable gaol".

KP closed its doors September 30th, 2013 but today I am pleased to learn she did not follow the sad conclusion of the BC Pen, and fall prey to the wrecking ball. Shortly after its closure, it re-opened to host public tours with proceeds going to the United Way and Habitat for Humanity Canada. I understand that while there are redevelopment plans much of the old prison could be saved.

As our tours continued, Joyce would later accompany me on a personally guided tour of the famous "Tent City" located in the sweltering heat of the US Arizona dessert where it often reached triple digit temperatures.

This unique jail situated in the aptly named Sun City, acted as a remand centre for inmates sentenced to shorter terms, or those awaiting trial.

Joe Arpaio,[29] an 84-year-old sheriff, was stylized as America's Toughest Sherriff, and ran Tent City, but to many, simply known as Sheriff Joe. He ran the Mariposa County lockup with an iron fist. Inmates were housed in tents, and included the likes of Mike Tyson doing time for drug related offences. Tent City was not only famous for Sheriff Joe, but also the fact inmates sported pink underwear, handcuffs, coveralls and slippers. As we toured the Administrative Support division, I couldn't help wondering how the staff must have felt handing the disgraced "baddest man on the planet" his pink issue clothing fearing they might get their ear bitten off should the former boxer take offence.

Sheriff Joe felt, as did I, if the tents were good enough for serving US troops, then they were good enough for the inmates under his care. Inmates were afforded only the basics, no extravagant extras, no salt, mustard, or catsup with their daily meals. Those who would drive through the Arizona community of Sun City could on any given day see inmates from Tent city working on a chain gang picking the fruit from lemon, and grapefruit trees. The seniors within the community who owned the fruit trees would donate half the harvest to the inmates, select community groups, and keep the remaining fruit for themselves.

Since being elected in 1993, Sheriff Joe's tenure had been filled with varied allegations: from misuse of public funds, to his broad interpretation of the US immigration laws. These were often at the centre of lawsuits, and out-of-court settlements costing local taxpayers at last tally, $142 million dollars.

This right-wing, hard-nosed Republican Sheriff stayed the course, however, it was that hard-on-crime attitude that may have led to his falling out of favour with the voters. Nothing was forever, Tent City sadly falling to the wrecking ball in 2017 after 22 years in operation.

California Tour, 2003

The California 2003 tour as I called it, was the jewel in my crown of tours, and by now, the formula was tested, and true. I knew what worked, and what didn't. With just the right combination of extra-curricular activities combined with the exciting backdrop prison tours offered, we were assured of the best crowd-pleasing adventure. Some flew down, while others drove, and we would meet up before our first tour of Folsom Prison.

Opened in 1880, Folsom Prison[30] was reminiscent of a turn-of-the-century architectural design. It was one of 33 prisons operated by the California Department of Corrections, and was steeped in history. A welcoming to each inmate destined to the prison, saw a brass-plated Gatling gun perched over the main entrance (Sally Port) to the prison. This well-preserved relic from the prison's past could fire 700 rounds a minute. Urban myth, or a tour guard's tall tale, we were told that each Sunday morning guards would practice their shooting skills into the surrounding hills. As suburbia encroached ever so closely, residents would complain their beloved pets would go missing. Was their mysterious disappearance a result of target practice, or were they victims of the wild?

Unlike most of our modern Canadian prisons, Folsom had a past. Inmates who were executed, numbering 93, and like so many prison cemeteries across America found their final resting place in a cemetery called "Boot Hill". Boot Hill, the name, originated in a time of the US wild west in the 19th century where it became common for cowboys and gunfighters to find their final resting place in one of over 52 cemeteries named Boot Hill in North America.

Our final tour before arriving in San Francisco was a newer style facility situated in the middle of a California desert. Corcoran Prison was nothing out of the ordinary, but it was home to the likes of Charlie Manson[31], and Sirhan Sirhan[32]. Manson, their star resident, led a quasi–commune located in California in the late 1960s. Manson in and out of jail most of his life, was reportedly sold by his mother for a pitcher of beer to a woman wanting a child. His uncle had to find the woman so that he could get his nephew back. Manson had a history of manipulation, controlling behavior, and mental illnesses which included schizophrenia, and paranoid delusional behavior.

He was an unemployed singer/songwriter, friends with the Beach Boys, who never really found his mark in the music industry. Manson began his questionable criminal career incarcerated at McNeil Island Penitentiary (Washington State) at the age of 29 for cheque fraud.

At Manson's command, a small group of his most ardent followers brutally murdered Roman Polanski's pregnant wife, actress Sharon Tate, writer Wojciech Frykowski, coffee heiress Abigail Folger and celebrity hair stylist Jay Sebring in 1969. Also killed was Steven Parent, who was a friend of the family's gardener. The murders were committed by followers Tex Watson, Susan Atkins, and Patricia Krenwinkel. Linda Kasabian accompanied them as a lookout.

The Manson family killing rampage sent a chilling message of fear through a paralyzed community, and garnered international headlines. Manson believed in what he called "Helter Skelter" from a song of the same name by the Beatles, and was intended by Manson to spark an apocalyptic race war.

We made our trek across the Corcoran's burning sports field, on what seemed like the hottest day of the year. As Canadians from the great white north, we were not acclimatized to the sweltering heat, but were soon to understand the need for the two bottles of water given to us prior to the long, and painful hike. What seemed like a cross-country marathon really was a short stroll. It was on our final few minutes of our walk towards Segregation, we came across Charlie strumming his guitar safely behind the exercise yard fence. With him was Sirhan Sirhan, killer of Presidential hopeful Senator Robert (Bobby) Kennedy. They were unlikely tier mates in protective custody. Both inmates, albeit twisted, enjoyed a certain celebrity status within the walls. As we approached their unit, they chose a quick retreat, scurrying to the safety of their 9' X 6' cells not willing to put on a show for the likes of us.

Tired of all the glamourized media interviews, the California Correctional Peace Officers Association, wanting to silence Manson, petitioned the courts to prohibit anyone from making a profit from their crimes. Their successful petition put the brakes on the "Oprah style" interviews the public, and victims' families had to endure. Manson, no longer able to profit from lucrative musical recordings, and numerous media interviews, became a recluse of sorts. We were given a brief tour of their cells before their return, and told that to this day Manson still receives a large volume of fan mail. Our escorting officer explained Manson gets thousands of dollars along with nude pictures of adoring fans, tucked within each letter.

Alcatraz, and the Youngest Guard Hired on the Rock [33]

I first met Frank Heaney, the youngest guard on Alcatraz on my first organized tour of the isolated and mysterious prison known as "The Rock". We made our way down to our meeting point on San Francisco's tourist laden pier. As we approached, a pinniped of California Sea Lions, who claimed K-Dock as their home, would greet us. Were these barking self-claimed squatters offering a glorious welcome, or their ardent displeasure as we invaded their territory?

The smell of the sea was the appetizer to a menu filled with the crime-infested life of this once great prison. Departing from the nearby pier, "all aboard" was the call as we held on with anticipation. The 1.5-kilometre ferry ride across the frigid and unforgiving waters of the San Francisco Bay seemed to take forever as we were tossed about just like the inmates of a bygone era. As we approached the once-active prison, our eyes beheld the aging, and now crumbling foundation. Fortress Alcatraz as it was once called, built in the 1800s held many secrets just beneath the prisons underground. Holding the most notorious prison distinction, it provided front page headlines with each incident.

Alcatraz has been the topic of numerous feature films, and portrayed in a wide range of books, drawing millions of curious tourists each year.

It was on those very docks we met Frank, now in his 70s. He was a slender gray-haired man still active, and full of life. He had an infectious smile, and an unexpected laugh not characteristic of a man who survived so many adventures. He lived through two wars and later wrote a book detailing his life on Alcatraz. Frank's tours were truly unique as he took us where no tour had gone before and told stories never heard by the public. We climbed the steep and winding ¼ mile path to the main cellblocks making our way to the prison's kitchen. Sitting with Frank on the old benches, we wondered who had sat there before us. Over lunch Frank shared the more personal stories of how a simple poster on the post office bulletin board prompted him as a 21-year-old to embark on a life-altering career. Frank joined the Alcatraz workforce in 1948, but his distaste for the job caused him to quit a short three years later (1951). He would tell tales of those he worked with and his time on what was the last stop for many troubled men. He captivated us with his prison lore as we strolled the cellblocks leading to the big yard. Frank was the quintessential storyteller, weaving his dark and dangerous tales many clamored to hear. Through our groups consisted of 20 CSC employees, we would often have members of the public who overheard Frank's stories choosing to tag along.

Those years on the Rock were more than most could handle, and enough for this young man. As our friendship grew, fondly calling Frank my American Cousin, I was quick to realize he was so much more than just a prison guard. When his country called, he was quick to enlist in the Coast Guard, and served proudly in World War II, and later in the Korean conflict.

Once stateside, Frank, now a distinguished war veteran, had many options available to him, but clearly, he would have no part in returning to Alcatraz. He said there were just too many bad memories. He spoke of the mental harassment from some of the prisoners who were deranged and perverse.

Frank recited a list of famous convicts as we walked the darkened halls, talking about George Francis Barnes Jr, he remembered more like a bank president than bank robber. I think it is fair to say while everyone liked George Barnes Jr. aka Machine Gun Kelly no one, Frank said, liked Robert Stroud[34] a.k.a. the Bird Man of Alcatraz. Frank had a dislike for this man who had spent many years in the Alcatraz hospital's psych ward. He was a murdering pimp from Alaska who was convicted of manslaughter. He was known for being difficult to manage, expressing psychotic frustrations, and violently lashing out at staff at every opportunity. In 1916, while incarcerated in Leavenworth Prison, Kansas, Missouri, Stroud stabbed a guard in the mess hall, killing him in front of 1100 stunned, and cheering inmates.

It was solitary confinement in Leavenworth, not Alcatraz, where Stroud undertook the hobby of bird keeping, and maintained a lab for his studies. Stroud later penned two books on canaries and their diseases having raised nearly 300 birds in his cell. After many ground-breaking discoveries, officials found some of the scientific equipment in his lab had been used for the distillation of jailhouse hooch. Stroud's actions earned him a transfer to the dreaded Alcatraz in 1942 where his death sentence for killing a guard in 1916 was commuted to life. He spent his next 17 years on the Rock, with six years in the prison's pitch black and sound proofed solitary confinement.

In 1959, he was transferred on the final leg of his incarceration to the medical centre for federal inmates in Springfield, Missouri where he subsequently died of natural causes in 1963.

Burt Lancaster starred in the Oscar nominated movie "Bird Man of Alcatraz", and despite Hollywood's best efforts to glamorize Stroud's persona as a gentle man, he was anything but. Stroud never actually cared for any birds on Alcatraz despite tinsel town's imaginative storytellers.

Frank worked on the island in various positions, including tower officer, where the unrelenting cold winds would chill him to the bone. Frank also worked in the cold dark units, and supervised inmates in various employment positions. Over lunch, he relayed to the private, and captive audience his many frightening moments as we hung on his every word. Alcatraz, like prisons in general, had its exciting moments however, for the most part, was dull and lonely. It was boring, and repetitious work, surrounded by doom and gloom. Now stateside, back from the war, Frank felt it was time for a career change. While Frank was welcome to rejoin his fellow officers on Alcatraz, he instead chose to become a Bay area firefighter working for the Albany Fire Department, serving until his retirement 27 years later.

Never settling for the quiet life of retirement, Frank was quick to return to Alcatraz as a Park Ranger, then in 1980, he put pen to paper and recounted his many island adventures in a book titled "Inside the Walls". A published author, Frank now a tour guide would make the pilgrimage along with six million visitors a year as they glimpsed into the fascinating world of a turn-of-the-century prison. We would return two additional times for Frank's unique tours around Isle de los Alcatraces, so named by the early Spaniards, meaning the Island of the Pelicans.

After our privileged time with Frank and his very personal and unique behind-the-scenes tours came to a successful conclusion, we boarded our blue and gold ferry for our windy, sea-swept ride back to the mainland.

The ANGLIN escape in 1962 was the last straw for Alcatraz as authorities moved swiftly under Robert Kennedy's term (1963) as Attorney General to end her glorious, albeit troublesome reign.

Alcatraz would lay dormant before she would find herself once again centre stage when the American Indian movement, simply called "Occupation Alcatraz" who would claim the island as their own. In a twist of historic fate, it was now the island prison held prisoner by 89 Native American Indians that would occupy the federal land. The Treaty of Fort Laramie (1863) stated all retired, and abandoned property that belonged to the federal government would be ceded to the Native Indians of the day. Since its closure in 1963, the island had been declared surplus and several Red Power activists felt the island now qualified for reclamation. The protest lasted 19 months from 1969 to 1971 before federal troops stormed the island prison. During the occupation many of the historic buildings were destroyed, falling onto their foundations.

Through the numerous movies, Alcatraz was not far from our memories in blockbusters like Escape from Alcatraz with Clint Eastwood, and the Rock with Sean Connery to name just a few. In 1973 it became part of the Golden Gate National Recreation area, and the Rock became a protected park.

Sadly, while speaking with his daughter, I learned Frank had suffered a stroke in 2004. His mind sharp she said, he was no longer able to return to the island, and has now officially retired.

Frank Heaney, the youngest guard hired on Alcatraz.

San Francisco was a mecca where our officers could take in the fresh sea air, traverse the historic hills, experience the local cuisine, and sample the beer, wine and seafood.

As I spent my childhood summers with my sister in and around San Francisco, I relished a chance to return and relive my childhood memories. If I wasn't watching Batman with my sister's friends, I was bothering the old man at the corner store where Steve McQueen filmed the iconic blockbuster Bullitt. (located at 1199 Clay Street for any Steve McQueen fans).

One of my sister's early homes was just another street corner to this prepubescent youth, but was destined to go down in folk history as the birthplace of the 60s-hippy movement. While free love and rock music may have found its roots in this little neighbourhood, it was lost on this young kid who was more interested in playing marbles than hanging out at the corner of Haight and Ashbury.

MAXIMUM FUN

KENT STAFF TOUR ALCATRAZ, SAN QUENTIN AND FOLSOM PRISON

CSC employees representing Kent, Matsqui and RPC travelled south on the June 26th weekend Francisco on a truly "busman's holiday".

Recognizing Core Value #4, these Officers shared ideas with their American counterparts at San Quen Folsom Prison, with a stopover at the local F.B.I. office. Highlights included a special guided tour of A by the youngest officer ever hired on "the Rock", Mr. Frank Heaney.

As we ate our way through Chinatown, any number of us could be seen hanging from cable cars or sh at Fisherman's Wharf.

Pictured in the sportsfield at Alcatraz are:

Back Row (L-R): Carla Bartlett, Rip Kirby - Matsqui, Retired Alcatraz Officer Frank Heaney, Dwight Mater - Ke Cawley - Kent, Val Edmonson - RPC
Front Row (L-R: Neil MacLean - Kent, Paul MacInnis - Kent, Karleen Scott - RPC, Deb Mater - RPC, Wayne Pallet

Missing from the picture are Matt Brown, Wes Samuel and Bill Moirier.

Alcatraz, Kent Peeper.

Just across the Golden Gate Bridge in rich Marin County in the City of San Quentin was the fictional home of TV character Jim Rockford. Of course I'm talking about San Quentin State Prison. The oldest prison in California, San Quentin was built in 1852, and currently holds 4,223 inmates. The "Q" as she was called, rests on 432 acres of the richest real estate in the area, and valued at 664 million dollars. San Quentin maintains the largest death chamber in North America, and is the only facility for executions in California. Over its 164-year history, San Quentin had instituted death by hanging. The early 40s saw the introduction of the famed gas chamber. Although the gas chamber of San Quentin was a crowd pleaser, it was abandoned as cruel and inhumane in 1996. Inmates sentenced to death are now executed by lethal injection. A small sign within sight of the condemned inmate was advertising "Tombstone Pizza" either a tongue in cheek play on words, or maybe his last meal, offering dine in, and touting free delivery.

Deep inside the prison walls lay a secret only known to a few, the 20-foot high historic mural consisting of six separate panels that lined the kitchen mess hall that captivated our group. The murals were painted in muted sepia tones, and depicted the history of California, including the iconic San Francisco cable cars, and various Hollywood luminaries. No matter where you stood, the artist's cable car seemed to follow the unsuspecting visitor throughout their brief kitchen tour. The murals sophistication, and imagery of the working class brought rave reviews. A young unknown artist by the name of Alfredo Santos[35] was the son of a carpenter who encouraged his son to incorporate the socialist spirit into his mural. You look at the magnitude of the artistry of those walls that provided a kaleidoscope of people, places, and events shaping the nation's most populous state. It was hard to comprehend how the artist, of simple stock, with no formal education or understanding of geometric angles was able to create this great master piece. Sadly only staff, visiting media, a few privileged Canadians, and those who were incarcerated can view his historic work of art.

Santos never wanted to talk about the mural, shunning the media for fear his shameful past would have exposed this young man's sordid prison past, a period of his life that cast a dishonourable shadow on him, and his family. Like so many starving artists, Santos's story was no different.

From poverty, to a life of crime, he wound up spending four years at San Quentin (1951-1955) for human smuggling. Since his mural caught the public's attention, he had settled into a life of anonymity, and lived a quiet life in San Diego until his passing in 2015.

As we walked into the dining hall, the harsh realities of this "no star" restaurant became abundantly clear. Other than it's bigger than life size, the mess hall was nothing special. We were offered a sampling from the lunch menu: plastic trays filled with slop. Remembering our manners, we politely declined. What they called food would have made a dog sick with such delicacies as powdered milk, watery soup, and Spam, lightly fried, taking centre stage as their main entre.

San Quentin's mess hall would have been intimidating to average folk, having hundreds in one place, but to us we felt surprisingly at home. I think the inmates were just as interested in us, as we were of them. At the end of the meal line as many walked by our table they would stop to ask questions. They too, were surprised at these unexpected visitors. Feeling strangely at ease, we introduced ourselves as visiting correctional officers from Canada. The inmates were almost welcoming, smiling, with one inmate calling me sir.

As we continued our stroll around the grounds of this historic penitentiary, we learned of San Quentin's other claim to fame, a correctional officer by the name of Sgt. John Whearty.[36]

Sgt. Whearty was the longest serving correctional officer at San Quentin, perhaps anywhere. As the Movement and Transportation Officer Sgt. Whearty had almost 60 years on the job. He was well respected by both staff, and inmates, who acknowledged his unique approach to a very tough job. Staff would speak of his unorthodox disciplinary methods, and interaction with inmates. When dealing with an unruly inmate for example, Whearty had the inmates name each individual goose that roamed the back

40 of the penitentiary. At the end of the day, those inmates under "alternative punishment" would report the names given to each specific goose.

I think the coolest of his many nicknames was a badge of honour, calling him Officer Golden Sleeves. Each hash bar represented three years of service, so as you can imagine his left arm filled the entire uniform jacket sleeve. While he was doing well, and showing no signs of retirement at the time, I understand he suddenly passed away from cancer in 2005.

As my tours evolved, we were fortunate to visit McNeil Island Penitentiary located off the Washington State coast in Pierce County, early home to Robert Stroud and Charlie Manson.

Pelican Bay, a super max located in Crescent City California, home to the famed Gladiator fights, pitting inmates against each other. It was reported the guards took betting action on the outcome of these deadly fights.

Three times a charm, another visit to the infamous San Quentin Prison.

Los Angeles Police Department (LAPD) Ride Along, the Mean Streets of LA

Wanting to experience the mean streets of Los Angeles from the hot seat of a police cruiser I signed up for a ride along with the famed LAPD. After a routine records check, signing the ever-popular waiver saving them from harm, I attended the squad briefing, and received a warm reception wishing me luck before we hit the road.

Off we went to our Sergeant's car, a typical black and white unit, just like Adam 12 I thought. Ill equipped for the task at hand, I was informed I would not be given any basic body armour for protection, let alone a weapon for self-defence. The smart aleck sergeant handed me a Bic pen stating it was a fine point, "knock yourself out".

Hearing the constant chatter of the police radio, I listened anxiously for our call sign, and was ready to pounce into action. My host, a veteran patrol Sergeant, was a no-nonsense police officer with his gold and silver engraved badge hanging just above the breast pocket of his neatly pressed uniform. His stellar dress and deportment outwardly displayed his pride working for the police force after which many television shows were fashioned.

Our first stop, ironically was a donut shop. Sitting on the patio, eyes everywhere watching these sometimes-maligned crime fighters. Within minutes, not able to finish our coffee an ear-piercing tone startled me, "Hollywood cars a 211 in progress, (armed robbery) Code 3".

Reaching for the radio I answered with our call sign, "6 L 20, roger".

Returning to our unit, it was "go time", speeding though the tourist-laden streets of Hollywood, lights flashing, and the deafening multi-pitched siren blaring, we were closing in on the heels of the suspect vehicle driving a black Mercedes. Everything was a blur as pedestrians jumped from the normally safe crosswalks. Cars pulled over more so out of fear than respect.

I learned quickly the public had a healthy regard, or in some cases, fear of the no-nonsense attitude of the LAPD.

As we raced down the streets of Hollywood I could not help noticing out of the corner of my eye, the distinct shape of the Capital Records building that was on my tourist list of things to see. One of departments many airships, Air 1, was now flying overhead while other patrol vehicles were leading the chase.

The loud noise from the thundering ghetto bird, as residents called them, had become a regular fixture to those in, and around Los Angeles, and the 469 square miles they patrolled. Although we were well back of the lead pursuit vehicle, the squeal of the tires was deafening as we rounded the tight corners of the narrow streets. Disappointed, yet relieved we lost the stolen Mercedes in a city that personifies luxury vehicles. We terminated our pursuit and my heart rate returned to normal. We took a moment for small talk, my host seemed interested as I explained the history of the Royal Canadian Mounted Police.

Our next call on this hot and blustery day, February 14th was a domestic dispute, a fight in progress. Finally, I got a chance to see some action, as we rolled up to the three-story apartment building in the uncaring heart of Hollywood. This call took a sad, but funny turn as we entered the apartment, it was a full on domestic fight involving an underappreciated wife sparring with her husband, forgetting the romance of Valentine's Day. Once we separated the couple, and the language dissipated, this Canadian was now charged with taking the beaten and somewhat embarrassed husband into custody. Walking to the police car I thought I had no authority to arrest, or transport an American prisoner, nothing to defend myself but the Bic pen given to me earlier, should a fight ensue. We took a long walk through the dusty hall to the elevator, and then to the awaiting patrol car. As nothing was said, I assumed the male, this 60-something husband, seemed more ashamed from the day's events than any threat from me. I gently guided this soon-to-be ex-husband into the rear of the police car when he turned towards me, our eyes met, I knew what was coming, it was now or never, he made his ill planned bolt for freedom. Our bodies collided, crashing to the ground the fight was on. While his struggle was short lived, I had felt a hot searing stab like pain through my abdomen with a force I'd never experienced. It was a good tussle that I eventually won, but for a moment, I wondered if I had been stabbed. He was now returned to the back seat with less care than before. My hair disheveled, the pain unbearable. As the Sergeant returned, my host unaware of what had transpired we settled back into our crime-fighting routine, I discreetly looked-for blood, anything that would explain the horrific pain I was in. Not covered by Worker's Compensation, and not aware to the extent of my injuries, I finished off the eight-hour shift less enthusiastically than I had begun. Upon my return to Canada, I now had 22 staple marks from a hernia repair that today reminds me of my youthful misadventures with the Los Angeles Police Department.

Italy's Volterra Prison, "Pasta You Can't Refuse[37]"

As Joyce and I continued our around-the-world journeys, we always found time to include an occasional prison or fire department tour. I was surprised Joyce took to these prison tours like a seasoned pro, never showing the slightest fear, even though we sometimes found ourselves outnumbered, and crammed in amongst some of the world's worst killers.

The Fortezza Medicea, better known as Volterra Prison, was built in 1474, some 68 kilometres from Pisa Italy, and just steps from the medieval town of Volterra. It is home to many high security inmates serving no less than seven years for crimes that would curdle one's blood. What was unique about Volterra other than its status as the regions maximum security prison, was their internationally renowned culinary program. These mobsters-turned chefs represented the most notorious criminal organization in the world offering the public each month "Pasta You Can't Refuse," a marketing slogan to celebrate this popular program. They dished up some exquisite meals and wine from the regions wineries all served by mob killers dressed in tuxedos. It was rather trippy, and a memory not soon forgotten.

Our official letter of introduction had been given a heightened level of importance and traveled through the different government channels ending up at the Foreign Affairs office in Ottawa. Our simple request to tour Volterra got lost in translation, and we became "dignitaries of the Canadian Government". As we made our way from Pisa through the Tuscan country side, we managed to get lost. While we attempted to get directions from a "stazione di servizio" the ability to communicate was our next, and impossible hurdle. In a foreign country, unable to speak their language, we were faced with having to inform authorities of our dilemma. Within minutes and much to our chagrin three police vehicles with emergency lights flashing would greet us. This high-profile escort to Volterra prison was memorable, reminding me of a scene from a Bond movie, generating head-turning looks as we traversed the ancient Italian streets.

As we walked the 8th century cobblestone to the prison's main entrance and through the herculean wooden doors, we marveled at the forbidding prison's lime stone walls. We were ushered to the Warden's office where a middle-aged woman smoking two cigarettes greeted us. The dangers of smoking had not yet filtered down to Italian policymakers as we choked back the thick smoke. We waited for the translator to arrive awkwardly drawing stick figures on napkins in hopes of communicating with our hosts, while sipping horribly strong Caffe Americano.

By today's standards this maximum-security building was no match for anyone determined to escape. As we made our way up the wrought iron spiral staircase, a lone gunman with a machine gun-slung over his shoulder cautiously greeted us. As we toured around the gun walk the guard pointed out signatures etched into those 500-year-old prison walls. This ancient form of graffiti was testament to the prison's age, and history.

As we were escorted around the prison, most notable, was the lack of air conditioning that made living, and working conditions almost unbearable. "Pasta You Can't Refuse" was a tongue-in-cheek reference to Mafioso inmates who each month would serve up anything from tuna tartare in citrus fruit rinds, pâte with sweet wine, and couscous with fish. Part of a fundraiser for many of the local charities, the program taught culinary and service skills to inmates in hopes of assisting them in securing employment upon release.

Having missed the previous night's dinner, our host prepared an "intimate luncheon" in the enclosed courtyard. Washed in the afternoon sun, with olive trees throughout, our palates were ready to partake in the much-coveted Italian lunch (pranzo italiano).

Inmates for the various positions, from cooks, chefs, to sommeliers were carefully screened for suitability before they could participate in this highly-coveted program. Dinner guests were subject to the usual background checks, then admitted into the ancient prison, their cell phones, and bags checked at the door. The tables were draped in the finest Italian linen, and candles carefully adorned the many tables arranged to enhance the extraordinary dining experience. While the menu was top notch, officials would never lose touch with the realities of the prison environment, reminding visitors they were dining with plastic knives and cups for a reason.

The Italian Mob had evolved over centuries with their roots in ancient Sicily.

These inmates were the latest generation of crime families, the Italian Cosa Nostra. One inmate I remembered speaking with, Joseph, told us of his passion for cooking, and the break it provided from the restrictive environment of a maximum-security prison. No one would ever suspect this tuxedo-clad gentleman whose skin was leather worn from the sun, was in fact, a member of the Italian mob.

A courtyard lunch at Volterra prison. Many of the waiters were members of the Italian Cosa Nostra.

London's Belmarsh Prison, U.K.[38]

As the curtain was closing on the final act in what was a long history of prison tours spanning 25 years, and stretching around the globe, I was growing tired, and relieved Her Majesty's Prison, Belmarsh in the United Kingdom was to be my last.

In the place where Common Law originated, I was anxious to discover our roots, and compare policies, and procedures.

Known to some as "Hellmarsh", Belmarsh blended into the tiny neighbourhood of Thamesmead on the outskirts of London. Commissioned in 1991 it is situated on 60 acres of the British countryside. Unassuming in design, it was not your typical prison, nor was it how I envisioned a British prison would look.

This multi-level facility housed your garden-variety inmates sent from Magistrates Court, plus those from Criminal Court including some of England's very rich and famous. I was told Belmarsh served as the backdrop to numerous movies and television shows including my favourite, Coronation Street.

After entering through the front gate, the all too intrusive processing unfolded: Empty your pockets, put your rings, watches, wallets, and belts through the X-ray machine. Drug detection dogs were everywhere. I later learned contraband flooded the facility as the elite of society, many now incarcerated at Belmarsh thought nothing of offering big money bribes for a bottle of G&T. Officers on limited incomes could not resist these temptations, and a few fell prey to the "con set up". The Warden, or Governor as he was called, explained this over tea, and a rather dry sampling of English biscuits. It was for those reasons security was tight. Their high security wing was the home to the most closely watched inmates, with 51 cells reserved for international terrorists. Wooden truncheons still in use, hung from officers' belts, snuggly against their neatly pressed uniforms. From post to post the standard greeting was "Ay up Governor", offering me a typical English cupper along the way. My God I thought, trying to interpret their rendition of the English language. As I walked the halls of Belmarsh, it struck me how calm things seemed to be. Inmates in the units walked freely throughout the crowded tiers, casual in their presence, yet polite to this foreign bloke looking totally out of place.

Walking among the guards, past and present, Belmarsh was home to the likes of Ronnie Biggs (great train robbery, 1963), and Karl Bishop serving 20 years for the murder of Harry Potter actor Robert Knox. Knox as you may remember was a young lad of 18 and was set to reprise his role in the second Harry Potter franchise with his character Marcus Belby when he was stabbed outside a London night club. Another notable inmate was shamed Member of Parliament, Lord Jeffrey Howard Archer, Baron and English author who got caught up in a financial scandal that left him penniless. Archer was now a houseguest of Belmarsh for Perjury, and Perverting the Course of Justice. Prior to his meteoric rise in the Conservative Party, Lord Archer was, and is still a prolific writer, having penned some 40 novels along with numerous plays selling upwards of 300 million copies.

Getting closer to the finish line that I called retirement, I reflect on some good times with some great people who still thank me for hosting those rare behind-the-scenes tours that took us inside some very dark, and troubling prisons. While most are quick to criticize the Correctional Service of Canada, yours truly included, it was through these invaluable prison tours we were able to gain insight to our own system.

Say what you will, after 25 years of bleak and depressing prison tours, the difference in prison management was not lost on the likes of me.

Our claim to being "world leaders" in the complex world of incarceration and rehabilitation was not so farfetched. I believed our smaller populations, combined with a boutique style of prisons, made for a safer environment when compared to the US model of warehousing over 2.2 million inmates. While there are shortcomings in every system, there were, and continue to this day to be many success stories of those who managed to return to society, and become law abiding citizens.

Chapter 7

The Human Dynamic

Staff briefings provided a time to chat with co-workers and elicited many fond memories. While there were many unusual personalities, mine included, there were many kind people. You needed a thick skin as correctional officers were relentless with their teasing, and practical jokes. As we waited patiently for the commencement of a staff briefing, we had the opportunity to stock up with snack food found in the staff canteen. It was a great little money maker that provided the funding for our annual Christmas party.

We always had time for a laugh. Sending a rookie officer up on the tier to check out a cell call in # 213 always got a great belly laugh, given the unit cells were only numbered to #212. It was fun watching them search for the mythical, and elusive cell. At Christmas time we would always manage to find a new, unsuspecting officer and tell him about his free Christmas turkey at Bromley's supermarket in Sumas Washington. Just present your badge to get your free festive meal. While there was no free lunch, or in this case dinner, these kinds of gags provided endless hours of childlike entertainment.

The Raccoon Caper, and a Midnight Snack

It was the early 90s when one of our more colourful correctional officers on the graveyard shift shot a raccoon that was sitting harmlessly in an old garbage bin on the loading dock, back of the kitchen. Each night after the final lock up (10:30pm), an officer would patrol the exterior grounds to ensure doors were locked, and nothing was out of place. If there was a best time to escape, many thought the night would provide the perfect cover. The kind-hearted and well-meaning officer reported seeing a pair of eyes illuminating from the garbage bin. Quick into action, but failing to identify the owner of these incandescent green eyes as being friend or foe, he drew down on this unsuspecting little critter like an old west sheriff, blasting two lead bullets into his fur covered carcass. Following his demise, raccoon jokes were the order of the day and for months to come we harassed the "raccoon sheriff" at every opportunity (including raccoon tails left anonymously in his mail box). The ability to laugh at each other was an important part of who we were as a family, and while no one liked being laughed at, those rare occasions helped offset our rather serious prison moments.

The Great Camera Give Away[39]

I was an acting correctional supervisor at Kent, settling into my evening shift, I was annoyed to see that several disposable cameras had been left lying around the office. They had been there for weeks and I wanted to rid my in-basket of the clutter.

Each pay period inmates could purchase various canteen items, including their favourite cereal. The unsuspecting government food buyers had no idea inside the well labeled box of Froot Loops was a free camera. Technically, they were the property of the inmates, but we couldn't have inmates taking pictures within a maximum-security environment, so for security reasons the cameras were seized. I thought it was a grand idea to distribute the cameras to the staff with children, at the same time, decluttering the office. Win-win I thought, but the error of my ways soon became known. To avoid numerous inmate complaints, I scrambled to retrieve the ill-gotten gifts from the staff as a rather red-faced Neil groveled for their return. In the spirit of jail-house fun an everlasting cartoon would be my reminder.

The Great Camera Give away.
Original artwork conceived, and designed by correctional manager Pierre Bouvier. Froot Loops, the name, and its logo are owned by Kellogg's Limited.

Coast Guard Party Sails Off Course[40]

The calm waters off Cape Spear in the harbour of St. John Newfoundland provided the idyllic backdrop for a taxpayer funded booze cruise aboard the Canadian Coast Guard ship (CCGS), J.E. Bernier. The evening skies blackened the once bright sky; the party was about to begin. Twenty-four well-dressed men and women made their way across the old wooden pier, up the gangplank, to what would be a night not many would forget.

Lasting just over three hours, the cruise would ply the waters in and around the eastern-most point of North America. The privileged few dined on lobster, cod, crab, fresh salmon, and prime rib, paired with the finest local wines. The mystical night, would cost taxpayers just under $10,000.00.

What some believed was a harmless evening, would rock Ottawa, and provide the Official Opposition with a feeding frenzy of political embarrassment. Many partygoers were senior officials from the Correctional Service of Canada, along with federal bureaucrats from the Department of Fisheries and Oceans. A staff of four were serving, along with a qualified crew at the ship's helm. The date was September 15, 1999 when the Canadian public expressed outrage when they learned of the outrageous expense, as bureaucrats bellied up to the public trough.

The politicians were scrambling to respond to the damning government audit that landed like a bombshell on the desks of the Official Opposition, sparking a firestorm of political rhetoric. The spin doctors, taking a page from the Wizard of Oz, as the creative writers of the Liberal government tried to present the story as "a bite to eat for a few people".

Though originally built to serve as an ice breaker, the CCGS J.E. Bernier, once a proud ship with a distinguished history stationed in the St. John's harbour, now served in the capacity of search and rescue. That night her role would drastically change as she was shamefully reduced to a party boat filled with denial, and cover-ups, amid a fog of secrecy. At the height of the festivities an emergency distress call came in, from Bonavista Harbour, some 90 nautical miles away. In the midst of the party a man had been violently swept off the rocks, and swallowed up by the unforgiving sea. Newspaper articles later revealed that the ship's helicopter-landing pad was temporarily decommissioned for the soiree's dance floor, rendering her unable to respond.

I shook my head in disbelief upon reading this in the media who reported the blatant waste of taxpayers' dollars going towards such an outrageous party. I took it upon myself to write my Honourable Member of Parliament representing Fraser Valley West, Randy White. Sharing this outrageous story was the beginning of a political matching of our common goals. To most, he was a relentless pit bull, and house leader in the Reform Party. The story provided the necessary ammo to continue his attacks on the Liberal Government. When Randy responded to my work email, he said in his sarcastic, and ever-cutting tone, "The sad passing of the drowning victim could not have been prevented, as the staff most likely were too drunk to respond". (Author's note, in no way does the author suggest staff were impaired.)

Although filled with sorrow at the loss of life, I managed to find a gallows humour in my elected representative, and his unprofessional, but amusing response. I decided to forward his email to all users within the Correctional Service of Canada, which to my surprise reached the already irate, and sensitive government brass. While those in power chose not to act against any of the partiers, as was so typical, they went after me for exposing the embarrassing event further. The CSC demanded a pound of flesh from this lowly CO-II, and union troublemaker. In my response to their discipline, I cited "qualified privilege", my right to communicate with my duly-elected Member of Parliament. Further I had stated that I had not received training on the corporate email system, thus "no training equalled no discipline", an established and important labour standard.

In the early days of the UCCO-SACC-CSN, some managers would bully, and attempt to intimidate those whose only job was to protect their workers. In the end, the correctional manager tasked with the hanging of Neil MacLean returned a finding of "not guilty" in what was called a "fact-finding" investigation. Now angry, a senior manager now retired once again looked as foolish as his turn-of-the-century mustache.

The Kent Peeper, Staff Communique[41]

The "Kent Peeper", the brainchild of our warden's secretary was a monthly newsletter filled with the latest in prison entertainment including new staff arrivals, recipes, and subtle training articles. It was a joy to read, and provided a great way to while away the endless hours in a bubble. There were various columns of interest including the Editor's Chit Chat, and the "Warden's Monthly Message". Eager staff, looking to catch up on the latest gossip, would turn to the Peeper. As a bonus, I enjoyed researching the answers to the questions posed in the Peeper, for a chance to win a coveted up-front employee parking spot.

One Tough Inmate

To fully understand the dynamic makeup of the inmate population, I wanted to find a way to take you, the reader inside prison life in hopes you might understand the danger, the hate, and the true personalities of those we we're hired to manage, but many also loathed. I had my view from an officer's perspective, but I wanted more, to delve into the carefully guarded world of an inmate, from their perspective.

A career criminal now on parole, one such inmate afforded me just such an opportunity. "John" as we will call him laid out his life story one afternoon. His hope was to explain where he went wrong in his life.

John now a free man, and me retired writing a book had our first meeting since the unruly days at Kent. We met at a local chip shop, chosen for its open atmosphere, and safer for me, until I could gauge the situation. Still unsure, I wondered the real reason this con wanted to meet. John was now showing the effects of a life of incarceration, his long grey hair, slightly balding, and a craggy face that clearly showed the signatures of a hard life. As I glanced around the room, I noticed he looked like most, however I couldn't help wonder if anyone knew he was an ex-con. Does anyone know I was a guard? To "crack to the man" was a long-standing taboo, and could spell disaster for his tough guy image. Would he, or could he, provide a rare glimpse into the seedy underbelly I was eager to expose?

As we settled into the conversation, I gradually became more at ease, and willing to listen. Each wrinkle on this man's face, and there were many, was a road map of the pain of a life wasted in prison. While open and willing to share, he was still guarded about some aspects of prison life, protecting as it were the secrets that could harm those he left behind.

As a young boy, growing up on the dangerous streets of Vancouver's east side, he escaped a troubled, and abusive childhood at the violent hands of his father. Coming from the affluent side of the tracks known as West Vancouver I had grown up only a few miles away, but had little in common with John. When he spoke of his "crew", he would smile as he remembers how they shared similar backgrounds. He was in his comfort zone, within a gang that provided John with the trust he so longed for in close friends.

His young crew would commit break and enters (B&E) throughout the business community of Vancouver, behaving more like thrill seeking hooligans than professional burglars. Lacking appropriate parenting role models John rebelled, and lived on the edge during those formative teenage years. One of the gangs early B&Es involved pilfering several tires from a local tire shop, the sole purpose of which was to roll them down one of Vancouver's steeper hills, providing a moment of entertainment. This could have been the crossroads that led to the beginning of John's undoing. All the petty thefts were more about a journey into young adulthood than about being part of an organized gang for profit. They were young, angry kids, in their early teens, lacking direction, and living for the moment. His crew would huddle in the maintenance room, and soak up the heat from the boilers at the local pool. This quickly became their headquarters for crime, a haven away from troublesome home lives.

The transition from young kid to punk, into a hardened criminal was progressive. He graduated from petty crimes, to the selling of recreational drugs to his friends. His habit included inhaling nail polish to using Mexican pot, then eventually turning to the harder drugs, LSD, and Speed. He would sell anything to finance his own habit, mixing the roles of a drug user, with the business side of a drug dealer. Those around him would either die from an overdose at the end of a dirty needle, taken out by a bullet from a rival gang member, or wound up like most, in jail.

John became a successful participant in organized crime, and being part of a group was to his liking. Sometimes conflicted by his roll, addiction was his business. He grew hardened and cold, but he had boundaries. He didn't like getting new users hooked, but it was a business after all. He rolled with the bad guys, thundering down many BC roads on his Harley Fat Boy.

In his 30s, John was now in the fast-lane, fast action, motorcycles, and danger. He had a tough reputation to go with riding his "ape hanger" style bike including the worn leather, branded clothing, and a handful of finger bling.

As his drug use, and desperation to feed his own habit escalated, John became a collector of drug debts.

With collections, strong-arming, and eventual murder, the days of innocence, John would say, were forever gone. There was no room for compassion, or kindness, everything was about making money. Whether it was the need for speed, or the easy money being a drug dealer, each part had its inherent dangers.

The bonds of trust long since broken when he quickly realized there was no honour among thieves. His experiences told him there was more profit in cooking the product that allowed him to control the drug's quality. Cutting, or buffing, he would dilute his product with store-bought lactose, increasing his profit margins.

While John stated that his ego eventually would bring him down, his dependency on his product made him paranoid, developing a mistrust of his customers, and competitors alike. The strong bonds of life's many friendships were now torn asunder. He would see many of his former associates join him later in jail. Like most, discovering their pathway to the criminal underworld, John was introduced to pre-trial in Vancouver while awaiting sentencing for less serious crimes from his teenage years. First there was Wilkinson Road Prison (Wilky) in Victoria, followed by Burnaby's Oakalla Prison, and finally, Kent Institution. His crew was never far behind.

Convicted in the mid-80s of First Degree Murder as a killer for hire, he was only a short time in Oakalla before he arrived at Kent where we first met. Wakened by the Sheriffs one morning, they rushed him out of bed, as guards told him it was time to go. Hustled to the back seat of a waiting, Sheriff's van, his wrists were handcuffed, and legs shackled. It was a rude awakening to his start of doing federal time. His 25 to life "bit" began with his long ride to Kent. As he rolled up to the back of A&D, the van door slid open, not a welcoming word was spoken, rather an icy stare from a less than enthusiastic guard, ordering him to bend over, and touch his toes.

While we strived to treat all inmates the same, this was John's new reality, starting with the stripping of his personal dignity. After he was given his unit assignment, he would acquire those items to sustain him-white bed sheets (blue came later), a hand-me-down hospital style blue cotton blanket, institutional clothing, and a stained pillow that he would tuck under his arm. He would carefully walk down the corridor towards what he thought was his final, and pitiful journey to the units. As he walked through the two doors entering the unit, he was hit with the stark realities of prison life.

The smell of sweat was everywhere. Toilets in every cell added to the jailhouse ambience, and the acrid smell of urine almost made him puke. Even worse was the overwhelming odour of bleach used in a futile attempt to mask the smells.

Freedom was no longer his. He had a strict prison schedule to follow: when to eat, and when to sleep. All he had were a few items of personal clothing, family pictures, limited toiletries, and a small 14-inch television to while away the long monotonous hours. These were the sum of his life's achievements.

A simple thing like a TV that we take for granted was for him, his only connection to the outside world. He was surrounded by people with their own problems, ranging from drug habits to mental issues, to the unresolved anger, and deviant behaviours of his new tier mates.

Seeing old friends after he arrived was reassuring, and the thought of a prison reunion provided some level of assurance. There were many familiar faces at this reunion from hell; however, there were more questionable psychopaths to be wary of, inmates with insurmountable problems. Although John was in a unit with many other guys, he was alone, doing his own time. He came with a solid reputation, a force to be reckoned with that provided a level of respect, and protection. He was a leader, directive in nature, who was revered by inmates on the unit. Settling into the unit's routine, the movement schedule was going to take some getting used to, but for now it was glad-handing with those he knew would help him get the lay of the land before he turned in for his first night.

On the rare occasions that he reunited with the outside world for court proceedings, visits or hospital appointments, each began with hearing those bone-chilling words, "bend over and touch your toes".

John was as tough as nails, and by their measure, a stand-up con. Labeled a cold-hearted killer, a sociopath, it was during our first meeting on the street that he described himself a solver of problems, a renaissance man, who prided himself, accomplished in the art of writing.

Involved in the Lifer's Group, then Inmate Committee, President John would be in the mix of every problem, from unrest, to riots. He claimed to be the go-to-guy working for peaceful solutions. He was a limit setter, a label we used to describe certain inmates, and their behaviours, a "Type A" disposition, a man with a killer personality. I never doubted my memory of him as a troublemaker was more accurate than his, as peacemaker. Though most inmates tried, it was nearly impossible to do your own time, as everybody was into everyone's business.

John would say the young punks of today have much more violent tendencies, and while they may have been GP inmates, it was clear through their often-violent crimes that they were anything but stand up.

He reflected further, stating an inmate's job was to break the law, and ours to catch them. It was never personal, unless you made it personal, then they would retaliate in kind. John's day was busy, solving problems, making deals, or dealing with the daily drama.

Walking the sports field was less about exercise than it was about clandestine meetings. No different than the street, John had his fingers in every pie. Selling drugs, making deals, strong arming, all while under the watchful eye of the man. He had his go-to guys, some who would hold (drugs) some that would sell and deliver, others that would steal just about anything. If one inmate got along with a guard, he/she then would be utilized. Everyone had a job. The communications network through loved ones facilitated arrangements for the packing of drugs through visits. More complicated shipments were smuggled through Admission and Discharge (A&D) but smaller quantities of drugs could be tossed over in a drug stuffed bird. As the guards discovered their methods, inmates would conjure up new hiding places. Knowing our procedures for opening mail allowed them to hide drugs under the envelops flap, or under a stamp. As time progressed, a family member would dissolve their drugs into actual writing paper, which would be smoked later. In rare cases inmates would cultivate those staff that seemed vulnerable. Over time they would be groomed to pack cell phones to drugs, discarded after their usefulness was no longer needed. To some, the "con set up" was a game, using a staff member then, exposing the compromised employee when they were finished.

Idiosyncrasies that he developed over the years was the needed control, in an out-of-control world. Staking out a regular seat in the dining hall, cleaning his drum, to folding his clothes neatly, were part of his daily regime.

Now, for the first time in 27 years, John found himself free from the restrictive chains of incarceration. He would cascade down, eventually residing in a halfway house, and then his own apartment.

John recounts his experience as a free man. Traveling with his Native Elder on the BC Ferries, he asked permission to use the public washroom. Coming from a structured prison life for many years, it was understandable that using public washrooms was confusing. The technology of self-flushing toilets almost did him in. Remaining cool, his next daunting task was the self-defeating hurdles of the motion-detecting taps, and motion-activated soap dispensers. Swallowing his pride, John would ask the gentleman at the next wash basin to show him the secrets of their operation. Later, standing on the ferries deck, the wind blowing in his hair, he leaned on the guardrail taking in the fresh sea air, this was freedom.

During our meeting, John introduced me to his girlfriend. He said this was what life was about, the love he missed growing up, a partner for whatever time he had left. He got his do-over, now we shall see. While he admits his life was "fucked up", it's those experiences that made him who he is today. Still a bit tentative, John stays close to home, as feelings of an uncertain world cause him anxiety.

From the BC Pen to Canada's Top "Turnkey", the Career of Don Head[42]

He is a giant of a man, standing well over 6 feet, an imposing force that is until you meet him. Don, a veteran of Canada's Armed Forces, is also a skilled, and respected bureaucrat. While he knows his way around Ottawa, he is equally at home visiting with staff. He is an enigma. To most, he is simply Don, personable yet confident in who he is, and what he represents.

I have known of Don for years, but it wasn't until later in my career that we would finally meet. While enjoying lunch at my Abbotsford Wendy's shortly after he became Commissioner, I glanced up, and to my surprise, in strolls Don Head followed by his well-dressed entourage. Taking advantage of a brief respite between meetings, Don grabbed his burger, and like the wind, he was gone.

He is a husband, father, sports enthusiast, and an avid fisherman who freely shares his fishing antics on Facebook. He has a deep passion for our history, and its people.

Between 1978-1995 he added the experiences of four federal penitentiaries in BC to his resume, crisscrossing our country as Senior Commissioner visiting all federal prisons, and representing our interests worldwide.

Don would enter the Penitentiary Service at William Head Institution. He was somewhat surprised at the idyllic seaside prison, where the deer and antelope played. When the BC Penitentiary came calling in the form of a job offer, Don made the move as a correctional officer in 1978. He speaks of his long walk as a recruit from the parking lot up through the towering solid wood doors that welcomed him in what became a time-honoured career. It was a daunting fortress, dark and gloomy, but the history of the building was not lost on the rookie. As he walked through the main gates of the BC Pen, and through the halls, he could smell the despair, the tragic history devoid of hope.

Moving quickly to the new Kent, Don continued as a correctional officer working the very posts I would work years later. Don received the all-important job experience, a foundation that would serve him well throughout his career.

After many years as a dedicated public servant, Don was appointed our Commissioner on June 27, 2008.

Commissioner Head had received numerous awards throughout his illustrious career, including the Governor General Corrections Exemplary Service medal with bar (each 10-year period), the Special Alert medal, United Nations Emergency Force 2, United Nations Force (Cyprus) and the Queens Diamond Jubilee medal.

No matter how successful he became, Don would not forget his roots. Never afraid to be himself, showing his personal side to the delight of those who knew him. He is great at remembering staff, and had a deep knowledge of the history of the Correctional Service of Canada. These observations are in stark contrast to the role of an Ottawa politician, but a role that he manages quite well.

At the Matsqui 50th anniversary celebration, I would cross paths with our Commissioner once again. During his reflective talk to the throngs of celebrants, he spoke of "that one story". As a member of the Guard of Honour I listened from the crowded bleachers, interested to hear more about that "one story". Still curious, I asked Don to elaborate. Was it an inmate success story, or maybe a CSC program he was most proud? To my delight, the anticipated story arrived in my in-basket.

The taxpayers of Canada got their monies worth with Don as he most often did his greatest work pounding away on his laptop while waiting for a plane, or in this case writing the "one story" while flying to Europe for a corrections symposium.

> *Over my almost 40 years in corrections, I am constantly asked what stands out most for me. Was it a riot, a hostage taking, a death or some other security incident that influenced upon me the most in my career? Thinking back to when I started as a Correctional Officer in February 1978 and working through the ranks of CSC, in four penitentiaries, two regional HQs, NHQ and also working in the Yukon Territory and the province of Saskatchewan I can honestly say that there is one thing that sticks out for me more than anything else — it is the people that come to work for CSC. Each day I am constantly reminded of the strength, dedication, commitment, professionalism, resilience and fragility of the tens of thousands of staff across this great country of ours who come to work to contribute to changing lives and protecting Canadians. I am constantly energized by the innovative and inspiring ideas that the staff bring to their jobs. Although I talk about their jobs, they are really careers. The vast majority of the staff commit 20, 25, 30, and 35 years of their life to corrections. One only does this for a career, not a job. When you see the collective intelligence, energy, and commitment of many people day in and day out, you cannot help but be moved and impacted on a personal level. When you start to look at the people as part of the equation of our business, you are quickly reminded about what the focus of your efforts need*

to be as a leader, no matter where you sit in the hierarchy. Inspiring individuals to excel in their roles, empowering them to make a difference, and allowing them to innovate and bring forward the next best idea that will assist others— these are the roles of leaders in a people-centered and people-centric organization. When you see the challenges that the staff face day in and day out, and then see how they rise to those challenges, you cannot help but be amazed, impressed, and deeply moved. So when I am asked what stands out the most for me in my career, it truly is the people.

Don Head
Commissioner
Correctional Service of Canada

Rising through the ranks Don contributed 40 years of public service.

Claire Culhane, Bringing the Outside In[43]

No history of the prisoners' rights movement in Canada would be complete without mentioning the life achievements of Claire Culhane. A story of incredible courage.

Claire was many things to many people; she was a mother, grandmother, great grandmother, volunteer healthcare provider in Vietnam, union organizer, and Canada's foremost peace activist. Born into a family of Russian Jews in Montreal in 1918, Claire later became a member of the Communist Party of Canada. Her front row seat to Canada's participation in the Vietnam war drove her passion. At issue with Claire was the exportation and funding of military supplies including ammunition, Napalm and Agent Orange to the United States for use in the wholesale killing of innocent young children in Quang Ngai, South Central Vietnam, site of the wars Tet Offensive and some of the wars worst atrocities.

At war's end, returning to Canada, Claire focused her humanitarian efforts on those she felt were incarcerated in a Canadian prison system she believed was inhumane. She would speak for those who did not have a voice, and by some accounts, could not be silenced.

She cared deeply, and had utter contempt for a system she felt was dangerous, and anything but rehabilitative in nature.

While she taught incarcerated women as far back as 1974, she didn't come into her own until June 9, 1975 with a hostage-taking at the British Columbia Penitentiary. The events over those 41 hours ending in the death of Mary Steinhauser (see Chapter I, the Mary Steinhauser Story) gave her a cause, and now a platform in which to protest the abysmal conditions in Segregation units within our Canadian prison system.

Claire was arrested at the BC Pen, and later charged with trespassing in 1977 after staging a passionate sit-in of the warden's office. She wanted access to the over-represented native inmate populations within Segregation, however her aggressive stance often saw her requests bound in red tape, or summarily dismissed.

In an attempt to become more transparent within the public, the CSC formed the Citizens' Advisory Committee (CAC) in 1976. The CAC are a group of dedicated volunteers tasked with representing the residents within the surrounding prison communities. Looking for an opportunity to work from within, she managed to secure a coveted position on the Board.

Claire if anything, was compassionate. After the closing of the BC Pen she found her way to Kent in 1979 where we would later meet in 1988. While her ego, and self-importance annoyed me to no end, there was no questioning her loyalty to the cause. To me, she seemed to love inmates, and hate staff; you could see the contempt on her face for the jailers. For the first time, she was given an air of legitimacy, and saw firsthand what she surmised as horrid living conditions. Over the months, and years to come, Claire would organize, and participate in numerous sit-ins, hoping to educate the public.

The in-custody death of Edward NALON in 1974 was but a single death however was instrumental in the formation, and her participation in the Prisoners' Rights Group (PRG). Placed in Segregation, NOLAN refused to work. He was given 30 days in the "hole" and placed on a restrictive diet. He later committed suicide in Millhaven's tough Seg unit. It was a pivotal event in Canada's prison history, and ignited a movement that was quick to gather momentum.

Each year on the anniversary of his death, inmates and community support groups observe August 10th as a day of remembrance of the harsh conditions within our penal system and those who had perished within. It was to be known as Prisoner's Justice Day where inmates would show support of their fellow inmates who had died in prison either to self-harm issues, or at the hands of an uncaring system. They would refuse to eat or work.

The organization of which Claire was a founding member, would help inmates with involuntary transfers, locating lawyers, filing grievances, and attending parole hearings on their behalf. The organization worked towards the abolishment of 25-year sentences, and what was once called solitary confinement.

The PRG over many years, she said was the best game in town as she fought for everything from better access to health care, to the philosophy of a world without incarceration.

Claire would attend the institution for the purposes of an inmate visit asking to see Jimmy or Steve. Calling an inmate by anything other than his last name created a level of familiarity that could blur professional lines. I think she knew this, and tried to provoke a response. We recognized the dangerous tensions between line officers, the system, and inmates, and like her or not, Claire Culhane looked at what she felt was wrong, and spoke out. With an icy stare, she could bring her most staunch opponent to their knees. She was a woman of enormous strength who some said could only be stopped with her death. While her marriage to Jerry Culhane was short lived, she raised a family, complete with grandchildren. She was a prolific writer who penned numerous titles including "Still Barred from Prison", "One Woman Army", "Why is Canada in Vietnam", and "No Longer Barred".

Her time as a prisoner advocate was stormy at best. She would say in her book Barred from Prison that the system was built to keep inmates on the inside, and the public out.

Claire was a cheerleader for change, and worked feverously to right the wrongs of Canada's troubled prison system. That in-your-face attitude brought about social change, albeit slowly. I believe our mistrust of her was justified, but she was a voice for those inmates who could not be heard.

Upon her death, I remember commenting about the ungrateful inmates who couldn't be bothered to show up to her prison memorial in 2002. The PRG that she loved, I understand, honoured Claire's memory with a park bench at Trout Lake in Burnaby BC.

Claire was tough as nails, and spoke for those who could not speak.

LINC-Glen FLETT from Criminal to Christ[44]

Glen FLETT was a career criminal, in and out of prisons most of his life, starting his first prison sentence when he was 19 years of age. In 1977, FLETT was on a Christmas pass from William Head on Vancouver Island when he failed to return. A fugitive from justice, he embarked on a string of armed robberies down the west coast of the United States, and across Canada.

The Brinks robbery of the Hudson's Bay store in Eglington Square, a Toronto suburb in Ontario went bad. As they fled the scene, FLETT, and his accomplice shot, and killed 40-year-old Theodore Van Sluytman, a Hudson Bay Company men's wear employee. He was captured three months later, and transferred to Vancouver Island Regional Correctional Centre, or Wilkinson Road Jail as it was known. He would face charges for being unlawfully at large while out on Christmas pass, and for not remaining at the scene of a hit and run. While awaiting trial, FLETT received a visit from the Toronto Police with an extradition order returning him to Toronto's infamous Don Jail, where FLETT would also be charged with the murder of Van Sluytman. FLETT now back in federal custody, he was assessed in the Reception Centre at Kingston Penitentiary, and later sent to Millhaven Institution where he would meet Sherry Edmunds. Sherry was a volunteer with the prison. In 1982 I met up with FLETT again after he transferred to Kent. Known as a "bomber pilot" for all the pills he was taking, FLETT said Kent was like a war zone. He was struggling with the violence of daily prison life, and carried a shank for protection most times. Another inmate saw FLETT's pain from the guilt he carried, and suggested that he visit the prison chapel where he met Chaplain Arne Jenson.

FLETT transferred three years later to Matsqui Institution, and subsequently to William Head Institution on Vancouver Island where he served out the remainder of his sentence after it was reduced to 14 years to life. FLETT found the Lord, and was baptized in 1982.

At William Head in June 1987, he would marry Sherry Edmunds. Born in the prison town of Kingston Ontario, Sherry started early in life amassing educational accomplishments, including a BA in Sociology, Bachelor in Education, and a Master in African Studies. To marry someone in prison was the last thing on her mind.

After he was granted full parole in 1992, he and wife Sherry co-founded the Long-Term Inmates Now in the Community (LINC) Society (www.lincsociety.bc.ca), an organization that believed:

1. that every person within society has a fundamental right to be safe and secure,
2. that everyone is part of the reintegration process where all people have an inherent value and dignity,
3. that the positive contribution of every person can have a meaningful impact on the spirit of justice, and on the sense of wellbeing, within the community,
4. that hope for the future lies in the potential of every individual to change, and in the willingness of others to support, and encourage that change.

At the core of the LINC philosophy is the belief in restorative justice. The worthlessness, and isolation many inmates often clouded by their denial of guilt. This guilt could be expressed in the form of anger, and a sense of victimization. In order for inmates to modify their behaviour, they needed to be held accountable for what they had done to their victims, their families, and the community.

Supporting victims of crime had become an integral part of the work LINC undertook, and has evolved over the years to where they now provide direct services to victims of crime through funding and organizing victim centered community events, victim peer support groups, assisting victims to attend conferences, and workshops.

It was 2007 unknown to FLETT, his wife Sherry inadvertently contacted his victim's daughter, Margo Van Sluytman, and a new journey of healing began. What started innocently enough with an email would bring together the most unlikely kinship. Despite the overwhelming success of LINC, FLETT was described as riddled, addled, and saddled with ghosts from his past.

The guilt weighed heavily on him, never forgetting what he had done in Toronto that fateful day. Meeting Margot was an unlikely opportunity, but provided a bond between a victim, and a killer. It was an important turning point for FLETT. To the daughter Margot, it was a lifetime of suffering as she went from job to job as she struggled with the memories of her father's murder. From drug addiction, her life of suffering was not much different than his. They have kept in regular contact since that initial meeting, and have become unexpected best friends.

Now 65 (when I last met with FLETT, and his wife Sherry at Emma's Acres), with grey hair, and a weathered face, he enjoys life as a husband, father, grandfather and servant to our community. Soft spoken, he has the rough hands of a farmer, a role he seems to flourish in. Sherry, the executive director of LINC, is a successful woman in her own right, working towards her PhD. I'm sure back in the old days I viewed FLETT as a con, and his wife Sherry as a con-lover. Times have, or seemed to have proven me wrong. After I retired, I saw Glen in a different light. He is nothing like I remember him.

Joyce and I were invited, and have attended each year the annual LINC Christmas dinner in Mission. Dining with 300 hundred people from the community each year has been a humbling experience, as most just needed a much-desired meal, a moment of warmth, a break from the cold and unforgiving street.

As I glanced around the room, I would see faces from my past, including several Kent alumni who years later earned transfers to lower security, and were eventually paroled into the community. Gone was the angry guard in me, I was open at least to say hello, wondering if they would recognize their former tormentor from many years gone by.

Glen has also found a small measure of peace, and now understands the magnitude of his actions that day. A healing journey that has lasted a lifetime, Glen, too humble to say he has found peace, gives back to the community through the efforts of his work, and the work of others in Emma's Acres, a small farm on the outskirts of Mission.

Glen FLETT, "Kent was like a war zone".

Summing Up My Family, the Social Dynamic

As I reflect back on my 25 years, it was the people I met during this incredible journey who had the deepest, and most profound effect on my soul. While you have read about the trials and tribulations of prison life, I want to convey my appreciation to the many kind hearted people I had the honour to know.

I suppose one of the coping mechanisms of dealing with prison life is to find activities, or people, and friendships to offset the physiological damage caused from work. Whether it was the gallows humour, or the endless practical jokes, whatever worked, we did, resulting in bonds that would last a lifetime.

I found my solace through prison tours, community service, or volunteerism from within. Others sought out the comradery of raising a few "day seven" beers at the Legion, or down by the river on a summer's eve. One memorable event that transcended the borders of Kent were the baseball games at the various institutions. The Kent Cutthroats along with the Kent Kokanees were, I understand, fielding the best in players, but also had the kindest human beings bar none. It was a different time back then, an innocence when compared to today. Staff were family. Administration staff worked tirelessly to dream up festive games, from "Angels and Earthlings" to "Secret Santa". I always enjoyed the Christmas season around Kent and Mountain, watching my peers compete for the best-decorated light show in a unit office, or staff cubical. Whether it was a children's Christmas party, or other events, staff were solid, and social events played an important role in the building of our solidarity. Kent was well represented in the various sporting events and teams, including a noon hour walking club, slow pitch softball, regional sports day, and organized gun competitions. There were also events honouring people: funerals of fallen staff members, the happier celebrations of a birthday, or anniversary. It was a joyous time that brought our dysfunctional, and most times funny family, together.

Now in retirement I am proud member of the Pacific Region Guard of Honour, and attend different functions at every opportunity. This is a hallowed honour that allows me to stay connected with those within the CSC, and pay homage to those sadly departed.

Chapter 8

From Unrest to Riots, The Violence of Prison Life

Courtyard Riot, The Loss of our Beloved Benches

A mere 25 days into my career I watched in disbelief as a fight between two inmates broke out in the dining hall, eventually escalating into the destruction of the kitchen, spilling out into the courtyard of Kent. Five of our correctional officers stationed at the kitchen entrance rushed in to help those officers trapped in the dining hall battling dozens of inmates embroiled in what was now a full-on riot. The kitchen gun walk officer managed to fire off a round providing a brief distraction, allowing our staff to escape the area when it was clear we were losing the kitchen.

I was in C-Unit on the evening shift, and had a bird's eye view when the inmates now in the courtyard continued their wave of destruction. I watched through the unit window in disbelief as they destroyed our beloved courtyard benches. Management was quick to call it an "isolated incident", a buzz phrase used repeatedly throughout my career to minimize many dangerous, and troubling situations. While the damage resulting from the riot was only $42,000.00, it had a direct impact on me, and my first month on the job.

I was trapped in the C-Unit office and like other officers on the GP side we were unable to escape from the inmates who were yelling death threats from behind the unit's sliding metal door. As luck would have it those in the courtyard decided to negioate with management through my office window giving me an upfront vantage point to the ongoing inmate demands. As was typical in prison the despirate inmates wanted drugs. The IERT advanced through the tunnel ready to strike, entering A/B and C/D control posts, waiting for the right moment to swoop in to rescue those of us remaining in each of the four unit offices. I couldn't believe the carnage. Broken windows, smashed kitchen equipment, plates and glasses scattered about our dining hall. The courtyard benches, once a place to rest our weary bones during movement times, were but a memory. Our comfort in a very uncomfortable courtyard now looked like kindling, sadly never to be rebuilt. Once safely in the control post, guns at the ready we supervised as those remaning in the courtyard were escorted back into their respective units and locked up. To watch an out-of-control riot from the beginning to the end had me questioning my choosen career. It showed me how things could change in the blink of an eye, and the potential for life threatening danger.

The Kent Riot, 2003 Like a War Zone[45]

The Kent riot of 2003 was by far the worst in the Institution's dark and dangerous history. It was the evening shift, and the heat from the summer's day was cooling, as day turned to night. Inmates were returning from the gym for what we thought was the evening's final count, and lockup. They could wear street clothing after day shift work hours, often putting on hockey jerseys, or other personal items of clothing. That day they were wearing the non-descript institutional issued jeans, and blue golf shirts that allowed them to blend in. This did not go unnoticed as staff became aware of the subtle warning signs of pending trouble. Earlier that day inmates were seen hoarding supplies such as extra canteen items, and toilet paper in what would normally be a clue of bad things to come.

As the events of June 16, 2003 unfolded, despite intelligence reports, staff had little time to react. Just prior to the final lockdown of the day (10:30 pm) A-B unit inmates, carrying makeshift weapons, and wearing balaclavas, refused to lock up, forcing staff off the tier, and into the unit offices. Activated PPA alarms, loud and frequent, echoed throughout MCCP-Central Control. Radio calls for assistance came in fast and furious. Gunfire could be heard throughout the prison as staff responded, the rifle's report, first sporadic, then every few seconds.

Later, one officer's wife at home said she was by the phone expecting her husband's all-clear phone call, a traditional practice many spouses made, their way of saying the count was clear, the inmates were neatly tucked away, and they would be home shortly. It was a call that never came.

The warning signs had been received by management in the form of an unsigned letter, we assume from an unidentified inmate. The "rat letter" for some reason, its existence denied, wound up in the hands of our Member of Parliament Randy White. The Institutional spokesperson discounted the thought of a sinister plot, going with the simpler excuse of a brew party gone awry.

Thanks to a volley of warning shots discharged by the A/B control post officer, the IERT was able to evacuate remaining staff from the unit, before the monsters came through the barriers, and down the stairs. Now covering the outside control post windows with blankets, the inmates effectively blinded the armed bubble officer. He shot intuitively, repeatedly. The first shot, then two, on and on, eventually he called for more ammo. The inmates were lighting fires, the noise unbearable. Flames engulfed the cinderblock walls, spreading their boiling rage across everything in their path. The unmistakable scent of smoke permeated my nostrils, scorching, and sweltering hot. Now with two correctional officers in the bubble adding support, the shift dragged on.

The inmates were smashing anything in their sight as unit chairs went crashing into the walls. There was no limit to the destruction as these rebellious inmates lashed out in very dangerous ways, trashing lights, breaking off sprinkler heads, smashing windows, and burning anything the flames would consume.

The IERT was set up and waiting for the Crisis Manager to authorize a signed Situational Management Emergency Action Communication (SMEAC) that gave legal authorization for their team to commence an all-out attack.

As smoke and flames billowed out of windows, Kent was burning. The Crisis Manager could see an out-of-control situation getting worse by the minute. With the Emergency Response Team Leader in the Command Centre, it was time. Taking control, the Crisis Manager would direct his managers to go to the unit's entrance door to read the Riot Act giving the IERT authority to use all means necessary, up to and including deadly force. The Criminal Code of Canada (CCC) states "a group of 12 or more who were riotously, and tumultuously acting, or assembled together constituted an unlawful assembly". An unlawful assembly occurs when at least three (3) or more persons assemble and form a common purpose, and there are reasonable grounds to believe that there will be a tumultuous breach of the peace. The disturbance had to be caused by a multiple of people and consists of more than just noise - then it may be deemed riotous.

Once the Act was read, inmates could be legally, and expeditiously dispersed, or face the consequences of injury, or death.

The Riot Act

Her Majesty the Queen charges, and commands all persons being assembled, immediately to disperse, and peaceably to depart to their habitations, or to their lawful business upon the pain of being guilty of an offence for which, upon conviction, they may be sentenced to imprisonment for life.

God Save The Queen

The legal requirements having now been met, as outlined in section 67 in the Criminal Code of Canada (CCC), the IERT now had clear jurisdiction, and authority to use all force deemed necessary.

Those inmates still in the units were trying to take control of the courtyard but were held at bay by staff. During the event, the danger was very real, yet one experienced correctional officer managed to extract a laugh from his colleagues as he discharged his shotgun towards a white flag flying in a unit window. The officer was heard yelling, "this is for 30 years of bullshit".

With the end of the riot in sight, the powder from Oleo-resin Capsicum (a type of pepper spray or dust) still lingered in the courtyard air. Staff stood their ground, preventing the inmates' advance. Fifteen armed members of the IERT, now in position, converged on the units, one at a time they entered, guns at the ready. They proceeded cautiously, one step followed by another, as they waded through the ankle-deep bloody water. These intimidating officers, dressed in black, with night sticks they banged their shields, capturing each of the instigators who by now realized continued resistance was futile. Those identified as participating in the riot were escorted to Segregation, strip searched, and placed separately in a cell. When Segregation was full, the remaining instigators were ushered back to their units, and locked tightly in their drums. It was deadly quiet; the melee was finally over. The smoke had cleared, as we all stood in disbelief, we assessed the carnage. Flooding, and the smell of the burnt prison walls left an indelible impression. Staff would learn the price tag for these outrageous acts of defiance would reach a staggering $500,000.00.

The first victim of the riot was 39-year-old Darrell Vance SHANOSS who was found dead in his cell, stabbed through each eye. He was stabbed a total of 52 times. His murder described by staff as savage, showing no mercy. Was this a sick message from others we thought? While there weren't many tears shed over his death, there was the shock at his very violent demise. The IERT removed his body to the courtyard as they cautiously moved forward looking for survivors.

SHANOSS, we were told, was young boy who grew up on the reserve. His deep-seated anger would manifest itself in ritual killings of small animals as he lashed out against others in a show of power. SHANOSS had been sentenced to life in prison for Second Degree Murder, Robbery and Assault. He was from British Columbia's north, a victim of the residential school system, and had been the product of a troubled childhood.

The next victim was Inmate ROBINSON who was severely beaten and stabbed for refusing to take part in the riot. He was found under his bunk bed with multiple stab wounds, and a plexiglass shank protruding from his head. Despite his serious injuries, ROBINSON survived.

The worst riot in the history of Kent, unnerved even the strongest old-time guards. I often wondered how those who knew of the warning letter, who uttered the more convenient version, could live with themselves. Staff knew the truth, but were powerless to hold management accountable. Only Member of Parliament Randy White, and a follow up investigation would expose the truth.

Six GP inmates were eventually charged, including inmates O'HERN, BIEGA, CHAPPEL, GREGORY, ANAKER, and DEAN, with willfully destroying government property. A select few were charged with assaulting five peace officers.

The slow return to a "new normal" was orchestrated with safety in mind. Each phase of feeding was carried out by members of the IERT, most of whom had little, or no sleep. With each passing day, they would be seen sleeping in their so-called turtle shells of armour ready to respond at a moment's notice. The exhaustion taking its toll, not seeing their families, sleeping in their sweat, most too busy to shower. The hours turned to days, they were exhausted.

Inmates were locked down for 10 days before returning to a new operational routine which was slow, and methodical. There was no more lounging in the courtyard. Point "A" to Point "B" freedom was gone.

Not your typical day at the office.
B-unit office 1982

Kent Riot.

Anonymous letter warned prison officials about riot

Stories by Sarah Young
Staff Reporter

Kent prison administrators were warned last week in an anonymous letter from an inmate that a riot was about to break out but didn't take it seriously.

The letter warned prison officials they should "assume a pending protest . . . assume a full-scale riot [with] millions of dollars damage, assume hostage-taking . . . assume murders and deaths."

But Kent institution warden Alex Lubimiv, noting the complaints in the letter, said yesterday "we didn't feel it was an appropriate context for a riot."

WHITE

On Sunday, three days after the letter was found, a riot broke out resulting in the fatal stabbing of murderer inmate Darrell Sha-noss, 39, the non-lethal stabbing of another prisoner and about $500,000 damage to the prison.

Lubimiv said administrators knew prisoners were upset with recent changes in how prisoners were fed, but didn't think a riot was in the offing.

"There were constant threats for three or four months," he said, "inmates don't like regulations."

But because of the note, prison managers closed down the institution, guards were issued with pepper spray and handcuffs — not part of their normal gear — and an extra

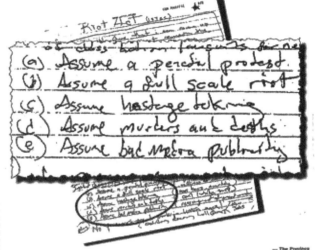

The two-page, handwritten letter titled 'Riot Act' details escalating tensions in the prison.

— The Province

officer was assigned to a control post. "I'm confident in saying we did everything we could," Lubimiv said.

Andy Reekie of the Union of Canadian Correctional Officers said yesterday that managers should be charged with criminal negligence for ignoring the letter.

"The administration knew and they didn't do anything to prevent the riot," he said.

The two-page, handwritten letter titled "Riot Act" details escalating tensions between protective-custody inmates and general-population prisoners. It says those in protective custody feared other inmates were contaminating their food supply, said Reekie.

He said that since Lubimiv took over Kent in late February, general-population prisoners have been forced to eat meals in their cells, like protective-custody inmates. The letter demands that regular inmates be allowed to eat meals in the dining hall.

Alliance MP Randy White renewed calls for a public inquiry into the institution, saying taxpayer money is being wasted again after prisoners trashed government property.

The prison guards' union, which is conducting its own probe, is also demanding an inquiry.
— with Lisa Morry

Killed inmate was merciless

Darrell Shanoss, the 39-year-old inmate killed in a riot at Kent Institution, was 23 when he was sentenced to life for second-degree murder in the stabbing of Ross Morrison, assault with intent to steal and armed robbery.

Shanoss and three others had been drinking in a field in Kispiox, northeast of Prince Rupert, when they assaulted Morrison and stole his truck. Morrison's throat was slashed and he was stabbed 14 times in the back.

At the time of the sentencing, Justice H. A. Callahan described the killing as "a particularly savage murder" and said Shanoss's response to Morrison's pleas was "show no mercy."

After serving 15 years, Shanoss was denied full parole in May 2002.

Documents from the parole board's decision showed that although he had a "fragile" understanding of the impact of his crime, they said Shanoss had made only minimal progress in determining the root of his violent behaviour and had yet to address his substance abuse issues.

Shanoss attended several aboriginal healing programs for violent offenders, but the board felt he remained a high risk for reoffending in a violent manner.

During his third attempt at the intensive treatment for violent offenders program, Shanoss was discharged when he displayed little motivation and his aggressive behaviour caused native elders and program staff to fear for their safety, said the documents.

Shanoss's criminal history began at age 19 with property offences. Noting his family's proclivity to drinking, vandalism and theft, the board characterized Shanoss's history as one of social isolation.

The board also reminded Shanoss of his history of violent and sadistic behaviour, including his own admission that he had used his hands "to kill small animals in order to demonstrate your power and prove the adage, 'Show no mercy.'"

Riot letter.

Jennifer Lutz Attack, a Christmas Party Gone Wrong[46]

Only a handful of stories in my career had ever touched deep into our souls as a Christmas party gone horribly wrong. It was December 2003 when Inmate Earl NANTAIS an inmate from Kent attacked Jennifer Lutz, his young bride.

Prior to the writing of this story, I reached out with a brief text conversation to Jennifer. Not sure how I would be received, I was cautiously optimistic. She agreed to speak with me, and we met a few days later in an undisclosed location where we sat down over coffee. Not wanting to trigger any troubling flashbacks, I asked a few basic questions. Jennifer told of her fondness for staff on duty the night she was attacked, whom she was told, saved her life.

NANTAIS, a 53-year-old PC inmate at Kent, had a violent, and troubled past. At the time, he was serving a life sentence for stabbing his previous girlfriend, who was only 16 at the time. Based on historical data, and a violent, and troubling criminal history, NANTAIS was labeled a psychopath. Violence was tightly woven into the troubled fabric of who he was, and if his past was any indicator, he would most likely strike again. As it turned out, officials should have been more aware, but it seemed his right to attend a social would outweigh the safety of his visitors.

The CSC holds various socials throughout each year in federal prisons in hopes of providing families with opportunities to strengthen broken ties, often torn apart by incarceration. It was a Christmas celebration; the invitations were sent out. Mothers, fathers, brothers, sisters, wives, and girlfriends were preparing for a seasonal visit once called a "Christmas Social". Guests started cuing around 12:30 pm. They were processed like any other visit into a maximum-security facility. Inmates had worked tirelessly to clean away its dirt and grime; however, all the elbow grease in the world could not erase the memories of the most popular killing zone in the prison. To most, it was your typical gymnasium, but staff knew the shocking history each room held.

Presents were wrapped as Santa eagerly waited in the wings for his adoring fans. The thought of a PC inmate bouncing children on his lap created a stir amongst staff, however we were quick to learn the show must go on.

Kitchen staff had prepared a wide selection of seasonal morsels, with refreshments being served as families walked around the gyms interior. The decorations, while pedestrian in nature, offered an opportunity to bring a small piece of normalcy to an otherwise dysfunctional family relationship. While the big house was packed with 30 eager guests, only one family was destined to be remembered.

Earl NANTAIS was an inmate at Bowden Institution, a medium security facility located in Innisfail, Alberta when he first crossed paths with 16-year-old Jennifer Lutz. It was a telephone relationship at first, then progressed to what could only be described as a fairy tale romance. Jennifer said, "the warning signs were there, but I was in love, or stupid I guess". Visiting daily, four times over the weekend, Jennifer fell under his controlling spell. In one specific month NANTAIS was reported to have called his bride a total of 180 times in one month alone, a fact lost on the case management team. He knew the system, and seemed to be a master of control of those in his life. Jennifer returned to Chilliwack for a brief time to be closer to her family, and away from NANTAIS's controlling reach. There were warning signs, but they were ignored. The volume of telephone calls from Bowden to Jennifer's home should have set off alarm bells, but they rang silent. They had reconnected after his transfer to Mountain Institution where Jennifer could visit her boyfriend almost daily for the next three years. They eventually became husband and wife on August 21, 2003 tying the knot in a jailhouse wedding. His time at Mountain was short-lived as staff, searching NANTAIS, and his cell, found two razor blades secreted in his mouth. Was this the precursor of things to come, or a missed opportunity to lash out? For his actions, NANTAIS was involuntary transferred across the street, to Kent. The emotional wheels now in play, Jennifer unaware what would transpire for her, and her three boys.

As the visitors arrived, the children were filled with innocence, excited at their festive surroundings. They ran to the Christmas tree that was surrounded by colourfully wrapped presents.

Jennifer had believed NANTAIS to be a good role model reading to her children, and ironically, teaching them to respect women. Jennifer said he had a strong Native spirituality, and was the perfect stepfather to her children. Families settled in, including NANTAIS, his wife, and her three boys, they choose an inside seat to enjoy the warmth of a hot chocolate before going outside. As they shared their dreams, he said he wanted to build their home after his release. He spoke of his recent parole hearing only three days prior where he had been denied his freedom. Jennifer claimed NANTAIS slipped an unknown drug into her hot chocolate under the guise it would relax her. Her blood tests later indicated levels of Tetrahydrocannabinol (THC), the principal psychoactive constituent of cannabis (pot) and Gamma-hydroxybutyrate (GHB) a club drug commonly found in victims of date rape.

Like many other families, they ventured outside, enjoying a walk around the sports field coming to rest at the bleachers next to the tennis court. Overlooking the festivities was the looming guard tower only meters away. NANTAIS and his wife seemed to be enjoying idle chatter, catching up on family stories while the children played nearby.

Completely unaware NANTAIS was holding a jailhouse shank, he would reach for the cold steel, reported to be hidden in his shoe. Pretending to comfort her, he reached around stroking her hair, whispering softly in his bride's ear, "are you ready to go see your Angel baby"? (A reference to Jennifer's four-month-old boy, Collin, who died of crib death). For anyone watching, they were just two people in love, sharing a private moment. Nothing could be further from the truth when without warning, NANTAIS's quiet words turned to a blind rage as he reached to slit his wife's throat. The couple fell to the icy ground. A struggle ensued as Jennifer tried desperately to get away. NANTAIS was heard yelling, "die bitch" as he punched her face, inflicting almost enough force to achieve his killing goal. One officer remembers the radio call heard throughout the prison, "839, this is the gym gun walk, NANTAIS is beating his wife in the sports field". As staff responded they heard the boys, now covered in their mother's blood cry out, "daddy, stop hurting mommy" as they tried in vain to stop the horrific attack on their mother. The gun walk officer would "put one up the spout", charging his rifle for psychological effect; however, he couldn't risk further casualties firing random, and dangerous shots, a decision for which he would later be commended. Staff responding to the radio call for help, stormed the gym, and were praised for their professional response as they weighed in, pulling NANTAIS away.

Jennifer's almost lifeless body lay on the frozen ground. She had life-threatening puncture wounds about her torso, and staff feared the worst. Separating the two, NANTAIS was quickly escorted to Health Care while staff in the sports field would tend to her wounds. Quickly moved to Segregation, NANTAIS was strip searched, and placed in the lower range shower cell, and placed on a suicide watch. NANTAIS was uncooperative, and showed no emotion. Meanwhile, back on the sports field, it was a hectic scene as the children, screamed "mommy was dead". The correctional supervisor called for an ambulance as the nurses struggled to minimize the blood loss from 28 puncture wounds, one narrowly missing her right eye, seven slashes to her throat, and a brutal attack on various parts of her body.

The attack was so violent, staff had reported seeing her intestines. Clinging to life, Jennifer was not expected to survive the 30-minute ambulance ride to the nearest hospital in Chilliwack.

What was to have been the setting for a festive family evening, instead provided a haunting nightmare for staff, and a long, and troubling road of rehabilitation for Jennifer, and her three boys. While normally there was no room for compassion in our jobs, this situation was different. No one deserved this. They left the prison, sirens blaring, and lights flashing from the ambulance as it made its way into the dark night. Staff tell the story of the long ambulance ride, during which they tried to offer any kind of hope for Jennifer as she lay bleeding, the shock of trauma setting in. The paramedic desperately trying to stabilize Jennifer, applying pressure bandages to suck up the blood. In the hours and days to come it was a daunting task facing doctors as they worked tirelessly to save her life. She was called the miracle survivor.

What went wrong? Where, or how did the system let Jennifer down? Before any social was to take place, visitor applications were meticulously reviewed by dedicated institutional parole officers (IPO). In that process was NANTAIS's violent history overlooked? Was NANTAIS' 1994 Attempted Murder charge of his then 16-year-old girlfriend, the denial of the honeymoon PFV, or the Parole Board's denial just a few days prior, not enough of a pre-curser to the danger, or were we once again handcuffed by Canada's liberal laws? Could the CSC not see his risk to reoffend in such a violent manner? Risk assessments on inmate behaviours are at the very core of what we do as correctional professionals. Court documents in the attempted murder trial of NANTAIS told a story of trauma that would follow her, and the three boys forever. The Public Guardian of BC, a public agency mandated to protect the legal and financial interests of children under the age of 19 years were looking out for the interests of

Jennifer's children, and would seek damages on their behalf for future lost wages, and counselling. The family was seeking compensation for the boys' pain and suffering, along with medical and rehabilitation expenses. The children, like their mother, suffered deep emotional scars.

A year following the attack, Jennifer found living in her parents one bedroom home untenable. The $610 she was receiving from welfare was insufficient to sustain her family. Two of the boys, fought the symptoms of Post-Traumatic Stress Disorder (PTSD). The battles Jennifer, and her children faced included alcoholism, drug abuse, and an unimaginable range of emotional issues.

The court documents filed, claimed the CSC was negligent when they failed to take steps to properly supervise NANTAIS, and to protect the children from the dangers he posed. Once again the CSC minimized their responsibility, and while the settlement with Jennifer was confidential, she pointed to her old truck sitting in the parking lot, and stated, "I'm broke".

Most, if not all inmates have poor impulse control, a lack of coping skills, and anger management issues. Anything could set them off, at any moment: a single disagreement with a loved one on the phone, or the loss of control that incarceration brings. I've seen it, as have others. At the time of visit reviews, staff were reported to have submitted computer files of casework records outlining their concerns fearing NANTAIS would lash out, and commit another violent act. Staff say their warnings were ignored and their reports no where to be found.

From my arm's length view, the denial of parole should have received more attention by the decision makers. While his behaviour seemed normal from all accounts, despite a history of violence against women, his application to attend the social was given the green light. In the lawsuit, counsel for Jennifer claimed CSC management should have known the risks involved.

Management's response after the media frenzy died down was to deny knowledge, or minimize staff concerns. They simply placed the socials into a state of moratorium until the public outcry lessened, allowing them to put into place new policies, and rename the "social" a "Special Visiting Event".

The spin-doctors in the CSC Media Relations Department worked overtime, and issued a desperate news release in hopes of counter-acting all the bad press, titled "A Christmas to Remember". It touted the efforts of both staff, and inmates to raise funds in support of Jennifer, and her family.

Inasmuch as the ill-conceived release was a transparent effort to exonerate the system, the intent, and efforts of those offering help was sincere. One correctional officer donated a freezer, and then filled it with food. Coming together, ignoring our differences, inmates and staff raised over $3,000.00. Gifts for the children, a lit tree, and a gold necklace to replace the one Jennifer lost in the attack were all part of the spectacular, and unprecedented fund-raising effort.

Jennifer was told that she was in the Intensive Care Unit (ICU) for 12 days. Now her next challenge was to face her attacker in court, her once loved husband, as he sat in a glassed prisoner's box. It took three long years to bring him to trial as she struggled to recount what she could of the painful events of December 13, 2003. Before announcing his findings, Justice William Grist heard from NANTAIS's defense counsel how he was sexually abused as a child, and watched in horror as his father killed his mother. Newspaper reports claimed NANTAIS could not speak until he was seven, undoubtedly from all the upheaval he had witnessed throughout his youth. His defense attorney claimed he suffered from a condition related to autism known as Asperger Syndrome.

NANTAIS pled guilty, in hopes his plea would provide some sort of closure. He was given a 16-year sentence for attempted murder.

Now 13 years later, Jennifer still struggles with the day-to-day tasks, normal for many, impossible for her. She has trust issues, as the wounds are as fresh today as the family tries to forget. The Christmas season for her and the boys is the most difficult time of the year, as it is now filled with fear and pain.

Jennifer brings our conversation to a close by saying she equates love with "I'm going to kill you", admitting her attraction to bad boys provides many sleepless nights. She now sports a neck tattoo, covering one of her scars. It depicts an eye; she says watches out for her.

As a correctional officer, I could not be prouder of the actions of those brave officers who, without fear responded to Jennifer's aid. I saw the heroes putting their own safety in jeopardy. The officers' actions that day were described as phenomenal, and with a level of care that was exemplary.

Jennifer Lutz.

The Mountain Riot, 2008[47]

The level of violence that night has never since been surpassed. It was one Saturday night that would change Mountain Institution forever, its innocence lost.

For the most part Mountain was a quiet prison, staff were professional, but many were young, and inexperienced with the level of violence soon to befall them.

Now my third riot, I understood the fast moving and dynamic process. One can never fully prepare for the human aspects of a riot. I had many friends among the staff, and while you were expected to act professionally, it was difficult to remove the personalities from the decisions you had to make.

As I arrived, I was unaware of the magnitude of the riot that was in progress. Briefed by the correctional manager on duty, I took over the operations desk. The Crisis Manager, and his team were in the Command Centre, so my responsibilities were relegated to processing information, directing staff, and briefing the Crisis Manager throughout the night. A well-experienced, and respected leader, the warden was capable of handling just about anything. The riot started in the prison's gymnasium around 9:45 pm as inmates looked for weapons in the equipment room. It would quickly spread to the units, and later, up the hill to Health Care. Now armed with baseball bats, and other makeshift weapons, balaclavas concealed their identities. Staff had only seconds to escape. Other inmates in unison, broke windows, as they swept through the units in a sea of terror.

As with any prison emergency, the correctional manager makes the initial determination, and notifies the warden of the details as they unfold. Once an emergency was declared, the warden would instruct staff to start setting up the Mountain Command Centre. The correctional manager would take on the role and title of Interim Crisis Manager until the warden, in this case Alex Lubimiv, or his delegate arrived. Telephone lines would be set up establishing Regional and National Command Centres, and a scribe would record decisions as they were taken. RCMP, or the military often would sit in as needed, along with members of the Citizens Advisory Committee who represent the concerns of those in the surrounding communities of Agassiz and the Village of Harrison Hot Springs.

Organized confusion was the best way to describe the situation as inmates attempted to breach the flimsy doors of the gym. Other inmates stormed the units forcing officers up an escape ladder to the unit roof. One officer who thought the end was near, managed to telephone her mother and children in what she thought was going to be one last conversation. This correctional officer thankfully made it out physically unharmed.

Officially, the root cause of the riot was a misguided sense of self-righteousness by inmates who wanted to protest being housed with sex offenders, or was that just an excuse? The lone victim that night was the son of a former co-worker from my time at Kent, and was reported to be one of BC's most notorious sex offenders. He was a sexual deviant, and prolific child pornographer who was caught up in a police sting by US Customs years earlier. GIBBONS Jr. was later convicted of sexual interference with the young children he was babysitting in the community.

Once he was killed, inmates continued their late-night rampage. Despite the best efforts of staff to stop them, inmates were able to access medicine cabinets in Health Care, looking for a desperate fix, feeding their dirty habits. One inmate identified as Trevor Wayne O'BRIEN would later die from an overdose. As the night wore on, the IERT was called in. Pounding their haunting beat with their nightsticks against their shields, the men and women bravely marched into a war zone, the fog from the O.C. dust so thick you could barely make out the next building.

With the mass exodus of inmates to hospital, I chose to reposition myself within the front gate area to address issues around the questionable paperwork known as a Temporary Absence (TA). Our parking lot became a wash of red flashing lights as ambulances from Agassiz, Boston Bar, Chilliwack and Hope assembled as they waited their turn. As each ambulance departed into the dark of night, sirens told the tale. The unsuspecting public must have been shocked at the armed presence, and the sea of blue uniforms that invaded Chilliwack's emergency room that night. In total, 11 inmates were transported to Chilliwack's only hospital approximately 30 kilometres away.

Later, with inmates either hospitalized or locked up, I visited the crime scene and witnessed the gruesome sight of GIBBONS' battered, and bloody body. My work friendship with Mike Sr. and a promise I made to look after Mike Jr. promted me to visit. While I had the best intentions, seeing him, and the horrid scene of his death, was deeply disturbing. The little piece of my pre-retirement heaven was now a faded memory.

In the weeks and months to come, a committee comprised of staff and management looked for operational ways in which to make routines safer. Gone were many of the trees that interfered with the sight line, removing the once pristine environment.

On the way to a "new norm", I thank God it wasn't worse than it was. A little piece of me was taken away that night knowing many of my friends and colleagues were so profoundly affected.

Chapter 9

Around the Region

Matsqui, the Ridding of Neil MacLean

The next chapter in my career found me at Matsqui, a medium security prison on the outskirts of Abbotsford BC, 70 kilometres east of Vancouver. I was not there of my own volition, rather a much-needed break from the barrage of union pressure I had heaped upon the management of Kent. As the union movement continued to grow, the CSC was under relentless public scrutiny—not a desirable position, as management looked for a way to break up this powerbase of union trouble. I was viewed as a rogue union leader whose behaviour was unmanageable. The deputy warden had found what he believed was a good excuse to rid himself of this troublesome union leader in the form of a fabricated inmate threat against me. On the pretense of caring, he had me transferred to Matsqui. I was told the risk to my personal safety was too great, and could not be managed at Kent. It was a flimsy excuse at best, as many staff have problems with inmates. I was never informed of the specific threat, level of concern or the inmate involved. Historically, we would be more inclined to mediate, or move the inmate to another institution, but this was an opportunity not to be missed. Get rid of the likes of Neil MacLean in hopes labour relations would simmer down.

Matsqui Institution was a three-storey prison, and home to 350 GP inmates. Opened in 1966, Matsqui was known for its vocational programs. Auto body, and mechanical repairs that were popular not only with the inmates, but also staff, and members of the public who could bring their vehicles in for servicing at substantial savings. Whether it was a brake job, or complete makeover, this program was a hit.

It was during correctional officer training, I remember sitting around the boardroom table with my CORE mates as we watched the CBC TV coverage of Matsqui's 1981 riot.

Nineteen recruits watched in horror as helicopters swooped in to rescue staff from the prison roof. By this time, all we could see was a burned-out shell with billowing smoke pouring from cellblock windows. I remember thinking to myself, hell NO.

My first day at Matsqui I was cornered by one of those correctional officers not enamored with the change in unions. Most days were endless arguments. On a good day, I got the cold shoulder. I refused to take over-time from the Matsqui correctional officers, nor would I take an existing position away from their regular staffing assignments. Once again, what to do with Neil MacLean was on the lips of managers. Doing what was considered a favour to Kent, turned out to be a continuation of union rabble rousing, now at Matsqui. Stationing me at the front gate to simply greet incoming employees was not an efficient use of their resources so I knew my days were numbered.

International Jewel Thief Gerald BLANCHARD[48]

Like any prison, they all had their stories, and Matsqui was no exception. The old Fraser Valley prison was centre stage with a spotlight on an inmate by the name of Gerald BLANCHARD.

His story began in Europe on his whirlwind honeymoon, puddle jumping from London, Rome, Barcelona, the French Riviera and finally Vienna. While in the Austrian capital of Vienna, his bride, and wealthy father-in-law, posed as tourists, walking the 500-acre property of Austria's Imperial Schonbraun Palace. Schonbraun had been the home of aristocracy playing host to visitors the likes of Napoleon, and Marie Antoinette. The self-taught computer and security systems expert, BLANCHARD videotaped their experience, getting lost among the throngs of tourists. BLANCHARD was more than sightseeing; he was checking the windows, video camera locations, and audible alarms, looking for that vulnerable back door to their security system. Using his father-in-law's wealth and stature as a world-renowned German construction mogul, BLANCHARD was able to arrange access for a personal tour of the palace's private art and gem collection. When the docents weren't looking, he was able to unlatch a single window, disabling the alarms, then he, his bride, and father in-law would saunter off the palace grounds unnoticed.

Security was tight as armed guards were everywhere, walking the grounds, and through the hallowed halls.

BLANCHARD readied himself for what must have seemed an impossible task. Was it the arrogance of youth, or the precision of a skilled thief? Befriending a German pilot, BLANCHARD hired his services, and chartered his small-single engine Cessna to fly over the palace, using only the glow of the bright incandescent security lights to mark his seemingly impossible landing zone. June 1998 was the second warmest month of the year, a typical Austrian summer. The plane leveled off, about one mile above the target. BLANCHARD prepared himself. While an experienced parachutist with over 100 jumps to his credit, there was nothing quite like this. He checked his straps, his left boot vicariously perched on the peg that protruded from the side of the plane. He hung onto the strut waiting for the precise moment and when the time was right, he took a leap of faith, and plunged into the dead of night. Though it took only a few seconds to clear the plane, it seemed like forever. Taking a deep breath, he intuitively pulled his ripcord. Relief could not have come soon enough as the chute deployed, and the silk canopy filled with the night air. The skies were black, and the wind calm, as if Mother Nature understood the duty at hand. While he was a veteran paratrooper, he landed hard, his body slamming onto the 15th century copper-tiled roof. His parachute still filled with the night's air, dragged him to the roof's edge. BLANCHARD paused momentarily to ascertain if his landing had awakened the guards. After unhooking his chute, he pulled a rope from his backpack, cautiously lowering himself down from the roof of the four-storey building. With a cat like stealth, he entered through the window left unlatched from the previous day's visit. Once inside, he was careful to maneuver the maze of corridors. He figured should he hear the guard's approach, he would hide behind the thick floor-to-ceiling draperies that lined the hallways. Eluding the Imperial Palace guards, he would eventually find his way to the isolated, cavernous vault room. There it was, his greatest challenge, in its entire splendor, the 10-point jeweled star surrounding a single white pearl. This magnificent jewel-encrusted broach was an important artifact of the Austrian people, as it represented royal nobility. Sitting behind bulletproof glass, it lay helpless on a red silk pillow-BLANCHARD, had to have it.

Princess Elisabeth, or Sisi as she was known, was the wife of Emperor Franz Joseph I and thus Empress of Austria, Queen of Hungary, Queen Consort of Croatia, and Bohemia. During her reign, Sisi commissioned similar pieces, each worth 2,000,000 French francs. Today we believe only two remain, as she would randomly present these jewels to her friends, ladies-in-waiting, or foreign dignitaries if she so pleased. She had a Princess Diana-like figure, and lived through an unhappy marriage. She struggled with anorexia, and was killed by an assassin's knife in September 1898.

As BLANCHARD approached the awaiting prize, he was careful, loosening the screws to the plexiglas lid, and holding the two rods in place so as not to trigger the motion-sensitive alarms. The final task before him was to gently lift the jeweled broach from its weight-sensitive spring-loaded platform that held the sparkling gem in place. As if to mock authorities, he was careful to substitute a cheap replica purchased the day before from the palace gift store. Only 3.5 centimetres in diameter, the priceless gem fit snugly into his jacket pocket. He made his way down the darkened hallways, around each corner, and out the back door. Now almost home free, he crept through the well-manicured gardens to the last leg of his adventure, a high stone wall to freedom. BLANCHARD was able, using his rope to climb over a back wall of the palace, making his hasty retreat to his upscale hotel room only a few kilometres away. In the morning, he could not resist returning to the scene of the crime, his sole purpose to see if authorities had caught on. Staff who found his discarded parachute in a nearby trash bin didn't connect it to the yet undiscovered theft. In fact, it would be weeks before authorities would identify the gift store fake.

His departure was more like a getaway, hiding his secret in the regulator of his scuba gear for its journey back to Canada. Knowing he would never be able to fence the stolen gem, BLANCHARD hid the broach in his grandmother's Winnipeg home, overlooked by its unsuspecting residents for over nine years.

His six-month whirlwind European honeymoon was quickly followed by an international manhunt. He was alleged to have been the linchpin involving an international fraud and theft ring, credited with the theft of millions from Canadian and US banks, and various financial institutions around the globe. The case grabbed international headlines involving Interpol, a flurry of warrants, and the allegation that BLANCHARD had links to Kurdish rebels.

It was a cold case team of Winnipeg Police detectives in 2007 and their dogged pursuit who finally caught up with BLANCHARD in Vancouver. Police later would describe him as charming, and uncommonly gifted. A criminal mastermind they would say. Canadian police authorities could not help but notice the similarities between the 1964 film Topkapi staring Maximilian Schell, and Peter Ustinov.

The criminal organization made millions as they lived flamboyant playboy lifestyles, jet-setting the world, and visiting the most exclusive resorts in Jamaica, the Turks and Caicos Islands.

BLANCHARD's technical prowess was only one aspect of his many talents. He was a chameleon and could turn himself into an identity of his choosing. Thirty-two aliases in all, he was able to create a new persona, dying his hair, or matching his stockpile of uniforms to fit the job. When BLANCHARD wasn't casing a job, he was using his new identities to portray a reporter, creating VIP passes to NHL playoff games, or taking a spin around the Indianapolis Motor Speedway with racing legend Mario Andretti. During a yacht race in Monte Carlo, he would meet the Prince of Monaco, and later interview Christina Aguilera at one of her concerts.

BLANCHARD was alleged to have been behind a $500,000 bank heist of the Winnipeg branch of the Canadian Imperial Bank of Commerce, where he unabashedly walked into the building's construction site, walking out with the blue prints. As the bank was being built, he frequently visited the site during the day dressed as either a delivery person, or construction worker.

He was able to plant his own security devices during construction, giving him an inside view of the build, and the opportunity to research and understand the various ATM locking systems as they were progressively installed. He would later order an identical lock on line, allowing practice in reverse engineering from the safety of his home. When the building construction was complete, he was ready. The money was placed in the site's ATMs on the Friday, before the bank's official opening on the Monday.

The Winnipeg Police Major Crimes Unit saw the similarities between the Winnipeg heist and others being perpetrated in Ontario, Alberta, and British Columbia. Despite the intense police manhunt, and the hours invested into the investigation it was an observant employee of Walmart who reported a seemingly out-of-place blue Dodge Caravan in the parking lot adjacent to the bank. Making note of the license plate numbers the unknowing witness would bring down this massive criminal empire with one telephone call to police when he heard of the break-in on the news.

Not only did BLANCHARD rent the panel van under his real name, he forgot to wear gloves, leaving tell-tale finger prints that would eventually end his criminal endeavor. This is what police needed to crack the case, tracing it back to BLANCHARD. Gathering information, and armed with 275 pages of evidence, police were able to secure search warrants based on the wiretap information from BLANCHARD, and his 18 cell phones. Police would gather enough evidence as they listened to secretive conversations in the hope that one slip of the tongue would make their case. BLANCHARD was surprisingly loose-lipped, planning his next caper with his team, describing in detail, a product-return scheme targeting the popular retailer Best Buy.

Now armed with search warrants, police made their long overdue, and highly anticipated move on numerous high-end properties owned by BLANCHARD. It was during one property search police unearthed the incriminating honeymoon video that unwittingly linked him to the cold case file. The video recording provided indisputable evidence of BLANCHARD's involvement.

Arrested in 2007, he was charged with 41 criminal offences in connection with his brazen crime wave. His co-accused 83-year-old Carl Bales of Vancouver, and 21-year-old Lynette Tien were alleged members of a nefarious crime group from western Canada, however they were never charged.

BLANCHARD on the other hand was charged with Fraud Under $5,000 (X 7), Fraud Over $5,000 (X 11), Break and Enter, Commit Offence for Criminal Organization (X 5), Traffic Credit Card Data, and Trafficking Ammunition.

During the coordinated raid on several Vancouver properties, police seized over 60,000 documents, cash in various currencies, smoke bombs, firearms, silencers, 300 electronic devices, and thousands of rounds of ammunition. Police also confiscated 10 pallets of materials from various homes, and warehouses throughout Vancouver, including elaborate card printers, card readers, and a wide selection of the latest surveillance equipment. In BLANCHARD's own home, they discovered a hidden room stocked with burglary kits, along with numerous fake identities.

He was now facing serious jail time, as much as 164 years in prison. BLANCHARD, unable to fence the stolen property, he concluded it was time to make a deal. Austrian officials were as desperate to retrieve a symbol of their country's honour, as he was to avoid a life behind bars.

Shackled in leg irons, BLANCHARD was driven to his grandmother's home where he would expose its secret hiding place in their basement.

Despite the Crown Attorney's flattering description of BLANCHARD calling him "cunning, clever, conniving and creative", he plead guilty to

16 charges, agreeing to sell his four condominiums, and pay restitution to the Canadian government. BLANCHARD was sent unceremoniously to the Prairie Region's toughest prison, Stony Mountain where he spent the first year and a half of his eight-year sentence. A GP inmate, he enjoyed a certain celebrity status, and after a brief interrogation by his fellow inmates, he was accepted into the GP fold.

BLANCHARD, would then transfer to Matsqui Institution in Abbotsford, and was quick to gain employment in the Lifers' kitchen, preparing meals for the GP inmates. He was regarded as a high profile bad boy, and stand up con, who seemed to fit in well. He eventually transferred to Kwikwexwelhp, (Kwi) located in the hills between Mission and Agassiz, and later paroled.

Once free, BLANCHARD choose Vancouver as his home. Ironically, he reinvented himself as a security consultant installing video surveillance equipment cameras in a Fraser Valley financial institution where I do my banking. Like an inquisitive reporter I ventured into that very bank years later. A manager quickly ushered me into her office, and was quick to close the door as if their embarrassing story might be exposed. Intrigued, she denied any knowledge of the story, choosing, I think, to forget that embarrassing day.

It was during a visit to China, he would meet, and fall in love with a woman he would later marry. He still lived life in the fast lane of exotic cars, (two Lamborghinis) and resided in a multi-million-dollar condominium in Vancouver where this unassuming young man started a new life, establishing new friends. BLANCHARD was now 44 years of age when I spoke with him.

He recalls that as a youngster, raised by a single mother, one of his early childhood memories not having a lot of money he grew tired of dry cereal every morning for breakfast. He would sneak onto the neighbours porch to steal the occasional bottle of milk for his dry cereal. Was poverty the genesis of his life of crime?

Despite severe dyslexia, and a speech impediment, he was a genius with his hands, and achieved a level of criminal brilliance rarely seen by police. BLANCHARD started building his "criminal empire" in the suburbs of Winnipeg, emptying an entire Radio Shack on a holiday weekend. By the age of 16 he purchased his first home for $100,000 cash with the aid of his lawyer.

Rather than work part-time after school like most kids, BLANCHARD chose the more financially lucrative option of fencing stolen goods. Enlisting the help of employees from a local department store, they would steal valuable merchandise, paying .25 cents on the dollar. Stacking shelves vs. fencing goods…the option was obvious.

I was attracted to BLANCHARD's intriguing tale as it represented a back story one doesn't often read in files, or hear about from those who walk the tiers.

Gerald BLANCHARD.

The famed Sisi diamond and pearl encrusted
broach stolen by BLANCHARD.

Mountain Institution and the Doukhobor Movement[49]

Mountain Institution was designed as a medium security facility in early 1962 at a cost of $294,000. It shares federal reserve land next to Kent, which was built in 1979, and rests on 80 acres of farmland. Mountain was built to house the increasing number of "domestic terrorists" called the Sons of Freedom Doukhobors, one of three spiritual Christian religious groups of Russian origin who lived in communes throughout western Canada, and later in British Columbia.

Escaping the tyranny, and oppression of the Russian government they immigrated to Canada in 1899. They dreamed of a land that would allow them to follow their religious principles, eventually settling in Saskatchewan. Their beliefs put them at odds with the Canadian government whose authority they rejected in areas of declaration of war, private ownership of property, compulsory education, and registering births, marriages and deaths. In 1907, the government reneged on a promise of lands they had gifted the Doukhobors, and encouraged the 7500 disgruntled pheasants to move west, eventually settling in communities throughout the Kootenays, including Nelson and Cranbrook. It was the Doukhobor's unusual protest methods that found them at loggerheads with lawmakers, protesting government policies with nude protests, and random acts of arson. Their unique methods were a statement of sorts, saying "you've taken our land, and everything we own, you can take the shirts off our backs".

In the early 1930s, the Doukhobor men convicted of mass acts of lawlessness included the bombing of a power station, burning bridges, and schools. They were convicted, and sent to the BC Pen, the first leg of their very long journey. Those incarcerated were unmanageable, and became an ongoing problem as bureaucrats pondered their fate. As quickly as they arrived at yet another prison, their families would set up makeshift cardboard camps in what is now Glenbrook Ravine Park, in New Westminster.

Burning their cardboard and wooden homes just outside the fences of the BC Pen, the Doukhobor inmates were eventually moved down the hill, and shipped from the BC Pen wharf to the nearby Piers Island in the Strait of Georgia.

Their protests showed no signs of letting up as they continued to use arson and nudity as their trademark method of protest. Deemed incorrigible, the Sons of Freedom Doukhobors were moved throughout BC. It was time for something more permanent to house these contemptable prisoners. Mountain was a provincial prison in 1962 and built to discourage acts of arson. Mountain Institution's buildings were metal in construction, with concrete cells, metal bed frames, and flame-retardant blankets, bed sheets, and included the use of flame retardant materials used in the construction of their furniture.

As the movement's supporters made their "trek" to be close to their loved ones, followers set up camp a few steps from their latest home, just outside prison gates of Mountain in what is now the District of Kent's gravel pit. One family, numbering 16 would live in a small 9'X12' (108 square feet) tent, slightly bigger than a modern-day jail cell. As their movement gained popularity, their numbers grew between 1000 and 1500 residents.

I sat down with one of the original protesters in 2016 still residing in Agassiz, Helen, girl number 85, a numbering brand from her days in the residential school system, and title of her new book. It was a hard life, but to this young, innocent 16-year-old, it was an adventure. She knew of nothing else, and went along with her family. Her early recollections were of a damp tent, living in close quarters, the human smell was rank. Harvesting horseradish from the swampy fields was a chore assigned by her father, but also a distraction away from an over crowded site. While they had food, her family for the most part were vegetarians, and she remembers rare feasting on borscht, perogies and corn bread, all traditional Russian fare. Times were tough, she recalls, the late-night bathroom trips up the winding hill to the outhouse near the cemetery.

The Doukhobors I would learn were a common folk, wanting only the necessities of life. Whether there were times of sadness, or times of joy, singing was part of their lives. As a group, they formed choirs to represent what was deep within their souls, promoting peace and justice through their songs.

A community within themselves many found employment in and around the District of Kent, with their children eventually attending local public schools.

Other families were torn apart when the men and women protesters were separated from their loved ones, who now resided behind the prison fences. The children were placed in foster homes throughout BC, and in some cases across Canada.

As the cause wore down, the last prisoner was transferred out from Mountain, and finally disbanded, they were gone in 1964. Many of the Doukhobor sect that died during their incarceration can be found in the Valley View Cemetery overlooking their former home.

As the camp was vacated, rumors abound that hippies were interested in taking up the now abandoned shacks outside the prison. Local residents wanting none of that, are said to have torched the remaining ramshackle sheds to prevent the onslaught of the hippies, their drug use, and free love. It was a rather ironic ending to a camp, once filled with arsonists.

As time marched on, Mountain would house an aging community of inmates. In 1969 inmates needing protective custody, in part due to their heinous crimes were gradually introduced into the prison population.

Mountain had a long history as a sex offender prison, and try what they may, officials couldn't shake its reputation for housing those convicted of sexual offences, making it difficult to introduce GP inmates in the future. In 1999, the Correctional Service of Canada undertook an extensive rebuilding campaign upgrading a tired prison, making more bed space available as the demand increased. Gone were the old partitioned dormitories, replacing the old Quonset huts with three modern living units. Mountain Institution now had a rated occupancy of 480, including 16 Segregation cells. Like most institutions, Mountain was a self-contained facility with a large dining hall, school, programs area, and health care department.

Mountain was ever changing, evolving as the need dictated, it became a program-oriented facility that focused on assisting inmates addressing their criminality through many different treatment programs. There were mandatory educational programs such as Adult Basic Education (ABE), General Education Development Program, (GED) Moderate to High Intensity Sex Offender Programs, Substance Abuse, and Anger Management Programs.

After 19 years at Kent, I felt my time was drawing to a close. I chose to transfer in 2007 to Mountain's more dynamic environment, a medium security setting that would provide a much-needed change.

I had the distinct pleasure of working with many of my former colleagues from Kent who, like me, sought relief from the maximum-security environment that weighed heavily on many great staff. Whereas a few before me were somewhat resistant to change, I was lucky to have adapted quickly. To understand why many loved Mountain was only to visit. Nestled at the foot of Mt. Agassiz, its open spaces, and fresh air was a break from the stifling security setting that occupied the early years of my career.

Prior to the 2008 riot, I enjoyed the walk down the gently sloped pathways bordered by the colourful flowerbeds to my assigned unit. It was a great way to start any day. An acting supervisor at Kent, my transfer to Mountain returned me to my substantive rank of correctional officer II. This was only fair as many Mountain staff were already acting in the supervisor's office, or on a waiting list. I needed to do my time, understand the dynamics of a very different prison setting before the managers would consider me for advancement.

Mountain provided a new challenge, one where I was forced to use my communication skills, different than the "no can do" attitude of Kent. Mountain management, and staff spoke to, and worked constructively with inmates. I had to relearn how to listen, and communicate more respectfully. Speaking with inmates in the very open units was foreign. The routine was tedious, range walks, searches, processing their frivolous requests.

After only a few months. I was pleased to be offered an acting correctional manager stint on the operations desk. I enjoyed the challenges, and the immense responsibility. We were tasked with staff and inmate safety, the "good order" of the Institution, its reputation and the multi-million facility. The warden once told me if you erred on the side of staff safety, you would never go wrong. Despite the "staff first" way of thinking, many were untrusting of anything in a light blue shirt.

Caring on the Inside[50]

Just as Canada's prison system aged, so too, do the inmates. An "older inmate" division in Ottawa, ensured the system provided adequate care for those who were fast approaching the end of their troubled journey.

While there were many spectacular employees, Joey Ellis, and her award-winning contributions were noteworthy. She moved to Agassiz at the age of three. Like most, she attended school, and graduated from the town's only secondary school. She was not your typical stereotypical prison guard, slight in stature, she joined the CSC, and immediately found herself in the middle of an "Old Boys Club". Women were new to the system, and in many cases, not welcome.

As a correctional supervisor, Joey, a strong woman in her own right, was championing a new program called the "Palliative Caregivers Program", or "Caring from the Inside". Originally referred to as the "Bleach Program", inmates were taught of the deadly risks associated with drug use. Her efforts at Mountain saw 45 inmates trained to provide physical, and emotional support to those inmates in need. The program recognized our prisons as small communities, and it was the inmates themselves who in many cases were the only families, and support system to their aging counterparts. As the population aged, many of those incarcerated would look to an uncaring system for health, nutrition, exercise, and quality of living assistance. Joey was a no-nonsense correctional supervisor who could hold her own. She rejected the usual military style uniform, choosing street clothes as her uniform of choice. She spoke with pride, saying this program was a natural. Inmates were trained in all aspects of patient care including understanding HIV-AIDS, pain management, attending to blood spills, and guiding others, helping them make informed end of life decisions.

Joey was honoured with the Meritorious Service medal in 2003 for her outstanding contribution to this valued program.

Although Joey had since retired, remnants of her once viral program remain. A newbie to Mountain, I was unaware that inmates pushing each other around in wheel chairs, and caring for aging inmates was part of Joey's initiative. It wasn't until 2012 that I would meet Joey at a Lions Club dinner when I spoke to her members about the importance of the Automated External Defibrillator, and their placement within our community. Now well into retirement, Joey remains active in the Lions.

Mission, Acting No More

Two years was enough to become attached to staff, and the idyllic surroundings at Mountain. It was 2009, a bittersweet time as I finally passed the correctional manager's competition earning an unwanted transfer, and promotion to Mission.

Although I was not happy at the prospects of starting over at yet another prison, this old dog was off to Mission Institution, and about to learn some new tricks.

Mission was an older town, rich in history as a once thriving logging community overlooking the mighty Fraser River. Located up a steep hill, Mission was by far my worst experience. Staff were somewhat cool to my arrival, or just suspicious of a new boss, and defrocked union leader. New relationships were hard to cultivate; however, most were pleasant. I think it was more about me than it was about staff at Mission as I just didn't want to be there. The long commute, a new unfamiliar prison, learning new names and the players was more than my weary mind could take.

First opening as a medium security facility in 1977, three kilometers from the city of Mission, it was built to house 324 inmates, and was broken into five separate units. Mission shared property with Ferndale (now called Mission Minimum), a minimum-security facility.

A Near Elvis Sighting [51]

Just prior to leaving Mission, sitting in my office, I glanced out my window towards the typical metal clad rundown buildings, collectively known as Industries.

Overlooking the never-ending construction zone stood a man, slumped over making himself appear shorter, and somewhat beaten down. Leaving the security of my correctional manager's office I ventured out to investigate the noise of the jackhammers that were invading my peace. His radio call sign was Baker 5, a construction escort officer, though most knew him simply as Morris.

After a brief introduction, I made what I thought was an innocent remark about him looking like Elvis Presley. Morris was a heavy-set man, 60 ish, his nose, those eyes somehow reminded me of the King from yesteryear. A rather innocuous, and unassuming comment I thought, brought a smile from this welcome recognition.

As his tale unfolded, I learned working amongst us, unbeknownst to most, was a faded star from the glitter days of Las Vegas. Morris Bates in what seemed another life, was the world's number one Elvis impersonator. Being an Elvis fan, I was gob smacked.

Hatzic Lake, just outside of Mission is where Morris now lives in retirement. I made my way to the back door of his rather unassuming BC box house, not befitting a celebrity. I was greeted by a woman in her 60's who would guide me a few steps inside, where I would have my audience with "the King". He extended his hand, and greeted me with that turned up lip made famous by Elvis. A little weather worn, slightly grey, wearing his signature fedora, his voice now raw and raspy, and sounded more like Rod Stewart. Morris said of his voice, lost to over 300 shows a year in his 10-year run. As I settled into a chair, my home for the next two hours, Morris sat perched on his throne, a make shift hospital bed. Around him was evidence of a sickly man who would spend most of his day in the living room of his basement apartment. I knew from the outset it would be a tough interview as Morris was frustrated, not so much with me, but life, and the life he so loved.

Morris referred to himself as an Indian. He was old school. He told me of his life growing up, but also about life after Elvis. His pain was no secret as he lashed out at what was an unfair ending to such a brilliant career. "Fuck them" he said, as I squirmed uncomfortably in his lazy boy recliner.

He had it all, the money, the women he called adoring fans, and a gold-flecked Cadillac, (one of six in total). He was a decent man, filled with good spirit in helping his First Nations people, but I could see the frustration the medical challenges were taking. No matter how tired he appeared, Morris was gracious enough to share his story.

Literally left unwanted on the doorsteps of a rundown motel, Morris was abandoned as a baby. Luckily for him, two people, his aunt and uncle, Phyllis and Pascal Bates took him in. His life as he would relate, was not an easy one, and like many aboriginal people, he grew up with an unfair, and cruel start in life.

Morris, a full-blooded Shuswap Indian, spent his early years on the Sugar Cane Reserve in Williams Lake, BC where his training as a ranch hand served him well.

He was "a cowboy", he laughed. Taking extra jobs, always looking for a chance. He was by no means lazy; quite the contrary; he was eager, and willing if not somewhat desperate to make money. He had loving parents, he had everything, and yet he had nothing. The remote location, living in isolation, with no road access, a plane would drop the weekly groceries to the awaiting families below. Rushing to gather the potatoes from the sacks broken on impact, his father would nickname him "Spud".

It was a different time back then, drugs were not as prevalent. He did however sneak an occasional beer as a youngster. With no opportunity for a higher education, Morris turned to music as his escape. It was his love, and a foundation he hoped would be his ticket out of an impoverished life. Playing the gin joints, and country bars he formed a hard rock band called "Injun Joe's Medicine Show", perfecting his craft as he went. His love of Elvis didn't come out until the late 60's. From his movies, he studied the King's every move. Though Morris didn't truly sound like the King, his mannerisms were pure Elvis, and his on-stage persona, was spot on. He had the moves he would say, and the fans went wild.

As he honed his skills someone suggested he was ready. Encouraged to take a leap of faith, he journeyed to Vancouver's hot spot on Hornby Street a place called the Cave Theatre Restaurant.

Over its 44-year run, the Cave was a cultural mecca for those "up and comers", featuring the likes of Mitzi Gaynor, Tina Turner, Tony Bennett and Ella Fitzgerald. Morris even in his early years was shrewd business man. He was a hit, now making $25,000 a week, he hired 28 body builders to oversee security at the doors as part of his mystique. One day when the Cave's owner Stan Grozina attempted to see Morris between shows, his bodyguards barred his access. Grozina protested, saying "I'm the owner". A quick thinking, and somewhat witty security guard corrected the frustrated owner, saying "when Morris plays the Cave, he owns it".

Morris had the confidence, but he wanted more. Packing up everything he headed to Las Vegas as a headliner at the Silver Slipper, and worked around the likes of Frank Sinatra. With fame, came the pressure, "you don't go to Vegas to sell records, rather, you fill seats "he would say. Now making six figures, he worked at a fever-pitch, rarely seeing a day off over the 10 years he worked the strip. When he wasn't on the Vegas strip, he was on the road traveling at the grueling pace of 70 cities in 71 days. Most times he didn't know where he was. It was all a blur.

He was billed as "Morris as Elvis" and he made a worldwide name for himself. The Los Angles times called him the "great pretender", and Morris enjoyed a certain celebrity status with all the additional perks, autographs to room keys, just like the real Elvis, a man he never met. He worked hard, and played harder.

It was 1977, the summer when the world got the news. Elvis was dead. While it was a shock to the fans, he became a nostalgic gold mine. As his popularity grew, he moved up to the Landmark, and given a $5,000.00 daily stake at the gaming tables. Over the years, band members would come and go, along with the houses, the cars including his six Cadillacs. His gambling addiction would take away his lust for life. Now bankrupt he returned to Canada, not as Elvis, but just plain old Morris, the neon lights were now a faded memory.

The downtown eastside of Vancouver, the regions poorest postal code was calling him home. It was a natural transition for a man with such deep passion, and native spirituality as Morris. Working as a Native Liaison Officer with the Vancouver Police, Morris became an outreach worker on the mean, and unforgiving streets. He worked with the kids, the lost, and forgotten, selling themselves, or anything they owned, to feed their habits. He saw the hopelessness; his people being destroyed. You can smell it Morris said; the desperation of the street was everywhere. His program closely resembled the popular "Scared Straight" program from the late 70's. It was called "Reality Check for Indigenous People" (RIP) showing aboriginal youth the dead ends of life, as they would walk down each dark and dangerous alley. His book, "Morris as Elvis, Take a Chance on Life", was to encourage aboriginal youth to avoid the pitfalls of drugs and alcohol. He became embedded into the downtown east side, and was quickly recognized as a "subject matter expert", and councilor on the "Missing Women's Task Force". The area's most vulnerable were going missing, the numbers were staggering, drawing him deeper into the tragic lives of his people. As the rewards grew to $100,000.00 he was fielding thousands of tips. Working through the Task Force, Morris provided comfort to the families. Over a year investigating the missing, and murdered women, he beat a well-worn path between his outreach offices on Main Street, to the PICKTON farm in Port Coquitlam. The evidence at the crime scene would seal Robert Willy PICKTON's fate, and in 2006, he was charged with six counts of First-Degree Murder based on DNA found on his Coquitlam pig farm.

As time wore on, Morris was almost penniless, taking a job with the Correctional Service of Canada, working at Mission Institution where we first met. Despite his issues, he was a kindly man, who kept in touch with me, encouraging me to write.

Reflecting upon his 14 years with the Elvis Tribute show, the thrill was gone.

The bright lights of Las Vegas had long lost their luster, and his neon sign, now dim, hangs sadly on his wall as a remembrance of his years past. "I have come to terms with my life, and its ups and downs, but now,

I have laid Elvis to rest", he would lament. For those who read the story of Morris Bates, its relevance to corrections was simply to spotlight our people. The take away for me, and I hope for the reader is everyone has a story. Many stories remain untold, or hidden between the 'corner stones of our endeavor'. The secrets of those who walk among us in many cases that go unnoticed; waiting to be discovered.

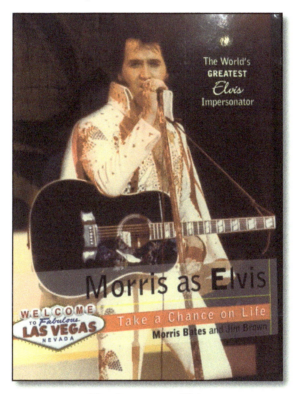

Morris as a young Elvis

Mission's senior management team, in my opinion was the epitome of everything wrong with our correctional system, who seemed to care more about their opinions, and their careers than those of others. Mission had its share of management ladder climbers, and the daily warden's meetings were nothing but a daily battle of egos. As I settled in, yet another warden was transferred in, with hopes I thought to rescue us from a not so transparent management tyranny. The incoming warden had line experience, and while

I had run in's with her at Kent, I had endless respect for her abilities. I no longer had the patience of a young man and decided to address a nagging arthritic knee issue that had been plaguing me for some time. Not wanting any more of the management team's foolishness, I underwent double knee replacement surgeries over the next two years, never to return to Mission. The years of sudden running on the unforgiving pavement had taken its toll, and the invasive, and painful surgery was a better option than the daily drama of Mission.

I went under the knife for the first knee operation in 2010, and the second knee replacement surgery in 2011. The pain from knee surgery was an enjoyable tradeoff as it provided much needed time away from a job I no longer loved. It was an easy way out of a difficult work situation, and what appeared to me as the desperate rule of those who wished to be queen.

After a two-year absence, and learning to walk all over again, I was given my final assignment, returning to Mountain in 2012.

Mountain, My Final Assignment

In my last two years, prior to retirement, I returned to Mountain and assigned to LU2 as a correctional manager. It was a busy unit that contained 60 cells, on six ranges. Most cells were double bunked, with the exception of the Pathways range where our native population, willing to "walk the red path", could live. My unit was an open concept that was intimidating at first, as inmates were wandering about at every opportunity. This openness was the core complaint from most staff, and protested the dangerous environment these larger populations created. The units were noisy, and in my humble opinion, unsafe for staff.

My own office, and my personal coffee maker, were comfort symbols, where I could close the door, and focus on the many daily tasks. I truly believed, with a few exceptions, I had the best staff, bar none. While I was not aware of it yet, my PTSD was slowly taking over, making the simplest tasks impossible. My memory was going, attributed to old age, I struggled.

Most staff were welcoming, relaxed, and truly enjoyed their jobs. Inmates I knew from my days at Kent now at Mountain tried to cash in on those relationships, in hopes of garnering favour in our daily interactions. "Hey, Mr. MacLean", they would say. "Remember me"? As they tried in their not so transparent ways, they would try to cozy up to the new Sheriff in town. What they had forgotten was most, if not all inmate relationships from Kent were steeped in a violent history, something I was hoping to forget. As the unit correctional manager, my role was more likened to a referee, listening to complaints over cell assignments, lack of work opportunities to debt mediation. Double bunking was a reality of prison life, and a daily challenge to match suitable cellmates. Endless file reviews taking into account each inmates crime and personal quirks made match ups difficult. After all, no one wanted a roommate to begin with, not to mention a creepy sex offender, or one with poor hygiene. I understood, but those refusing to cooperate were told, "You find a cell mate, or we will find one for you". This saved a lot of work and frustration, as inmates were now tasked with finding the ideal killer or rapist, to share their intimate accommodations.

One duty I enjoyed was presiding over Minor Court, often referred to as Kangaroo Court. "One's right to be heard" was an important legal component of the Duty to Act Fairly. Charges ranged from unauthorized visits on the unit, to those who hurled insults at staff.

I had a zero tolerance for abuse towards staff, and came down hard with monetary fines. No one who ever told a staff member to "fuck off" ever got a warning. If an inmate swore at a staff it was an automatic $25.00 fine, the maximum minor court would allow.

I often felt inmates had too many remedies at their disposal. They had the grievance process, the complaint process, mediation through the Chaplin, a chance to speak to the Warden, Prison Legal Services, the Office of the Special Investigator, or the Citizen's Advisory Committee. The Inmate complaint and grievance processes were time consuming, and for the most part, a waste of my time. The Claims Against the Crown process was vexatious in nature, a scam to dupe the system out of money, many complaints capitalizing on staff mistakes.

The different levels of security, going from the max environment to a case oriented facility was like night and day. The days of the 70's where the warden was law, to the late 70's where the law became our guiding principal. It was a casework driven system and paperwork consumed our day.

Lunch Time Serenade

The allure of Mountain cannot just be written about; it must be experienced. Imagine if you will, our lunch break, and time for a well-deserved rest from the chaotic world of inmates, staff, and endless meetings. One employee, Stephen Gallagher, a school teacher, and member of the Guard of Honour, was a talented player of the "pipes". Most days when the clock struck twelve, Stephen would practice his Scottish harp during his lunch, much to the delight of many. His music was much more than practice; it was, for a moment in time, a chance for peace. As the case with inmates, there was always one who would try to ruin it for others. Not everyone enjoyed the bagpipes, and like Haggis, the bagpipes were an acquired taste. One specific occasion, a prolific inmate complainer claimed the bagpipes were too loud, and destroyed his noon-time dining experience. I understand National Headquarters brought in sound engineers to measure the decibel levels. As it turns out, a government report would identify the passing mobile patrols more intrusive to the ears than the bagpipes themselves.

Stephen Gallagher.

Wrongfully Convicted, the Ivan HENRY Story[52]

An older man when we first met at Mountain, Ivan HENRY would find his way to my office in LU2, sheepishly looking though my office window in hopes of a coffee, or a chance to discuss the merits of his case, or the latest prison drama. Polite and unassuming, balding with grey hair, this soft-spoken man was not your typical inmate. As he never seemed to get in trouble, I hardy saw him but for occasional personal visits. My office I assume, was a non-judgmental, neutral zone where he could simply shoot the shit. Years later in a telephone conversation after his release Ivan said I was one of the good guys.

He was a good old Prairie boy he would say, born in a time of innocence. (1946 in Regina, Saskatchewan). Like many inmates, he claimed abuse at the hands of his stepfather, and was taken into care by the child welfare authorities. It was not an idyllic childhood as he was in and out of trouble, culminating with his first arrest at age 16. He was hardly the Godfather of the criminal world, convicted mostly of drug trafficking, and property crimes.

As we sat down over breakfast (2016), eight years after his release, Ivan told me his mother always said, "those who make you angry would eventually go away". How he survived four months short of 27 years knowing the truth, was a testament of who he became.

Now both free from incarceration, HENRY through parole, and me through retirement his story goes back to the 80s. The Winnipeg Police, Ivan says, punched and kicked him using a phone book to cover up the incriminating and violent evidence of crimes he would be charged. Don't get me wrong, HENRY was by all accounts a nasty human being in his youth. He loathed authority, and had a checkered, and troubling criminal history.

HENRY looked the part of a con, with little education, limited skills, who's future looked bleak. Listening to his version of his life I became enthralled. It was not like me to believe an inmate's story, HENRY would claim his innocence.

In the late 70s and early 80s, living in Vancouver, HENRY was married to his wife Jessie when she became suspicious of HENRY's late night, unexplained absences from the house. Fearing the worst, she called the Vancouver Police Department (VPD) and said she thought he might be the "Rip Off Rapist" who was terrorizing the city. Although they had their issues, Ivan never believed his late wife "rolled on him".

Nonetheless, it seemed that's all the police needed to close their case. If it looked like a duck, then it must be a duck.

HENRY may never have come to the attention of police if his wife, now deceased, hadn't called them. She would later provide clothing samples to police, and one picture of HENRY. The police would put him under surveillance, thinking, hoping he might be their man.

During an 18-month period, November 1980 to June 1982, VPD were investigating more than 20 complaints of sexual assault at various locations around the city. During these investigations, police obtained detailed, but unsworn statements, and collected exhibits that were submitted for forensic analysis. Police would obtain finger print evidence, and tool markings from some of HENRY's work tools that he had kept in his truck. All were sent to the crime lab for comparison to the evidence at many crime scenes.

Armed with a vast resource of investigative tools, the police would apply for warrants to use a Dial Number Recorder, (DNR) or wiretap, and the placement of a GPS on HENRY's vehicle. What screamed from the pages of his recent transcripts was that their investigation yielded nothing. Nothing to link him to any crimes. It would be the police lineup that would be his undoing, and what would later be his claim of unjust, and unfair evidence. One complainant saw surveillance pictures of HENRY, and was later shown the now infamous police lineup picture.

On the strength of that identification, HENRY was arrested July 29, 1982. The preliminarily hearing took over eight days on new information from 19 counts, naming 17 complainants. HENRY's jury trial would commence February 28, 1983, and was now reduced to 10 counts with eight complaints that included three counts of rape, two counts of attempted rape, and five counts of indecent assault.

The courtroom drama was getting underway. Over time, HENRY fired lawyer after lawyer, and eventually chose to represent himself. The courts routinely dismissed most of his procedural motions citing them as frivolous. HENRY was heading for jail for a very long time. During the police investigation of Donald Jones MCRAE[52,] HENRY's case became interesting. MCRAE by coincidence lived in the same Mount Pleasant neighbourhood as HENRY. MCRAE, now deceased, resembled HENRY in appearance.

The police were now looking at MCRAE who had a history of late-night predatory sexual behaviour. Surprisingly, it wasn't until 2005 that MCRAE pled guilty, and was sentenced on three sexual assaults that bore striking similarities to the crimes of which HENRY had been convicted.

Representing himself at trial was, he later thought, his biggest mistake, as he struggled to understand important legal avenues available to him. The Appeal Court Judge hearing the compelling evidence felt that had HENRY not represented himself, there would most likely have been a different outcome. Representing one's self in court was like having a fool for a client. Misstep after legal misstep, HENRY's fate was all but sealed. By today's standards, anything but full disclosure of the evidence would be looked upon as legal high jinx. It would have been seen for what it was, an abuse of process, or at the very least, a marked, and unacceptable departure from reasonable standards.

Now convicted in 10 charges of sexual assault, he received the stinging blow from the Judge giving HENRY an Indeterminate sentence. A "dangerous offender" status (DO) determined at the time of sentence, based on the dynamics of his crime (s) could see him locked up forever.

HENRY, came to Mountain in 2004, quickly snagging a job in the kitchen. Long maintaining his innocence, HENRY would read what he could. There weren't a lot of books in the prison's libraries back then, so he started with the very basics in law, the Canadian Criminal Code. Was he another jailhouse lawyer, or were his years of study enough to convince the lofty high Court of Appeal of his innocence? With the introduction of DNA gathering techniques, his sperm was found not to have been a match from any of the crime scenes.

After years of appeals HENRY eventually obtained the services of a lawyer who requested that his case be reopened.

The Vancouver Police, when asked, claimed they no longer had any physical evidence related to the case.

In 2005, a Crown attorney noticed similarities between MCRAE's crimes, and those in which HENRY was convicted. The Crown attorney suggested to authorities that a file review would be appropriate. In 2006, a Special Crown Prosecutor would be assigned to conduct an in-depth investigation of all materials related to HENRY's conviction that could lead to a possible miscarriage of justice.

In 2008, HENRY had already served 25 years of an unjust sentence when new evidence was uncovered that eventually would cast doubt on his many convictions. A Vancouver City Police review of cold case sex files brought to the attention of police a serial killer making his own killing debut, and was quite possibly responsible for the very crimes believed committed by HENRY. The same style of crime with the same modus operandi (MO) was being perpetrated on victims throughout the bedroom communities of Vancouver well after HENRY was locked up. Was this new evidence overlooked as a matter of convenience? Citing weak identification evidence, and the biased police lineup, the more significate pieces of the puzzle came together making up his appeal. HENRY's crack defense team was quick to accuse the Crown of withholding vital evidence during the original 1983 trial.

For the first time in many years, there was a glimmer of hope. In a carefully worded media release, the Crown said they would not oppose any application to the reopening of HENRY's case. A finding would rock HENRY's world, and would provide the potential final chapter in this troubling case. It was good news on a long legal journey, finally a hope of vindication. On June 12, 2009 a judge would set aside HENRY's application, pending a review of the evidence.

Now 26 years, 10 months and 14 days later, HENRY was granted bail pending his new trial, and would remain free for the first time since his original arrest. Ivan HENRY was a bad man, no doubt. He had a history of petty property crimes, and Attempted Rape back east, so it was easy to see how police jumped to conclusions, fitting the square peg into the round hole of prosecution.

The court findings were shocking, and concluded the identification evidence was weak. The photo lineup was unfair the defense would say, citing those in the police lineup, called "foils" were at least 10 years his junior, and HENRY was the only one with curly hair. HENRY's appearance truly stood out from the rest, making him the intended target to a solid identification.

HENRY's defense, with counsel by his side, would conclude that based on weak evidence the 10 verdicts in HENRY's case were unreasonable, and that HENRY should be acquitted. Was representing himself an open door for prosecutorial abuse? They would further claim the staff in the crime lab were self-trained experts, understaffed, and using makeshift equipment cast off by the RCMP. The sperm sample, using new technology, didn't match evidence found on any of the victims.

The judge would not go so far as to acquit HENRY, but ruled there was adequate legal information to warrant the reopening of his case. The

Crown seeing their case before them in tatters, stopped short of agreeing, but did not oppose a new investigation.

It was now 2009, HENRY was in his mid-60s, tired, but not beaten when he got to present new evidence before the BC Supreme Court of Appeal. Somewhat the wiser, HENRY had his day in court; this time with legal representation. Citing several legal errors, and a glaring and botched police investigation the BC Court of Appeals ruled that HENRY be acquitted on all charges, and was deemed to have been "wrongfully convicted".

The shocking police photo lineup showed a restrained HENRY in a headlock surrounded by what were believed to be plainclothes officers, all of whom were smiling. HENRY was seen in the picture causing quite a stir, fighting with police, yet only one person in the lineup looked over, or seemed surprised.

I look back at the miscarriage of justice in amazement, as Ivan, to his credit, never presented as a man filled with anger. Quite the contrary. He was frustrated at best, but never showed his disdain for our prison system, the police, or attorneys that put him there.

I had lost touch with him over the years as I transferred from Mountain in 2009 just before his release, hearing the most recent updates through the newspapers like everyone else. HENRY was seeking financial compensation for so many lost years. Not seeing his girls grow up, missing those ever-important birthdays, HENRY wanted his pound of flesh. Ivan had two daughters, Kari and Tanya, who were seven and nine when their dad was taken into custody July 29, 1982. Growing up in North Vancouver, they moved from neighbourhood to neighbourhood. Later the girls lost their mother Jessie to a drug overdose. In 2005, at 39, Ivan's daughter Kari also succumbed to an overdose.

HENRY, subsequently sought compensation for a breach of his Charter Rights, for prosecutorial misconduct, but was there proof? His lawyers stated the Crown's actions were a marked, and an unacceptable departure from the "reasonable standard." It was a different time back then; the Crown Prosecutor would say.

Although he was now free, his sparring with the so-called criminal justice system was far from over. The question was, how much was 27 years of his life worth? Was he entitled to compensation for breach of his Charter of Rights? These were the only questions remaining. Was there prosecutorial misconduct, and more importantly, could he prove it?

By 2016, Henry settled with the federal government, and the City of Vancouver, and now set his sights on the public purse strings of the BC government. Henry's defense attorney would argue that he deserved as much as $43 million, citing other cases including David Milgaard who received $10 million for 22 years, and Guy Paul Morin who got $1.25 million for 15 months. The defense would say these figures would equate to a staggering $42.9 million for Henry.

He had penned his own book, unlike his first novel, which he admits wasn't him. This time, better prepared, he takes control of his story, and tells it in his own words. His book titled "My Life After Being Wrongfully Convicted" is according to HENRY a more accurate account of his life. Filled with the minute detail of his life I could see his bitterness coming out in print.

Still adapting to his freedom, he has had a hard time adjusting to a life outside of jail. Ivan suffers from PTSD, and some eight years later he continues to be tormented by nightmares. He stays close to home worried police might take him away.

Ivan enjoys the simple pleasures freedom brings. For him, now close to 70, his goals include getting his driver's license, and writing. He says of his millions, only that he is comfortable. At the conclusion of this fascinating story, I asked him what he would remember the most about his time in jail. He said prison was devoid of feelings. To most, he was not Ivan Henry, rather simply inmate #45975A.

Ivan HENRY, Wrongly Convicted.

The Cat Program, Paws for Thought[53]

Who wouldn't love a cat program I thought as I learned of the greatest rehabilitation program known to humanity? The cat program, or as some would call it the "Little Lifers Group" was sadly not a sanctioned Correctional Service of Canada program, rather an inmate supported program that started quite innocently when cats wandered onto the prison grounds. I suppose these wild ancestors of today's felines were looking for a meal, or warm place to sleep, and quite by accident the Cat Program was born.

Mountain Institution nestled at the base of an evergreen lined Mount Agassiz, was one of the most idyllic work sites I had ever experienced. When I first arrived, unsure of what to expect, I thought I was free from the drama of Kent. It was not uncommon to be met by visiting deer, and on rare occasion a bear or two, sitting harmlessly on the roadside as I drove to work.

The view, the floral smell of the well-tended gardens was a dream for this tired old guard. As I wandered in on my first day, I could feel a presence, eyes everywhere, or was I just paranoid? From the safety of their shrubbery, behind the bushes, or hiding in the flowerbeds, the soon to be feline friends were holding court, and checking out the newbie with a cat's ever so judgmental demeanor.

As I made my daily trek to the living units, the succulent smell was the calm before the usual storm. It was, after all prison, and my false sense of peace and tranquility would most assuredly be interrupted with the boisterous clamor of a busy living unit.

With millions of dollars invested in today's correctional programs, and with all its great intentions, it took a simple cat program, and a can of tuna to sooth the savage beast. At first, I was skeptical. Settling into my new home, I had the opportunity to see its calming effect in an otherwise troubled environment.

LU1, a unit filled primarily with older inmates, was the official home to the cats in residence. As an avid cat lover, working on occasion in the cat unit was a vacation of sorts. With each shift I would be greeted at the entrance of the unit by a cat standing 6, acting as guardian, and overlord to the unit. I saw the immediate benefits as both staff, and inmates came together. Various cat programs around the world, including several prisons in Sweden, enjoyed a measure of success. Like them or not, the psychology of pet ownership was deeply rooted in study after study. A

Swiss study conclusively showed cats, with all their charm, could affect psychological change in an inmate's state of mind. Their research had shown medical benefits of cat ownership reducing the risk of heart attacks, and strokes, not to mention cats provided a feel-good factor.

Despite the CSC's best intensions, it was a cat program that left an indelible mark on my inner child.

The more pragmatic thinker could look to the practical benefits of "cats on patrol" as they were natural born mousers. Keeping the rodent population at bay only added to the value of the program.

The calming affect cats provided was an important tie to staff safety, and in part why I was an ardent fan. Those inmates from Kent, now over at Mountain, many in LU1, seemed to be more social.

Working with the Inmate Committee, Mountain's management team allowed up to 20 cats within the population. This popular program had a waiting list, and once approved, the inmate would agree to buy, and care for a rescue cat from a local shelter. The Cat Club would pay for associated expenses, and collect from the specific cat owner. Working in LU1 was a chance to work with, and around cats all day, and for this cat lover a much-needed distraction from the usual foolishness of prison life. Coming to prison most inmates had lost everything, through their own doing, but the Cat Program at least allowed some measure of responsibly and comfort. Monitored closely, the program had strict guidelines. In order to qualify, or maintain a cat, discipline and behavioural expectations were the lynch pin to the program.

I would chat with the cat owners while on range walks, and on more than one occasion had to scurry a cat back to his or her cell wagging their tail in what I assume was an expression of utter contempt. A former inmate whom I had worked with at Kent, was more approachable in part because of the cat program. While doing a stand to count, I came across a cat, sitting on a cell bed with an attitude only a cat could have. I informed the cat that a charge would be forthcoming unless he stood for count. This banter was healthy as we could relate to inmates on a more personal level making our job safer.

Transphobia, Life in Prison was a drag[54]

Though she didn't start the transgendered revolution, Synthia KAVANAGH was the highest profile male inmate living as a female in a Canadian jail. From the early age of two, until nine, Richard Chaperon was in and out of children's care. Chaperon was introduced to the violent life as a prostitute at an early age working the streets living as a female in a man's body until she could legally change her name at 19.

KAVANAGH went before the courts, and was convicted in 1985 of murdering her roommate and fellow transsexual Lisa Black. While the judge suggested KAVANAGH be placed in a woman's facility, the CSC rejected the recommendation, and placed him at Millhaven Institution in Bath Ontario. As with most, if not all transgendered inmates, KAVANAGH spent most of his time in Segregation, and was sexually harassed, and abused. Sharing a cell in a double bunk situation was a living nightmare she would later tell a Canadian Human Rights Tribunal. Gay or transgendered inmates sometimes became victims of other inmates as the cycle of abuse continued. Once incarcerated, a doctor working for the CSC reduced her dosage of female hormones, thus effectively reversing any progress she had made through the gender reassignment process. KAVANAGH's struggles had yet to begin when she was transferred to Kent. Fighting through the courts, KAVANAGH won the right to have the sexual reassignment surgery, and in 2001 was transferred to Joliette, a medium security prison north of Montreal, Quebec.

Though new policy was developed for transgendered inmates, some staff, including myself truly never understood the struggle. To many, it was a joke, or a sickness. In 2014 when I left the service, it seemed to me management at Mountain, still didn't get it, so the struggles for transgendered inmates continued. Although not officially a sex offender prison, Mountain had a large population of inmates convicted of various sex related crimes, and the reputation to go with it.

Discussing feminine hygiene products, and various lingerie purchases was more than this liberal thinker could handle. Under-the-breath giggles could be heard at one managers' morning meeting much to the contempt of the warden. Some managers went too far, and had less than professional pet names for female body parts. Some would call a transgendered inmate a "she", others would refer to them as "it", while others cruelly called them "sh-it". I think it was a form of humour. Transgendered inmates had their rights as they made their way through the prison bureaucracies, and the transition through to womanhood. Being incarcerated just made it more challenging, and sometimes impossible. New policies were implemented as the rights of those going through the change brought their demands forward. What saddened me was after 15 years of struggles, and the lessons learned from KAVANAGH, we didn't seem to have progressed in our thinking. Every step was reluctantly slow in the development of new policy for transgendered inmates and their accommodation needs. These accommodations included living as a woman in a woman's prison, the ability to acquire various make up, clothing and female hygiene products. One of the first challenges I had witnessed was the protocol for pat down searches. We needed a female officer for the top and a male officer below the belt. It was the basic of human rights, that is, to be treated like a human.

Not always was I so enlightened. While working at Kent as a CO-II in E block, I shared with a transgendered inmate daily make up and beauty tips, tricks and secrets all while keeping a straight face. Just prior to an important meeting with the warden, I suggested to this inmate that he get dolled up. After all, I said, the warden was somewhat of a lady's man. As our meeting was about to commence, in walks the devil wearing Prada, sporting a red silk dress cut up the thigh, shoulder length, flowing hair, a push-up bra, and the right amount of lipstick and blush to turn any man's head. I could tell the warden was uncomfortable with this situation; however, being the kind and non-judgmental person he was, he remained silent. After the meeting concluded, he saw the author of his discomfort sitting still, eyes watering, showing the slightest hint of guilt. He said nothing as he got up from his chair. Words were not needed as his cool stare sent his message of contempt.

Fiscal Restraint, Cutting the Fat

Escaping political interference in our organization was almost impossible. After all, we are part of this behemoth machine called government. The Food Services Division of the CSC responsible for feeding over 15,000 inmates three squares a day was about to be challenged once again. We knew with fiscal restraint came belt tightening in all departments, and at all levels. In other government agencies, cutbacks were uncomfortable, or inconvenient; however, in the correctional environment, the same cuts could have disastrous consequences, even death.

From the days at Kent, inmates dined on the finest cuts of meat, and copious amounts of bacon. The Conservatives in the last few years of their political governance would once again put staff in danger with their poorly crafted budgetary restraints, calling them a form of "menu adjustments".

Inmates were allowed every few months to withdraw money from their institutional bank accounts and order in fast food from local area restaurants. A party like atmosphere would envelope the units on food nights as inmates would place their glutinous orders for pizza, hot dogs, and burgers. While the funds came from the inmates, extra staff were usually put in place to pick up and monitor its distribution. Inmates would gorge themselves, ordering enough for up to three meals. Many would use the food as a form of jailhouse currency to pay debts. The public was outraged when they found out about inmate food night. What was next? Budget cuts became the norm; the kitchen, like all departments were striped to the financial bone. Money was tight, and there were no more "free lunches". We were told to make due with less. The problem in the prison environment was if you take away too many privileges the resulting action could be a riot.

They lost "socials", food nights, and now night trays. Gone were the endless rations of peanut butter and jam for the inmate's evening snack. Bread, butter, fruit and juice, gone.

"Central feeding", and "Small meal preparation units" were on the CSC's menu of budget cuts as they looked for ways to further trim the fat from an already lean budget. The CSC in their infinite wisdom went to a centralized commissary style of preparing and feeding inmates. The "off-the-shelf" delivery of food, offering tighter inventory control, while maintaining menu and "recipe management", was the latest brainchild. Gone were the extras, as most meals were prepared, and packaged in the Matsqui prison kitchen, and transported to the various institutions.

Back in the Day, the RCMP and Carolyn Lee[55]

A day that touched so many: April 14th, 1977 when 12-year-old Carolyn Lee disappeared from the streets of Port Alberni. As a broadcaster, I covered the story. As an auxiliary constable, I was privy to the investigation, and as a family friend, I shared the tears of a community.

A chance meeting with an inmate in Mountain's LU2 turned into an unexpected reunion with the convicted killer of 12-year-old Carolyn Lee. As a young auxiliary constable, too many years ago, I was aware of the ongoing dynamics of the investigation into the young girl's disappearance. Carolyn's half-naked body was found on a country back road near Cox Lake the day after her disappearance. She had been raped, beaten, and left to die alone. The small island community was devastated that the little girl had been snatched off the street on the way home from dance class, her life snuffed out seemingly without a second thought. This case puzzled police for years, and though they had some sketchy leads, the case eventually went cold. The impressions made from the tire casts from the scene left three dimensional, and indisputable evidence that would identify them as Seiberling 700/15 heavy lug tires. While it was early in their investigation, their person of interest had a 1977 Blazer with the same matching tires. A single boot mark left on Carolyn's jacket was also linked to their suspect. One eye witness within the community remembered seeing a Chevy Blazer driving down the city's main street on the evening of her disappearance with an East Indian driving, a Chinese child and unidentified male in the back seat.

Though police had tire and shoe print evidence, it was 1977 and Deoxyribonucleic Acid (DNA) tests had not yet come into its own. It was not until 1984 that DNA would become a monumental discovery. It wasn't until international scientists were able to identify the remains of Nazi war criminal Josef Mengele that they knew they were onto something. Provisions for mandatory blood testing became law in Canada in 1995; but under very stringent guidelines. Testing later identified 48-year-old Gurmit Singh DHILLION as Carolyn's killer. This case was personal, as I knew the Lee's, owners of the Pine Café next to the radio station on Third Ave where I had worked. The whole town was turned upside down.

While their suspect had an alibi, witnesses could not agree to specific times he was at the bar. Now brought in for questioning, DHILLION passed the polygraph; however years later, he was eventually arrested, and charged with First Degree Murder.

During the trial, the cold case felon sat quietly in the prisoner's box, hanging his head in shame, saying nothing. In what was called one of the most sensational trials lasting over four weeks, the jury only took three days to deliver a verdict-guilty.

He was sentenced to 25 years in prison with no chance of parole. Though there was solid circumstantial evidence, it was the DNA that ultimately tipped the scales of justice. Police thought there was a second suspect; however, to date, no others had been charged, or convicted.

As with every child killing, it robbed the community of its spirit. Working at CJAV Radio, only a few doors down, I dropped in, and quickly became a regular of the Pine Cafe. I knew the owners personally, and remember a happy child who would visit her parent's restaurant after school, smiling, laughing, and dancing as she touched those lucky enough to know her. Years later, the Lees, now broken, closed their small-town eatery.

Getting through the grieving process was important to the family but never brings back their loved one, and while the conviction of this deviant came with a measure of satisfaction, nothing would replace the void in the families' heart.

Serving time in my prison, unaware who he was, I happened to be reviewing case files when I saw the name Carolyn Lee. Alarm bells went off, as I delved deeper, scrolling page after page on the computer as I took in the grizzly details. I connected his name with the tragic events from 1977. Now it was time to meet with him. I had to see the man who took this innocent life.

It was a personal memory that would haunt me, and I too wanted closure. Unaware of the purpose of my meeting, he sat comfortably in the chair looking puzzled. Making idle chatter, I questioned him about his time at Mountain. Easing into the conversation he was quick to open up. I explained my interest, telling him of my connection to the events that brought him to jail. I explained that I was a former RCMP auxiliary constable, and ever so familiar with his case. Now squirming in his chair, and less and less talkative, I ended our brief meeting with my final dig, citing our national police mantra, "the Mounties always get their man" a slogan that never meant so much as it did that day.

Mountain's new Warden arrived two years prior to my retirement. He was a personable guy who held his staff accountable, and called us when reports weren't up to his standards. It was hard to disagree with him, but we weren't used to this in-your-face supervision. Coming from an institutional parole background, he would review our reports with a teacher's skepticism, marking our mistakes with his condemning red pen. While I did not take a fancy to his management style at first, I think he was an outstanding leader with a good sense of humor, a bit mischievous when appropriate. A differing of management styles caused us to bump heads on occasion, but I respected his educational, and career achievements.

One would think after 24 years in the system I would have heard it all, and developed a hard crust, and a healthy level of skepticism. Not so, in regard to the case of the Canadian Border (CBSA) Guard who ran afoul of the law for his part in the smuggling of drugs, weapons and ammunition across the Canada-US border. As a guard at the Pacific Highway Border crossing, he worked with others in his criminal family, utilizing a burner cell phone communicating when, and at which booth he would be working. Convicted of conspiracy to import cocaine and guns into Canada, he was also charged with Breech of the Public Trust, and received 14 years for his foolish crimes.

Easy going, this guy was well groomed and articulate. He was smooth, and played the family man card telling me daily stories of how sorry he was, and how it affected his son, and wife. He was shocked, and disheartened at what he felt was an unjust prison sentence. He was a superb manipulator, and while he only bent my ear with discussions of Coronation Street, I was disappointed to learn that his version of his crime was in fact "alternate facts", used to garner sympathy.

The year 2010 saw another tragedy unfold in the name of Michael MCGRAY a serial killer recently transferred from Kent. MCGRAY who started his killing spree at a young age of 17, was given six concurrent life sentences. (25 years total) Doing his time, he convinced his casework team he warranted a transfer from Kent's Segregation unit to Mountain in 2010. A long-standing issue, and in his case at the root of many of our riots was double bunking. Single bunked while at Kent he was transferred to Mountain, and immediately placed in a double bunk cell with Jeremy PHILLIPS. With no specific issue MCGRAY and PHILLIPS seemed to get along. MCGRAY convinced PHILLIPS to partake in a hostage-taking scenario where MCGRAY stuffed a sock in his unsuspecting cell mates mouth as part of his strange and dangerous scenario, strangling him until dead. MCGRAY, a self-confessed serial killer pled guilty, adding one more concurrent life sentence to his existing sentence.

Staff once again were placed in a horrific situation dealing with the tragedy of a sudden death, and having to respond to an inmate who was in a hyper vigilant state, which placed staff at a heightened risk. While we love to bitch, and I did my share, when the chips were down, staff would come together, and responded like the professionals I knew they were.

One day while supervising the Principal Entrance (PE) a troubling inmate visitor came through my little piece of pre-retirement lighting up the alarm bells of the metal detector. Policy required our staff to determine the reason for the alarm. This rather busty female visitor had a chip on her shoulder, not to mention the possibility of something other than breasts in her bra. My job as the correctional manager was to support staff, but to protect them from all intrusions, or assaults against the prison. I was now tasked with conducting a risk assessment to determine whether we would allow the visitor access. Recognizing the delicate nature of the situation before me, I still had to do my job. Reviewing her visits history and speaking with staff was always a good move as they knew the inmate visitors more than anyone. I must credit the staff in V&C for this one, as they found a file notation detailing the visitor's previous attempt to smuggle a cell phone in her bra. Bam! I had reasonable grounds, so I explained quietly that I would require her to surrender her bra to a female officer for inspection. She was offered this option, or the opportunity, if too embarrassed, to leave, and return another day.

When her threats of job loss didn't phase me, she turned on the water works crying, I suspect to garner favour in this very awkward situation. Between her crying, and the staff snickering, I felt the burn. Notifying senior management of the delicate situation at hand, she was read her Charter Rights, and led into a private room by two female officers. Though she surrendered her bra amid protests, nothing was found. The front gate was the first line of defense in our ongoing war on drugs. Mountain's staff were handpicked for their professional and dedicated performance. No one had questioned the alarm notification that day preferring to explain it as the underwire in her brassiere. Visitors posed a barrage of threats against the integrality of our institution. It was a dangerous post requiring staff to be on their game. In the end, after the inmate also expressed his displeasure, the staff would nick name me "Brazilla".

Staff at the PE in my experience were professional, and the high standard of service set the bar throughout the Pacific Region.

One practice unique to Mountain was the "Mulligatawny Friday" (named after the soup featured on Friday's menu) lunch at the Agassiz eatery, the Horn of Plenty, a local favourite among CSC staff. Each Friday, the correctional manager group would enjoy a rare lunch together where we shared our stories. Say what you will about the closeness of those at other institutions, I found Mountain, and its comradery, second to none.

Working for the Man[56]

Our mandate was, and is, to provide inmates with meaningful employment which was a challenge at best. A shower cleaner job for example could take an hour each day, and yet inmates received a full day's pay. Range cleaner was a quick dust and mop each morning, followed by sack time in his drum (cell). Pay ranged from zero pay for refusing to take programs, basic pay level of $1.00 per day, an allowance rate of $2.50 per day for medical, D-pay of $5.25, C-$5.80, B-6.35 per day, to top pay of $6.90 per day. As the politicians called for tighter financial control through reduced budgets, the CSC had to become creative in managing their money. Anything less than perfect attendance, and a stellar job performance report from the instructors was a way to justify a drop in an inmate's pay level. Disciplinary charges were another. Inmates would take what little money they made to send out to loved ones, pay debts, and buy canteen items in hopes their treats would lessen the pain of incarceration.

While I speak volumes of staff and management entitlements, I would be remiss if I didn't speak of the shining stars that made my job worthwhile. The smiling faces when I walked into the unit, the practical jokes, or endless stories told by staff that made me laugh. The "go to staff", the problem solvers made it all come together. In 25 years, we tend to remember the negative when there were truly more positives than anyone could hope. Still, the mistrust of managers was in the forefront. I never went looking for friends, but I am happy to say I came away with a few close friends, and many that I was pleased to see on occasion in the community.

I never complained about the pay, it was a great wage no matter the risk. As retirement was looming, I came down with "A Fib", an irregular heart arrhythmia that put me briefly on the sidelines. Retiring from my volunteer position as a Lieutenant with the local fire department after nine years was tough, but now the writing was on the wall, it was time to retire. I will give the CSC credit, in my last six months, management didn't want me to have a heart attack, at least at work, so they assigned me to a perfect make work project to implement new fire plan drawings. This meant learning a new computer software program titled Computer Aided Design, (CAD) and was a challenge to say the least. For the first time in my career I was out of uniform, and working with a new group of non-security staff. Each morning we would meet for coffee and discuss the day's events. While it was a short six months, it was a welcome relief of the constant fighting with inmates. I wasn't aware the grasp that the mighty hand of PTSD had on me. Often faced with daunting learning challenges of this complicated software program, I would be hold up in my office, teary eyed as I struggled.

As the months turned to days, I would return to the Principal Entrance of Mountain.

My sole duty was to supervise staff and visitors as they came, and went. It was a make-work position for my last days that I enjoyed the most. Greeting those coming to work I would proudly announce the number of days to my retirement. Many would yell out "how many days Neil" as they walked by. I would wonder, were they looking forward to my departure, or just excited about a new beginning. Staff at Mountain were by far the best. Maybe the somewhat laid-back atmosphere was to Mountain's credit, but I would like to give them dues for being really kind souls.

Chapter 10

The Union Days

PSAC, Out with the Old[57]

From a rookie correctional officer, through my transition to a union shop steward, questionable union activities, to becoming a manager, I have worked with the best and represented some difficult, and personal situations that sometimes shook my confidence in my fellow officers. As a new officer, I was keen to fit in, and the union had an opening for Shop Steward. It provided a chance at critical thinking, and allowed me to participate in, and create solutions for our various safety issues in the work place.

The Public Service Alliance of Canada (PSAC) was the union representing over 170,000 federal government workers, and now was my chance to make my mark on a troubled, and deeply corrupt system.

Finding the Balance, Doing the Right Thing

It was a difficult challenge, balancing my job as a correctional officer, and that of a union representative. It was a constant battle defending the employment contract to those with little interest in upholding our basic rights. It felt like managers supporting managers, friends supporting friends. It became obvious to me early on, it was more about marching to the corporate drum beat than it was about doing the right thing. So much for the mission statement that touted "human relationships are the cornerstone of our endeavor."

It was always a fight, them versus us. Many grievances were ignored, or referred up to the next grievance level. They knew many grievances would be dropped as staff became disenchanted over the unnecessary delays. To emphasize this further, their approximately 4,000 outstanding staff grievances administered by PSAC waiting to be adjudicated were pushed aside, abandoned by an ungrateful union.

I have represented members with grievances ranging from simple pay issues, to the ever-troubling correctional officer caught in a compromising relationship with an inmate. Branded a trouble maker, or boat rocker, names that came early in my union career, I represented members "without fear", a mantra that would become my battle cry.

Though I began my union involvement as a shop steward over the course of my 10 years within the union, I would hold various positions including Secretary, Vice-President and Local President. While my work shift may have ended, the union work continued well into most nights as I would review grievances, complaints, and fielded numerous calls. It became my passion, and I learned from those before me. I was either on the phone, or attending endless meetings. There was a core of supporters that appreciated the union's work, while others would threaten parking lot justice, slashing tires, and late-night telephone hang ups. With the onset of our new union, UCCO-SACC-CSN, the die-hard PSAC supporters would give me a cool reception, others would whisper from the shadows.

I was always amazed at those staff and officers who managed the fine balance between the importance of family, and the job. Many focused on making a living, forgetting the importance of making a life. I attributed many staff problems to boredom, interspersed with the violence of prison. Politics in the work place combined with the relentless stress heaped upon our members was a troubling mix of emotions. Some could handle it, others could not. Many didn't recognize the signs, often calling it burnout, staff were told to "man up". Repeated incidents over a career, the violence, broken lives often contributed to broken marriages. Coping with the daily unrest, manifested itself in many ways, like personality disorders, drinking, excessive use of sick leave, or extramarital affairs as ways of coping.

My final years were marked with the diagnosis of Post-Traumatic Stress Disorder (PTSD). This diagnosis affected, and still affects me daily, albeit subtle. The stigma of PTSD often left us feeling unwanted, and unappreciated, left with a resentment toward the organization we so served. Others were tossed aside as useless, or terminated. Sometimes we were so busy just surviving our own lives, we didn't see the symptoms of our brothers and sisters, often ending in too many suicides.

From my union struggle, it seemed PSAC was by most accounts, in bed with the government; or at the very best, not an effective bargaining agent for the specific needs of correctional officers.

As the secretary of the union local my approach to most situations was reasonable, but I found middle managers would routinely run amuck, ignoring the contract, operating with only their interests in mind. I remember one such manager would determine what accommodation post would be most suitable for a pregnant officer. As if he knew. I organized stinging press releases, designed to shine a condemning light on the foolishness of everyday life in prison. They quickly despised this action, and took extraordinary measures to silence this troublemaker.

Television Protest[58]

At the age of 53 Brenda Marshall[59] became BC's first female warden (1997-1999) of a maximum-security prison. She was an experienced tough talking warden, and despite our oil and water relationship, she was fair and just. The early days of her time at Kent was dominated by the somewhat absurd media questions about her preferred genre of the books on her bedside table. It was an unwanted recognition who, like those before her, just wanted the chance to do her job. She was outspoken, with an in-your-face management style, but aware she was still living in a man's world. Though we had different roles, both honourable, we occasionally would disagree. When she wasn't yelling at me, she was asking about my health. She knew of my medical challenges without letting on that she knew the details-a truly classy individual.

Kent was under the gun to cut $500,000.00 from the prison's 1999 fiscal budget. These cuts would result in the elimination of inmate kitchen workers, but also a reported 24 senior correctional officers. Kitchen officers had to fill the resulting void, and thus bring us more in line with budget expectations.

With chest pounding threats of layoffs, Brenda brought down her decree. Knowing the public didn't care about the so-called overpaid government workers, I chose to put the focus on extravagant, and poorly timed expenditures in the form of television sets purchased for the inmates in the Temporary Detention (TD) Unit of Kent. The TD Unit (23 cells) within the segregation unit, was reserved for those inmates who had breached their parole conditions while in the community. Not officially Kent inmates, they were housed until their legal status was determined.

The thought of laying off, or "reorganizing staff", while buying TV sets that cost over $6,000, or $200 per inmate, was unfathomable. Taking on this tough as nails warden was a risk, but I was taught to represent my union brothers and sisters without fear, and despite the cannons across the bow attacks from management, I stood my ground. The view that public servants were overpaid was not an issue that would be well received, rather the message I wanted to convey was "TV sets for inmates", a theme that would better resonate with taxpayers. The scandalous uprising of the local union was an outrage, and brought a swift response from the desk jockeys, and politicians in Ottawa.

Next to the dreaded press release, management hated the information picket line. There would be no work slowdowns, just an opportunity to inform staff, and talk with the public through the media. It caused quite the stir, embarrassing the new warden, having to rethink the questionable reorganization plan. Bringing credence to my harsh words of corrupt governance, I was informed that despite our job saving efforts, the national PSAC ruled with a fearful hand: I was to be suspended from my duties as the union secretary. Although extreme, our information picket line proved very effective. Utilizing the media to get our message out became a successful formula I would utilize time and time again. Our efforts staved off the $500,000 "staff reorganization plan" but at what cost. Management's reaction was subtle but swift, "I wouldn't go anywhere with my attitude" I was told. Some members didn't like the in-your-face approach that became my signature.

Use of Force Defense [60]

Kent Segregation is a prison within a prison, and my partners in 1998 were Tom Vann and the late Tom Beeson. With the new Conditional Release Act and Regulations, inmate rights were clearly redefined and very specific. Inmates were entitled to one hour of yard (exercise) per day. The segregation area was more volatile than most areas of the prison, and staff had an elevated level of caution. It was a typical day shift in a not so typical unit. Inmates were returning from the J-side exercise yard. Inmates always looking for a way to express their frustrations, vigilant staff would be on the lookout for dangerous tell-tale signs. What we did, or what we said could have devastating results. Tom Vann, a no-nonsense officer, and myself, attempted to return an inmate to his cell. One at a time was the rule, but he wasn't having any part of our authoritarian direction. With the outside door being held in the open position by a careless officer, I could hear the control post officer yelling "close the fucking door." Things can change quickly for the worse; propping doors was just a bad practice. It was imperative to isolate the other inmates from becoming involved in this particularly dangerous situation, and we were forced to act quickly.

The inmate, his jaw already broken, and wired shut, carried on beaking off, as he refused to lock up, and return to his cell. Most of these situations are spontaneous, loud, and very dangerous, and we were now into a physical handling situation (fight). During the struggle, the inmate's jaw received further damage. In response to the inmate's complaint, and pending discipline, the local union (me), hired a "use of force expert", a 36-year veteran of the RCMP, Winnipeg and Vancouver Police, Sergeant John McKay.

After a lengthy investigation, Sgt. McKay concluded, based on CSC reports, that staff had acted within their scope of training, and within lawful authority using an appropriate level of force. Always pushing the union envelope, I was outraged at management's rush to judgement costing the union $750.00 for consultation fees, not to mention the anguish of a vexatious complaint. In a never tried before stunt, I filed a small claims court action in hopes of having the union's money returned. A certain level of showmanship was expected from Neil MacLean, and not to disappoint, I interrupted a warden's meeting, walking in, I delivered the subpoena. I said, "Hello my name is Neil MacLean, and I am here today to serve you with a subpoena for Small Claims Court." My grandstanding got their attention, but it was the Hollywood theatrics that they seemed to understand. I later learned that Small Claims Court action was no doubt an incorrect court of redress, but it served its purpose.

In the end, rightfully or not, I believe the CSC found it easier to approve the payment for Sgt. McKay's consultation fee than risk another public airing of our dirty laundry. This out-of-the-box thinking would become my specialty, and a source of great pride as we maintained our relentless attacks against the daily barrage of unfair labour practices. To this day, I have a copy of the cheque from the Receiver General for all monies incurred in defending our position.

With very few exceptions, the wardens were open, honest, and just trying to keep the lid on many difficult situations. Warden (s) Bob Lusk, Alex Lubimiv and Michael Boileau were some of the finest wardens.

The New Union, UCCO-SACC-CSN [61]

As time went on, we, as correctional officers, felt marginalized, not only at the national bargaining table, but also with issues specific to correctional officers. Being discounted as a troublesome group, we were often looked upon as spoiled children, and went shopping for a new union.

As a peace offering to the growing disenchantment by correctional officers PSAC offered an RCMP comparability study, if we would agree to continue with the old union. The study served us well in future negotiations; however, it was nothing more than a false comparison between the job of correctional officers, and the job of our national police force. Though I recognized the important, and difficult job of Canada's federal correctional officers, it was, in my opinion nothing more than a sham of disproportional comparison the union hoped would appease its unhappy members. To compare us to the RCMP was ludicrous. There were many similar duties including peace officer status, but we did not recruit like them. Shallow background checks allowed occasional unsavoury characters to infiltrate our ranks. We didn't train like them, or face the same dangers in volume, yet we demanded wage parity. Now don't get me wrong, there were, and are many real dangers that face correctional officers daily. Since 1835, and before Canada was a country, thousands of correctional employees dedicated to keeping Canadians safe through their work in the Correctional Service of Canada. More than 180 years, 34 federal employees–two women, and 32 men–have given their lives to protect our communities. Our fallen colleagues were working either as correctional officers, parole officers, managers, program officers, project officers, instructors or wardens when they died while carrying out their duties.

It was 1999, correctional officers were again becoming discontented, our problems it seemed were falling on deaf ears. While it was coming, and not without its challenges, the new UCCO-SACC-CSN was borne. It was a game changer for sure, and despite the drama, I was proud to be part of the organizing committee.

This Montreal-based union, CSN (Confederation des Syndicates Nationaux) was steeped in history, and celebrated a tradition of solidarity. Its strengths came from an "on your own, but not alone" system where membership offered its affiliated unions a strong, fearless representation. CSN was a surprising choice as they were largely isolated within Quebec. The second largest union in the province, a left-leaning, socialist organization seemed an unlikely pairing with the rough and tumble correctional officers.

The Battle Cry, Heard in Ottawa and Across this Land

The time had come for our national union's organizing committee to set the stage and bring together members from across Canada. Off we went to Montreal for a week of campaigning, and while there were 109 delegates, they were only allowed to vote for the names nominated in their respective regions.

After 13 years of working within the prison system, I understood the issues. My experience made me a viable candidate. I was ready to throw my "weight", or hat into the political ring.

I put my name forward, and ran as the Pacific Region's Regional President. There was a lot wrong with our system, and for the first time, I felt we had the right stuff to tackle the toughest issues. We were no longer going to remain silent. Each night after the day's events I would drag my weary body upstairs after a day of committee meetings, tossing around contract issues, and getting a sense of the hot button topics, important to the grass root members. I was proud of the outcome, and the support I had received. It was truly an honour to be part of this exciting and historic event. The room was filled with delegates from every region, representing correctional officers from across this great land. An upscale Montreal hotel was scene to some dramatic labour relation changes, and the convention room was filled with anticipation.

Our founding convention was near its historic conclusion and the time had come. Our newly elected National President, Sylvan Martel addressed our delegates at the convention's close. As he rose from his chair to address the new delegates, the room was steeped in anticipation. We were ready for change, and he did not disappoint. In his closing remarks, a well-crafted speech, Sylvan, a personable guy, was looking to stir the emotions brewing within. The crowd, normally rambunctious, was silent as he reached under the lectern dawning an army helmet, he said, "Ladies, and gentlemen, let's go to war." The crowd went wild. The war cry, I am sure, resonated all the way to Ottawa. One can only imagine how the senior managers sitting around their liberal boardroom table felt when word of Mr. Martel's speech leaked out. We had arrived.

The new UCCO-SACC-CSN was a member-based union, with membership finally in control of our own destiny. Who better to decide our fate than correctional officers who knew the issues?

Our initial action plan was carefully scripted with our nationally elected president being guided by CSN handlers every step of the way. Each meeting, we presented our principal issues from the new uniform, to a flurry of contract demands. Nothing happened overnight, but this tough new union was making groundbreaking progress. It provided, through our dues, access to union lawyers for adjudication proceedings, and very experienced grievance personnel to deal with each level of the process.

Upon my return from Montreal we settled into finding a new office. I remember the organizational meetings that were carefully planned to represent our correctional officers and, our specific needs. Press releases were the order of the day, and as long as we acted in good faith, our "qualified privilege" allowed us to speak to the public. This untested position could have gotten me fired. Indeed, when my position of President became threatened, I would shoot back with a stinging press release. We embarked on an education campaign as we took to the picket lines explaining our issues, and the role of today's professional correctional officer.

For the first time in our history, we had a legal defense fund set up for our members. It was time to build on our public image; we were guards no more. We were correctional officers who demanded the tools of the trade, and a pay raise commensurate with our new, and professional standing.

I was a hard-nosed, Regional President however I found every day a struggle, battling for the most basic security issues. The CSC, while normally in a rush to judgement, was slow in concluding our members' guilt or innocence, delaying a paycheque while the wheels of justice turned slowly. Most cases would take months, and in some cases years, which to me, hardly seemed fair to the families of an officer waiting for his or her day in court.

Abuse from inmates was not uncommon but there was also, sadly, abuses from within our own rank and file. I wanted to offer a balanced view of prison life, but also speak of the dynamics, and how it affected our lives. The workplace remains a revolving, and changing culture, fostering discrimination, and in my opinion unfair labour practices. Stalling tactics, or repeated violations of the contract that demoralized personnel. The due process model was anything but. Many managers were afraid to uphold the contract in fear of the consequences, so there was considerable consultation with the Human Relations Department to ensure mangers, and their positions would be in line with past grievance decisions, and their puppet masters. The CSC had full time personnel, and a labour relations department that would spend countless hours looking for justification, and a reason to say no. If you stood up for your members' rights, you were branded a troublemaker. There was no room for speaking "truth to power" in a system claiming to be transparent, that was both secretive, and protective. I was proud to be the National Chairperson for the Status of Women bringing the much-needed protection for our female officers. There were issues of harassment, sexual harassment, accommodation during pregnancy wage equity and respect for those working in a male dominated profession.

Those times were a blur to me, looking after nine institutions, supervising the grievance process, attending regional Labour Management meetings all while doing my job as a correctional officer. While my time was rocky at best, hated by some, I had a measured success including the fight for body armour, handcuffs, developing a "needle stick protocol" bringing about the introduction of leather search gloves, and representing those accused in email-gate. Better communication with our members was important to me, establishing a regional newsletter to ensure our officers were up to date on the latest bargaining challenges and our many successes.

As I grew into my own, this union confidence was referred to as "going full Neil MacLean". This in-your-face union leadership bucked the former union hierarchy that was seen by some as corrupt as the zoo keepers themselves.

Randy White, My New Best Friend [62]

Our Canadian political system represented by a Prime Minister and Members of Parliament (MP) are elected to speak for all Canadian citizens. The system, filled with political rhetoric, seemed more like a three-ring circus than an esteemed chamber of elected MPs. The Federal Reform Party, which had been around since 1987, became the Official Opposition.

Member of Parliament Randy White, the Opposition Justice Critic was like a dog with a bone, and would become my new best friend. Randy was a tough as nails politician, and as such, came with his own soapbox. He was relentless in his efforts to hold the Liberal government accountable, or as many did, seized an opportunity to forward his own agenda through public embarrassment. No matter what Randy's true motives were, he stuck it to "the man" every chance he could. From victim rights, the release of inmates to the street, Randy was on it, and in the news almost daily. I think his greatest moments were when he exposed what he called the soft prison life, and privileges not afforded our regular citizens. Randy awarded Kent the dubious honour of the second worse prison in Canada, but never told me who held the number one spot.

Jimmy Hoffa, "You Hurt One of Mine"

As the Pacific Region's Regional President, I extended a personal invitation to our Regional Deputy Commission to drop by for an inaugural meeting. A one-story walk up, our new office had an institutional freshness about it. The formaldehyde present in the carpets screamed new, but it represented the realization of our dreams. I thought it would be appropriate to invite Mr. Alphonse Cormier, our Regional Deputy Commissioner, to our new office. I was pleased when he graciously accepted. His visit went down in our history books as one of the funniest meetings to date.

Mr. Cormier was a tall man, well-groomed, and all business. As the Atlantic Region's Regional Deputy Commissioner, now transferred to the Pacific Region, he was preparing to retire.

I wanted to send an appropriate message of welcome similar to our president's message at the founding convention. Now into our meeting, small talk was the order of the day, both unsure of each other's agenda. Sitting back in his chair, he glanced around the room. I was hoping he would take the bait. Not wanting to be outdone by our glorious leader in Montreal, I strategically placed two pictures of Teamsters boss Jimmy Hoffa on my office wall. He fell into the trap, posing the question, he asked the significance of the pictures. Bursting inside, I said with a straight face that I shared the philosophy of the late union leader Hoffa, to wit, "you hurt one of mine, I'll kill 10 of yours." Despite his sincere attempts, I don't think Alphonse was able to fully recover from those remarks, he would never return. I believed those early remarks were in keeping with how many of us felt as correctional officers. The message was received loud, and clear. We were angry and full of contempt.

Reporting to work at Kent, like any other day, I was sporting our new union lapel pin. One manager, was quick to demand its removal. Refusing his demand, I was sent home, not unlike a child being sent to their room. Showing up for my next shift, I walked through the front gate, passing my co-workers along the way. Many shook their heads as I showed up sporting the letters UCCO shaved into my hair. A short time later, like many other unions, we were allowed to wear our pin on the exterior uniform jacket.

The Verville Decision, Handcuffed No More[63]

One of the first issues that garnered our attention was the right of our officers to carry handcuffs. Later known as the Verville Decision, after Correctional Officer II Juan Verville. As Regional President I encouraged the Health and Safety Chair, a bright young officer, to head up our union's advance. "No" was the CSCs response, citing the use of handcuffs would be confrontational, and a road block to building constructive relationships with the inmates. It was a casework driven system, and those in the ivory tower were living in their own little world. Out of touch with the realities of prison life, many actually thought it appropriate to call inmates by their first name. There were no relationships, professional or otherwise. The inmates hated us, and no amount of fancy uniforms, would change their hating ways.

Dynamics can change in a moment, most times without notice. Whether drug related, or simply anger issues, inmates can be volatile. The ability to control an inmate from lashing out, physically, was from a union's standpoint, a safer position for both staff and inmates. The logistics of having to run to the control bubble to retrieve handcuffs and return to the incident was not only unworkable, but dangerous. Calling for a movement control officer to bring the needed restraint equipment, often delayed our ability to take control. The delay could translate into injuries to our officers, and presented as an unacceptable risk.

While we had a grievance process to express our displeasure with policy, it was most times slow, and didn't address the immediate dangers within the prison environment. Our federal law makers introduced the Canada Labour Code (CLC) as part of our redress. A Section 128 of the CLC could be invoked by any staff member who felt they were working in a dangerous environment. Work would cease while the workers and management presented their positions. More often than not, the so-called independent review committee would rule "no danger" resulting in a return to work order.

Canada Labour Code 128 – In part…

(2)   An employee may not, under this section, refuse to use or operate a machine or thing, to work in a place or to perform an activity if

(b) The danger referred to in subsection (1) is a normal condition of employment.

The architects who penned the Canada Labour Code most assuredly were lawyers, and had clearly never considered the prison environment, or even stepped into a prison to witness firsthand the violence correctional officers faced daily before writing into law the nonsensical dribble of the CLC Section 128: refusal to work.

The "normal condition of employment" was at issue. In a prison, the very existence of inmates created a "normal condition" of danger. There was no question on that point, but it was management's refusal to issue handcuffs to our front-line officers that became our sticking point.

Officers in the A-H units expressed their dissatisfaction, refusing to work due to the very real dangers of prison life. Let's be honest, you have read that many inmates carried shanks, others called Kent a war zone, so was it a stretch to convince anyone that there was danger?

The chance of spontaneous outbursts, and violence toward officers often would precipitate a use of force. To me it seemed management thought it was better for us to intervene using physical handling, with the potential for officer injury, than using a lessor level of force like verbal and OC (pepper spray) intervention strategies. By the very nature of a maximum-security prison, inmates at Kent were violent, and no match for the correctional officer trying to gain control, hoping someone would bring handcuffs. Once again police wore them, security guards could wear them, yet we were denied the same basic right of protection.

Sporting legal representation from the CSN, our dream team led a group of 12 officers from Kent, offered testimony in the ensuing legal battle. Management would drone on with their arguments that just didn't make sense. Why were Segregation staff, and Movement Control Officers allowed to carry handcuffs, but not the very unit officers who were usually first on the scene of a fight?

In one of the strangest moves yet, management went so far as to place different coloured "mood circles" in the correctional supervisor's office window, and when reporting to work, we could better gauge the environment. A green circle would indicate calm, a red circle translated to an elevated level of hostilities. If the inmates were acting out, the red circle would be displayed allowing correctional officers to carry handcuffs. Ridiculous! These coloured circulars were just another of the many ill-thought out policies. After days in adjudication, I was ecstatic at our victorious outcome, Canadian correctional officers were now allowed to carry handcuffs.

Body Armour, Our Families Think We're Worth It[64]

Prison violence goes hand in hand with the diverse inmate populations throughout Canada. Over the years, I saw an escalation in violence from the mature, established con, to the young punks populating the prisons. Though some attacks were well-planned acts of revenge, others were spontaneous. Jail-made weapons were everywhere. Their ingenuity was confounding. As fast as we could find one, a dozen more would be fashioned using metal parts from various file drawers, or a simple toothbrush.

My work as a correctional officer gave me a unique insight into the daily prison violence.

With the advent of a new union, it was time to introduce differing levels of self-protection. We wanted the very basics of safety equipment, no more, no less. The self-aggrandized experts would spout all kinds of rhetoric why slash and stab-resistant body armour was not suitable for the prison environment. It would be hot, they would say, creating further danger to the correctional officer, or the assailant would simply aim for an unprotected body part. The most ludicrous response was that body armour would act as a barrier to building trusting relationships with inmates. Calling them offender, clients, or residents didn't lesson the risk to our officers. We wanted protection for all officers and staff working in direct contact with inmates. Simply put, we wanted equity with other law enforcement agencies. The basic right to protect myself, and others was laughed off as senseless, and rebuffed at every opportunity. After all, police wore them, our American prison counterparts consider them on the normal scale of issue, so why not the CSC?

Purchasing my own body armour, I hoped to make a point, and put the rumour out that I would attempt to wear the low profile concealed armour under my regular uniform. Frustrated and dumfounded at CSCs lack of concern, I launched into a media campaign in hopes of securing public support. I said, "our families think we're worth it". During my many presentations, we brought forward different issues, including the fact First Nation inmates were allowed various carving tools including so called "gouging tools" as part of the many dangerous tools available. With a hobby room, where carving tools were kept under lock and key, at least we could isolate their use, and ensure they were locked up for safekeeping. It was a reasonable balance between their rights, and our safety, I thought? To no one's surprise, management insisted it was an native right to be able to practice their carving anywhere they pleased, including in the units, and in their cells. Once again, the CSC felt body armour would send the wrong message to inmates who by definition were not incarcerated for good behaviour, once again Ottawa said NO.

I joined the ranks of management in 2004, and proud when the union continued with their efforts to have body armour placed on the scale of issue. It was ironic, despite my founding efforts, I never actually got a chance to wear body armour.

Some hated the new body armour, and many complained. They blamed me for their plight, citing the vests to be uncomfortable and hot. Each summer, even in retirement, I suffer the unflattering remarks from a few ungrateful officers who still hold a grudge despite the armour's life saving properties.

Visionaries Need Not Apply

I think one of my final protests was our chance to show utter contempt for a local manager regarding our dangerous working conditions. Knowing what worked, and what got under their skin we staged the ever-popular information picket line. We were all set up, huddled around a burn barrel when to everyone's surprise a visiting clown in a tri-coloured wig played by the late Matt Brown arrived.

Fed up with management's uncaring style, we were looking for any way to rid ourselves of a warden who seemed to many, uncaring. The warden of the day was not well liked by some correctional officers, and this controversial protest would surly send the message to him. He seemed to have a different agenda, and I was at the helm of what many thought was a sinking ship. We saw a wide variety of work grievances routinely denied, the rule of law ignored, as he seemed more interested in breaking the new union's back, and destroying morale. We added a roadside sign to our protest announcing the warden's position as vacant, and "visionaries need not apply."

Email-Gate[65]

Email-gate as it was called, was by far the most threatening attack on correctional officers and staff. It touched over 850 employees in all institutions throughout Pacific Region, and I understand, some institutions across Canada. Kent was the epicentre of trouble, and came with management's heavy-handed penalties in dealing with questionable emails. Let me clarify: no one ever said having pornographic material on government computers was appropriate, quite the contrary. It was embarrassing to say the least. We as a collective union felt terminations were too severe, and many of the penalties were excessive for inappropriate pictures, jokes, and hockey pools.

The police were quickly summoned in to investigate staff, I assume to punctuate their dramatic point. What was pornographic and what was in poor taste? There are no secrets in cyberspace, a hard, and painful lesson to learn. Two correctional officers were dismissed, and 107 disciplinary actions were taken, including financial penalties equalling between 1-5 days worth of pay. If there ever was a need for union representation, this was it. The investigation showed numerous irregularities. Some managers, equally as guilty, were overlooked, and those in receipt of inappropriate emails fell victim to a vengeful management.

We needed a regional approach to ensure consistency in the application of progressive discipline. To deal with the sheer numbers several managers were tasked with hearing each case, many offering different and inconsistence findings. I had to laugh as I was representing my member before a prim and proper female manager who was shocked at what she saw. I insisted that if they were going to determine one's guilt I wanted to see each and every picture. She would stew as each picture came on the computer screen, uttering "oh my goodness" or "oh no".

Sending inappropriate emails was one thing, but receiving inappropriate emails treated with the same harsh discipline I believed a miscarriage of justice.

One of my first cases as the Regional President of the new UCCO was testing the strength, and resilience of our members. It wasn't a role I took lightly. One such case that was one of many was an officer's wife sending her husband, an Easter bunny greeting card to his work email address.

I was confident that our right to be heard would be a chance for a fair hearing, away from what I felt was an unfair prosecution.

It took a few days, but we had won another battle. Those who lost their jobs were reinstated. Those receiving excessive fines, had them rolled back. It seemed to me that the new union was racking up some very impressive wins. I was thankful that I was never caught up in the dragnet of this unfair investigation.

Don't Leave Home Without Them

During a Labour Management Consultation (LMC) in 2000, the warden beamed with pride as he announced a new federal government program to give correctional officers a government sponsored American Express[66] card. Staff escorting inmates on Escorted Temporary Absences (ETA) in the community, or on compassionate escorts, could offer up the travel card to secure reservations on hotel, or car rentals if needed. Based on a sound and practical financial foundation, the bean counters did not factor in the end users, the ever so clever and resourceful correctional officers. A few ended up going bankrupt after maxing out the card for personal expenses. One event probably had the managers reeling in disbelief when two married officers took a cash advance on the card to place a down payment towards breast implants. Soon, government bureaucrats saw the error of their ways, and withdrew the credit card from staff before incidents like this bankrupted the country.

Like most labour complaints, we fought long and hard over suspensions without pay. In a country with the highest labour standards in the world, this "guilty until proven innocent" model was a contradiction, and a blemish on our international image.

One ground breaking legal case of Larson v the Treasury Board would be game changer. Larson was a correctional officer back east involved in what I understand was a case of arson. He was suspended without pay pending the outcome of a court trial. Whether you liked the behaviours or not, the union's mandate was to represent, or defend its members. Right or wrong, it didn't matter, it was about a process. Was it legal? I would ask myself each time. Suspensions from work, and the loss of pay while waiting through the grievance process was patently unfair, not to mention the financial hardship this draconian law inflicted on the families.

When management refused to listen to reason, the next course of action was not always a grievance, rather to embarrass. This occurred more often during the fledgling years of UCCO. Press releases were an effective way to get their attention as they scrambled to answer up the chain of command.

When management threatened me with termination for unauthorized press releases, I would threaten them with more. As a union representative, we enjoyed what was called "qualified privilege", meaning any authorized duly elected union representative could reach out to the public through the media as a form of public education. The grievance system was an effective stalling tactic for management. Most times it could take years for a grievance to be heard by the commissioner, or his delegate. It wasn't about following the contract, or the rule of law, it was about maintaining their position, right, or wrong. At the onset of the new union with thousands of grievances stalled, it was decided for the sake of expediency we would reach a mutually agreed upon position that would allow us to start anew, with some closure to those long overdue complaints.

At the end of a long career, now eligible for the Exemplary Service medal, I was temporally disheartened to learn my manager, too lazy to fill out my application, insisted my personal assessment would stand the best chance if I completed it. The deputy warden not liking my rendition, choose to pepper the appraisal with my more colourful union activities. Although this was typically illegal to use one's union participation against an employee, the heartless managers had what they needed to exact their final revenge. Another union member also felt the wrath of management for his union involvement concluding it was a reflection of his dedication, and service to our members. These were tough times, and despite complaints from a few staff, tough times required tough measures. I was proud of our many victories, and in retirement I make no apologies.

Harm Reduction Program[67]

In or around 2000, the CSC introduced a Harm Reduction program. It was a well-intentioned program to combat the increasing spread of HIV-AIDS and Hepatitis C among the inmate population. The concept was based on solid medical data, but the implementation was difficult at best, considering our inmates would now have unfettered access to bleach. The thought was to reduce the number of active medical cases by the introduction of bleach for needles, condoms and dental dams for those more intimate moments.

We couldn't stop the drug use, so let's help them clean their needles. Sex was in many cases not consensual, or a means of paying debts, so let's give them protection.

We were in the trenches. Few cared about inmates becoming infected, and many staff felt the drug use would likely kill them long before infections could set in. Initially the union would have no part of this ill-conceived program. Inmates would use the bleach not for its intended purpose, but to clean their cells, do their laundry, or on occasion throw in a staff member's face.

Part of the Bleach Program was the never-ending fight to catch inmates getting tattoos in hopes of preventing infection and disease. Nothing says, "I've been in jail" quite like a body covered in tattoos. Swedish studies have shown that half of the current prison population get tattoos while incarcerated. As in most jails around the world, tattooing is illegal, which caused the jailed artist to go underground, performing the prison artistry in the shadows. A whole prison industry emerged as a result. On many a search, I found cannibalized radios, CD and tape players, faded gifts from loved ones, now scrap plastic destined for the landfill. Resourceful inmates would remove the small motors to be used for their tattoo guns. The ink made with anything that gives off a dark liquid, including the burnt renderings of a harmless styrofoam cup, soap, or shoe polish mixed with oil, and yes, even black ink from a pen.

During 2005 the CSC introduced a pilot project which established in-house tattoo parlors. Disease was on the rise as a result of sharing dirty tattoo needles, and while the program made sense, the optics of inmates lounging around getting "tats", spelled its demise. Medical experts cited study after study and identifying the rising costs of treating the deadly disease, saying it was cheaper to control the use of dirty tattoo needles through prison tattoo shops than it was to treat and care for someone infected with Hepatitis C.

As a union rep, I could not support this out-of-the-box thinking. More appropriate on the street, I thought. I was pleased when the program was quickly shut down by the Conservative government.

Uniform Changes

The evolution of corrections in Canada borrows considerably from both the American and British systems. The khaki colours, and styles were reminiscent of those uniforms worn by many of our veterans in wars past. The old-style uniforms served a purpose in the day, providing sub-liminal cues as to the professional values of the wearer. As the Canadian penitentiary system changed, so did many of its policies.

A study from the Menlo California Police Department concluded that a more stylish blazer would see a reduction in officer assaults, and would increase the public's acceptance of their officers. As anyone could tell you, we seemed to follow our American counterparts. Picking up what they discarded, we embraced a more casual, runway style uniform that was void of any rank bars. To top off this fashion nightmare, we were given a generous selection of three different blue shirts. Dark blue, one with stripes, and a very translucent style light blue, not popular with the female officers. Each uniform had a selection of contrasting ties. For the most part, this radical uniform change did nothing to enhance our relationships with inmates, and only caused snickering when we were out in public. After years of embarrassing uniform changes, thanks to UCCO-SACC-CSN, we were to receive the well-deserved professional uniforms, cargo pants with dark blue shirts, and light blue shirts for correctional managers. Numbered badges were later issued in 2005.

Chapter 11

Stories at a Glance

Melanie Carpenter, a System Breakdown[68]

A future filled with hope, would sadly end tragically. In a typical week of BC rain, the weather was finally letting up when Melanie was abducted from Island Tan, located in Canada's fastest growing BC municipality of Surrey. Born and raised in Surrey, Melanie loved animals and life. Melanie Carpenter 23, a bright young girl was planning a future with her fiancé.

Island Tan was a means to an end as Aaron Bastien, her fiancé was saving for the down payment on their first home. It was January 6, 1995 when Melanie kissed Aaron in what would be their last farewell as they both headed off to work.

There was nothing unusual about the day as it unfolded, the usual clients came, and went until a troubling telephone call was received by Melanie from a man claiming to represent a group of Japanese executives. The unidentified man stated they wished to purchase an Island Tan franchise, and wanted an appointment. He requested the studio be closed to allow his clients an opportunity to look around.

It was only moments after the troubling phone call, the franchise owner would soon receive yet another call from a confused client stating the tanning salon was vacant.

Melanie's boss rushed to the strip mall in the Fleetwood district of Surrey where he was startled to find the back-door open, and no sign of Melanie.

After the police arrived, an intense investigation and man-hunt got under way. Within hours, as part of their investigation the police reviewed the CCTV film footage of a local ATM where an unidentified man was observed withdrawing $300 from Melanie's account. Police, through the media announced they had a clear picture of a suspect. He was later identified as Fernand AUGER, a former inmate from Bowden Institution out on statutory release. He was once again a fugitive.

A server at a local restaurant, his employer would say AUGER was one of his best employees who got along with almost everyone. On New Year's Eve 1995 AUGER served customers, and treated friends to dinner until closing. Leaving the popular bistro just after 3 am, AUGER was never to be heard from again. He had a violent past, including armed robbery, but more troubling was his sexual assault and buggery-related charges. The burning question, what was AUGER's plan? He rented a red Hyundai and ventured west from Alberta. Investigators asked why he would travel so far. Was it planned, or a crime of opportunity?

The investigation into Melanie's disappearance stalled after a few days, when they would receive a call from a local realtor in High River Alberta, that would break their case wide open. The realtor, while showing the home, noticed what appeared to be a man sleeping in a car, inside the closed garage. He was a balding man, 37 when he was found alone.

Authorities converged on the house only to find a lone occupant with a crudely fashioned garden hose leading from the tail pipe to the vehicles interior which provided the carbon dioxide that would tell his story. AUGER had left a suicide note addressed to his wife on the back of the vehicles rental agreement. In it he asked for forgiveness, and stated the person on the credit card used to rent the Hyundai was not complicit in his heinous crime.

> *"This vehicle was obtained fraudulently by me, Fern AUGER. Do not hold the credit card holder liable. Jan 9, 1995. My death was chosen my way, my choice, my place, and time. To my family, and ex-wife, I love you, but it is better this way".*

Sadly, the note was more about him, and offered no clue as to Melanie's where abouts.

Her family, understandably devastated, were quick to organize a non-profit society in the name of their beloved daughter. It would be known as the "Bring Melanie Home Society". A reward of $20,000, was offered, and later rose to $50,000. Her father, Steve Carpenter made a personal plea to bring their daughter home. The police readied the family to expect the worse. As the desperate hunt expanded, our Pacific Region ERT joined hundreds of volunteers as they searched every bush, gully and back road. Sadly, her remains were discovered by two men, 20 days after her disappearance. The once vibrant Melanie Carpenter was found wrapped in a blanket on a deserted side road near Yale BC. Now lifeless, police identified the body of a young women with golden hair as that of Melanie. AUGER would leave her by the Fraser River, 160 kilometres east of Vancouver. The coward had raped, and stabbed Melanie, leaving her remains on the road side.

The devesting news came late one night. Three weeks after she was snatched in broad daylight, Melanie was finally coming home. The family, and close friends sobbed at their loss, and were quick to call for tougher laws to keep dangerous criminals in jail longer. Although it wasn't the outcome the family had hoped for, it was a relief. The grief quickly turned to anger as Steve, Melanie's father, called her killer a coward. Mother Sandy, father Steve, sister Cindy, half-sister Tina, grandmother Enid, and fiancé Aaron were shaken. The "Bring Melanie Home" campaign, and her burial was a very public event held at Vancouver's Pacific Coliseum.

The police investigation revealed that the troubled Fernade AUGER had been diagnosed with an advance case of anti-social behaviour. Steve Carpenter said it was a better end for him when compared to what would have awaited him in the criminal justice system.

An ex-con on parole, AUGER kidnapped the girl causing both embarrassment for the CSC, but also unwanted media attention for this very sad situation.

Bounced from foster home to foster home, AUGER's sister understood her brother's troubled past. Living on welfare, AUGER was always looking for an easy escape from his grim past. Drug addicted, he suffered with his inadequate sexual tendencies, which played a major role in his dysfunctional, and troubled life. His gambling obsession led to his financial problems which in turn led to his committing an armed robbery of a Calgary gas station which would ultimately land him in Bowden Institution.

I am reminded of our connection to this sad tale, the pride shown by an already giving ERT, and a life that touched us all.

A Team Films at Kent[69]

There is always a positive side to the low Canadian dollar. In this case, Hollywood North would host the 2010 filming of the "A Team", a movie based on the TV series by the same name. This block buster starred Liam Neeson, Bradley Cooper, Jessica Biel, Sharlto Coley and Quinton Jackson and filmed within the 96-man unit of Kent. It was a perfect location for this $110 million-dollar undertaking. The production came with its own unique set of challenges, as care had to be taken as each crew member had to be personally escorted throughout the prison. Filled with anticipation of our visiting guests, their safety was our main concern. No detail was left to chance. One misstep could have brought the wrong kind of attention to the movie, and our institution. In the end, despite its moderate success, appealing to die hard fans, it gave staff lasting memories, and for some, their few seconds of fame as a movie extra.

The Little Devil Standing 6

My day started like most in Segregation, walking the four tiers of J-Unit. It was on one of my many routine range walks that I sensed I was being watched. My eyes scanned the area, left then right, up then down, when much to my surprise I spied a small voodoo doll standing "6" outside an inmate's cell. Inmate creativity could not be stifled, even in Segregation. This little devil's stringy hair was formed from an institutional blue blanket, the white cotton cloth t-shirt made from bed sheets, and paper fashioned into feet and hands, with a pencil connecting it all together. When confronted, the inmate denied ownership. Sensing a cool keepsake, I was quick to scoop up the artistically creative demon that today adorns a special place on my home office mantle.

Little Devil.

Volunteerism and the Community Spirit

My parents instilled in me from an early age the importance of giving back to the community; lessons I proudly carried into adulthood. As a sickly child, the medical challenges from cancer helped mold me. Good or bad, I got through many doctors' appointments, and hospital stays. From as early as 13, I would venture down to the dog kennels of the West Vancouver SPCA later becoming their youngest, or youngest looking Special Constable. As a cub scout, member of the Junior Chamber of Commerce (Jaycees) and as an Auxiliary Constable I obtained valuable skills that would be complementary to many job requirements in the future.

As a new correctional officer, I would look for opportunities to occupy my time, and hopefully stave off some of the boredom from the job.

The CSC was the perfect place to volunteer. Whether it was an in-house special project, or representing the CSC in the community, I was their man.

Working 25 years in our system, I was fortunate to have met many great people. They were like a family to me, and I, their "special" brother. Those were exciting times, and while I'm sure I will be remembered for my union rabble rousing, or prison tours, there were many volunteer projects that gave far more to me than I had given to them.

I was immensely proud to be a uniformed peace officer, and enjoyed speaking with the public at various recruiting venues regarding the many opportunities offered by the CSC. This enthusiasm for the job was off-putting for some, but I loved it.

My first interaction with Variety Club Telethon came in the mid-70s while working as a disk jockey for CKCQ Radio in Quesnel. I had the privilege to represent not only the station, but the residents in Quesnel encouraging them to call in with their pledges. I have held many positions with Variety over the years, from stamp licker in the back rooms of Varieties administration offices to answering pledge phones at the historic Queen Elizabeth Theater. Thirty plus years, and well into retirement I continue organizing our contingent with Variety Club as the plethora of memories continue.

Looking back, a slight smile cracks this old guard's tired face, remembering many fun times. While my prison tours were the ultimate in my volunteer achievements within the CSC, they did not solely define me. Researching our history, guiding college students around Kent, offering an insider's view of the many headlining incidents from Kent's troubling past was my passion.

Each year employees would look forward to Public Service Week. It was a time when managers throughout Canada's federal public service came together to recognize our staff, and their valued contribution. Prior to a shift we would serve up coffee, and morning snacks along with motivational speeches. We would present awards at the various meetings throughout the day, a small token of appreciation. I worked a job that rarely received positive reviews from the public, and it was frustrating sometimes as we were looked upon in such a negative manner. Approximately 19,000 federal public servants go to work within the CSC each day and are filled with the best intentions of doing a good job. Due to the unpredictable nature of prison, good things seldom happened. Riots and killings had a tendency of ruining what was hoped to be a good day, quickly turning into a PR nightmare. Despite the negative stories, public service was truly an honour.

The Tale of the Three Bears

Joyce brought forward the idea of a charity teddy bear that would see these cute and huggable bears, the updated version of the once popular "Custeddy Bear", conceived and developed by staff at Edmonton Max as a fund-raising project. It was our passion, and we spent countless hours developing a design, and marketing plan. We embarked on a tour of the factory in China we hoped would breathe life into our bears.

A limo was provided to transport us from our hotel to the factory. The cultural gap from the very rich to the very poor was alarmingly evident along the way. Driving the streets of the sparsely scattered Xiangcuns (villages), we were humbled at the gut wrenching poverty of the Chinese people. Upon our arrival in 2007 we were escorted to a small factory in the suburbs of Shanghai. We walked the shop floor to ensure there were no children working in the so-called "sweat shops". China was rich in cultural heritage, but the poor's very existence was threatened by encroaching modern cities with their towering skyscrapers. The old ways, and its people we were told were the carriers of folk culture, and customs that were dying with each new generation.

The birth of our bears was a project near and dear to our hearts. It was the absolute attention to detail that made these lovable little bears an instant hit. A correctional officer I (CO-I), CO-2, and keeper bear; all copied right down to the minute stich of the shoulder flash, the miniature hand cuffs, and bear ID showed our love in design. Our bears were one of a kind as only a prototype of each rank was ever produced. This self-funded, non-profit fundraiser for CSC sanctioned charities we hoped would further the CSCs professional, and public image. At the day's end, management dealt us a narrow-minded NO. For us it was devastating news, as their story would never be told. Our three bears that sadly, were destined to take centre stage on our bookcase, never to be appreciated outside our home.

The Three Bears are the property of Neil MacLean and Joyce Seidel.
Photo credit Lynn Amaral.

You served me well.

Conclusions

I hope the reader understands the real-life trials and tribulations that befall those who work in the trenches of the Canadian prison system. The daily going off to work was different for us, as no one truly understood what we had signed up for. Each day was filled with the unknown; daily working conditions were rarely as we had anticipated.

As with my career, my story comes to an end. I have mixed emotions: happiness, filled with anger, good memories, and some very bad ones. Most memorable were the individuals I called my colleagues, and work friends.

I choose to remember the good times, and special moments with each of those I had the honour to work. To me, the Correctional Service of Canada was not just a career, but a life experience that provided endless opportunities for growth.

There are many untold stories that needed to be told, lost souls forgotten, who needed to be remembered, and credit given to those of us who worked the toughest job I ever loved.

Stay safe, and thank you.

Neil D. MacLean, 2017

Acknowledgements

Thank you to the many individuals whose efforts, commitment, and expertise helped make this book better with every turn of the page. To the officers now retired, who sat through countless hours of interviews, with 104 gracious people without whose memories this book would not have been possible.

- To the editing services of Joyce Seidel, Terrill Scott, and Valerie Edmondson.

- Legal services graciously provided by John Conroy, QC, and Don Sorochan, QC.

- The graphic designs of Sharon Cinnamon, Hallmark Promotions, and Greg Laychak.

- The men and women in blue who are the forgotten heroes, the keepers of the kept, and who do their part in the criminal justice system.

- The Correctional Service of Canada, despite my musings, thank you for steady and most times challenging career.

- Thank you, Commissioner Don Head for your leadership, valued friendship, and support of this project.

- Retired Regional Deputy Commissioner Peter (Pete) German a dedicated and proud public servant. Your leadership and love of history motivated me in my writing.

- Mike Boileau, Regional Deputy Commissioner for believing in me when others did not.

- Alex Lubimiv, retired Warden Kent and Mountain Institutions for giving me my career break in the Correctional Manager's Office and stallworth leadership through some very bad times.

- To Brenda Lamm, everyone's favorite who showed a kindness not often found in managers.

- All other staff, valued members of our family.

- Lastly, to UCCO-SACC-CSN for your tireless efforts in improving our working environment.

The End

Citations

1. Author unknown-CSC Let's Talk-Vol 5, No-9-May 3, 1980.

   Author unknown-Correctional Service Web
   Site. www.csc.scc.gc.ca/resources/history.

2. Jack David Scott-Four Walls in the West Retired Federal Prison Officers'.

   Robert Belyk-Death Sentence, the New Westminster Penitentiary-British
   Columbia History-Vol. 39-No. 1-November 23, 2005.

   Association of British Columbia-1984.

   Len Norris-The Vancouver Sun-45,000 Say Goodbye to BC

   Penitentiary-May 1980.

   Dave Stockand-Vancouver Sun-Crowds jam Pen for closing open house-
   May 5,1980.

   Susan Taylor-Update on Demolition at the BC Penitentiary-
   Vancouver Sun-1984.

   Author unknown-Closing of the BC Pen-BC Pen Collection-wordpress.
   com New Westminster Heritage Society-1975.

   Author unknown-Closing of the BC
   Pen-BC Pen-Collection-wordpress.com-1975.

3. Jeremy Deutsch-Marysteinhauser.com-June 12, 2013.

   Ron Verzuh-Gunfire kills woman hostage-AQ-Simon Fraser University
   Magazine-Mary's Song. Vancouver Sun-June 1995.

Author unknown-Inquest Opens into death of Mary Steinhauser-Vancouver Sun-May 25, 1976.

The Farris Commission Transcripts-1975.

Author unknown-Albert Hollinger-Obituary-Ladner United Church-June 2015.

4. Verrenca, Tereza. Old Boot Hill Cemetery Could Receive New Life-New West Record June 2015.

5. Author Unknown-Official Opening of Kent-CSC publication Lets Talk-August 1, 1979.

Author unknown-The Vanguard for change-The Columbian-1979.

Author unknown-Kent's Opening Day Handbook-CSC-Let's Talk-1979.

Author unknown-Kent Nears Completion-CSC-Let's Talk-1979.

Author unknown-Kent Taking Shape-CSC-Let's Talk-1978.

Dave Stockand-Kent Prison has Gala Opening-Vancouver Sun-1979.

Author unknown-A New Era Begins-CSC-Let's Talk-1977.

Author unknown- First Inmates Arrive at Kent-Chilliwack Progress-1979.

Lloyd MacKay-No Andy BRUCE Types at New Kent Prison-Chilliwack Progress- 1978.

Author unknown-Living Unit Officer Help Wanted-Vancouver Sun-1978.

Photo Credit Neil MacLean-Inmate Handbook-CSC-Kent Maximum Security- 2004.

Dave Stockand-Larger Kent Prison Adds to Agassiz-Vancouver Sun-May 1980.

Author unknown-Killer of Two Slain in Prison-Vancouver Sun-July 1980.

Author unknown-Faith Helped Him Through Hostage Ordeal CSC Let's Talk-1982.

Author unknown-CSC Remembers-CSC Let's Talk-Vol 7, No 15-Date unknown.

Author unknown-Kent LUO Cited for Exceptional Bravery-CSC Let's Talk-1984.

Susan Taylor-Segregation Unit Opens-CSC Let's Talk-1984.

Larry Pynn-Steel and Tile Cell Replace Hole-Vancouver Sun-June 1984.

Author unknown-Toothbrush Weapon Nets 3 Years-Agassiz Harrison Observer-1985.

Author unknown-Citizens Discuss Female Guards-Agassiz Harrison Observer-1985.

Author unknown-Inquest Set Inmate Acquitted-Agassiz Harrison Observer-1989.

Author unknown-Kent Riot Under Scrutiny-Chilliwack Times-1988.

6. Correctional Service of Canada website www.csc-scc-gc.ca/mission statement.

7. Author unknown-CORE Program Brochure Outstanding Recruit Correctional Service of Canada-October 17, 1977.

   Author unknown-Black Hole of Calcutta-Solicitor General Warren Alman-Correctional Service of Canada-1979.

8. Author Unknown-Dean THOMAS LANGFORD-Kent's First Murder-Vancouver Sun-1979.

   Author unknown-Robert Mohr, William Smoke, and Adam Norris Charged Jointly in His Murder-Vancouver Sun-1979.

   Author unknown-Police Suspect Foul Play-Vancouver Sun-1990.

   Rian Maelzer-Murder Case Tough-Vancouver Sun-January 2, 1990.

9. Author unknown-Agassiz Harrison Observer-December 31, 1989.

   Author unknown-Police Suspect Foul Play-Vancouver Sun-1990.

10. Author unknown-John Melvin Ritchie-Vancouver Sun-Date unknown.

11. Author unknown-Dr. CHARALAMBOUS-Vancouver Sun-Date unknown.

    Holly Horwood-Wife tells of Affair, Fear-CHARALAMBOUS Defense Paints a Gold Digger-Province-November 2, 1994.

    Neal Hall-Doctor Escapes Procuring Charge-Vancouver Sun-Date unknown.

12. Motorola brand is the sole property of Motorola Canada Limited.

13. www.en.m.winipedia.org/driver

    www.theglobeand mail.com/news

    www.murderpedia.org

14. Robert Freeman-RCMP investigators-probe woman's death at Kent-The Chilliwack Progress-November 7, 1993.

    Robert Freeman-Murdered Woman pal-The Chilliwack Progress-May 26, 1995.

    Robert Freeman-It was like she'd gone to sleep-The Chilliwack Progress-May 26, 1995.

    Robert Freeman-Prisoner's Private Visits-The Chilliwack Progress-May 31, 1995.

    Author J.H.-Community Assessment Private Family Visit Correctional Service of Canada-2003.

15. Author Unknown-Inmate Gary ALLEN Killed at Kent, Killing Under Investigation-Vancouver Sun-1994.

    Jason Cormier, Parliamentary Relations Officer-Government of Canada-House of Commons Briefing Book-March 12, 1998.

    Author unknown-Inmate Gary ALLEN Killed at Kent-Vancouver Sun-1994.

16. Dan Scott-Convict Poet Launches Book From Behind Bars-Vancouver Sun-Date unknown.

    Stephen Reid-Stop Watch Gang-Novel-1999.

17. Jim Hutchison-A Week Inside a Max-Readers Digest-February 2007.

18. Author unknown- Shaughnessy Escape-Vancouver Sun-February 27, 1980.

    Author unknown-Guard cited after Escape-The Chilliwack Progress-February 27, 1980.

    Author unknown-Escaper Locks Guards in Shower-Vancouver Sun-July 22, 1980.

19. Personal memories of Steve Hall-BUTLER-MARTIN Box Escape-email-2016.

20. Personal Memories of Steve Hall-STONECHILD-BUTLER Escape-email-2016.

21. Personal memories of Steve Hall-Box Escape, Landry-email-2016.

22. Holly Horwood-Escape Incredibly Well Organized a Precision Job says Officials-Province Newspaper-Salim Jiwa-Date unknown.

Holly Horwood-Province Newspaper-Guards Charge Officials Alerted to Kent Breakout-June 21, 1990.

Author unknown-Helicopter Escape-The Gazette-June 1990.

Vancouver Court Registry-Court of Appeal-Regina v Robert Lee FORD January 26, 1993.

Correctional Service of Canada-Board of Investigation Report-Vetted and received through ATIP-File 1410-2-158.

K.P. Peterson-Escape Potential: Helicopter-Correctional Service of Canada-memo-December 14, 1989.

J. Croft-Helicopter Escape News Release-Correctional Service of Canada-June 18, 1990.

Deborah WILSON-Copter Didn't Come out of the Blue-Vancouver Sun-Date unknown.

Deborah WILSON-BC Inmates Flee in Helicopter-Globe and Mail-June 19, 1990.

Michael Jackson-Canada's First Helicopter Escape-Justice Behind the Walls-August 1, 2003.

Kim Pemberton-Escaper was Courteous, Helicopter Pilot Tells Court-Vancouver Sun-May 10, 1991.

Author unknown-Hijacked Chopper Pilot: My Ordeal at Gunpoint Plucking 2 Cons Out of Prison Yard-National Enquirer-June 1990.

Kim Pemberton-Anatomy of a Helicopter Escape-Vancouver Sun-December 8, 1990.

Robert Freeman-Pilot Settles in Kent Escape Chilliwack Progress-Date unknown.

Author unknown-Kent Helicopter Escape-Province Newspaper-June 1990.

Michael Jackson-The THOMAS Case-Justice Behind the Walls-August 1, 2003.

Author unknown-Two Use Helicopter in Daring BC Escape. Toronto Star-June 19, 1990.

Robert Freeman-Outside Escaper Sentenced for His Role-Chilliwack Progress-July 10, 1991.

Peter Baily-Pilot Flew at Gunpoint-Chilliwack Progress-June 20, 1990.

Photographer unknown-Get Away Car Identified-Chilliwack Progress-June 20, 1990.

Author unknown-Two Convicts Captured After Escaping from Prison in Helicopter-Associated Press-June 21, 1990.

Mark Nielson-Mystery Accomplice Captured-Province Newspaper-Date unknown.

Author unknown-No Wires Over Prison-Agassiz Harrison Observer-January 11, 1995.

Douglas Quan-Full Parole for Murderer Who Once Orchestrated Helicopter Prison Break in Agassiz-The Province Newspaper-May 16, 2016.

Author unknown-Fred Fandrich Interview-Vancouver Sun-Date unknown.

Tom Arnold-Bronson Film Inspires Daring Prison Breaks-Vancouver Sun-June 19, 1990.

23. James Kwantes-Here's Something New: Con in a Box-Chilliwack Times-June 1995.

    James Kwantes-Prison Population Booming-Chilliwack Times-June 1995.

    James Kwantes-Con was Carver to the Stars-Chilliwack Times-June 1995.

    James Kwantes-Kent Escapee Captured in Vancouver-Chilliwack Times-July 1995.

    Robert Freeman-Accomplice may be home for the Holidays-Chilliwack Progress-July 1995.

    Robert Freeman-Prison Moves to Prevent "Con in A Box" Escape-Chilliwack Progress-August 1995.

    Court of Queen's Bench of Alberta-Transcript-Kenneth Joseph Bronicki Sentencing Hearing-March 5, 1992.

    Supreme Court of Canada-Denzel Libonati v Department of Justice-October 17, 1997.

24. See Box Escape, citing 23

25. The Mission Statement is a registered copyright of the Correctional Service of Canada.

26. Claude Demers, Neil MacLean, Stan Beacon, Brian Buhay-Washington State Penitentiary Tour Report-1992.

    www.odmp.org

    unusualpunishmentbook.com/sergeant-William cross/

    www.12news.com

    www.//en.wikipedia.org

27. www.csc-scc.gc.ca/edmonton

    www.globalnews.ca/news

    www.edmontonjournal.com

28. www.en.m.wikipedia.org/kingston

    www.kingstonpentour.com

    www.penitentiarymuseum.ca

    www.globleandmail.com/news

29. Tim Mak-Sherrif Joe Tent City-Washington Examinor.com-April 8, 2014.

30. www.cdcr.ca.gov

    www.folsomprisonmuseum.org

31. www.cnn.com/2013/09/30/us/manson-fast-facts.

32. www.cnn.com/manson

    law2.umkc.edu/faculty

33. Patricia Elliott-Correctional Service of Canada-Kent Peeper-Date unknown.

34. Greg Machedo-Inside the Walls of Alcatraz-Frank Heaney-July 28, 2012. Patricia Elliot-Trip to Alcatraz Penitentiary-Correctional Service of Canada-Kent Peeper-Date unknown.

35. Michelle Locke-Associated Press-San Quentin www.semissourian.com- July 7, 2002.

    Alfredosantos.com

Christopher Hall-A Prisoner with a Brush, a Legacy at Risk-New York Times-August 19, 2007.

36. Turns 150, The John Whearty Story.

    www.corrections.com

    John Whearty-find a grave.com

    wikipedia.org/wikiHM.

    guardin.com

37. Marie Louise Guminchian-Globe and Mail-A Pasta You Can't Refuse-May 23, 2008.

38. independent.co.uk

39. Digital art work provided by Correctional Manager Pierre Bouvier.

    Froot Loops, the name, and its logo are owned exclusively by Kellogg's Limited.

40. Michael MCDONALD-Audit Reveals Violations During Coast Guard Party-The Canadian Press-January 2000.

41. Patricia Elliott-Kent Peeper-Various dates.

42. www.csc.scc.gc.ca/about/Don Head

    www.wikipedi.org/Don Head

43. Author unknow-Claire Culhane-Prisonjustice.ca

    Author unknown-Culhane to Appear in Court-The Advance-January 20, 1982.

    Lori Culbert-Parade of Uniformed Mourners Bid Farwell-Vancouver Sun-December 31, 1997.

44. www.lincsociety.bc.ca/Glen FLETT

    Glen FLETT-My Vison of Restorative Justice.www.lincsociety.ca-January 29, 2015.

    Howard Zehr-Changing Lenses: A New focus for Crime and Justice-Waterloo, Ontario: Herald Press, 1990, pgs. 49-50.

45. Author unknown-Kent Riot-Victoria Times Colonist-2003.

    Author unknown-Kent Riot-Vancouver Sun-2003.

Sarah Young-Jack Keating-Booze Fueled Jail Riot Leave an Inmate Dead-The Province-2003.

46. Mike Chouinard-Prison Party Turns Bloody Chilliwack Woman Stabbed repeatedly at Kent-Chilliwack Times-2003.

    Samantha Cater-Correctional Service of Canada- News Release-December 17, 2003.

    Author unknown-BC Boys Who Witnessed Prisoner Stab Their Mother Sue Federal Government.

    Author unknown-Globe and Mail-September 2010.

    Surrey Crown Counsel Statement-V.B.-January 2, 2004.

    Author unknown-Yale Man Acquitted on Sex Charge-The Chilliwack Progress-February 4, 1994.

47. Andy Ivens-Sex Inmate Killed in BC Prison Riot-Province Newspaper-2008.

    Anonymous-Two confirmed dead in Mountain lockdown-Agassiz Harrison Observer-March 31, 2008.

    Lorene Keitch-Two Dead Following Prison Riot-Agassiz Harrison Observer-April 2, 2008.

48. Winnipeg Media Release-June 1, 2007-Project Kite Arrests-http://winnipeg.ca/

    police/press

    Joe Friesen-Jet Set Thief's had designs on gems, police Say-Globe and Mail-January 2, 2007.

    www.en.mwikipedi.org/topaki

    www.Imdb.com/topkapi

49. Helen Chernoff-Freeman-Girl 85-Frieson Press-November 2013.

    Robert Boyd-The Doukhobor Camp-The Advance-August 13, 1980.

50. Kathleen Harris, Suzanne Bird-The Greying of our Prisoners-The Ottawa Sun-Date unknown.

51. Eli McLaughlin-Morris as Elvis-Morris Bates-July 5, 2010.

52. Joan McEwen-Innocence on Trial- September 27, 2014.

Author unknown-City of Vancouver says Wrongfully Convicted Ivan HENRY Not Innocent-Vancouver Sun-Date unknown.

Scott Brown-Five things you should know about Ivan HENRY-Vancouver Sun-December 1, 2015.

CBC News-Canadian Press-Laura Kane-December 10, 2015 Ivan HENRY wants $43 million for Wrongful Imprisonment for 27 years.

www.en.m.wikipededia/milgaard

www.aidwyc.org/milgaard

www.en.m.wikipededia/morin

www.aidwyc.org/morin

53. Lorene Keitch-Cats Bring Motivation to Inmates at Mountain-Agassiz Harrison Observer-December 16, 2008.

54. Tracy Tyler-Half a Woman-Synthia KAVANAGH-Toronto Star-March 1991.

55. Gerald Young-Carolyn Lee Murder Times Colonist-Regina v Dhillon-Transcript-

August 1999.

Canadian Broadcasting Company-Gene Squad-1999.

Unsolvedcanada.ca/Carolyn Lee

Wikipedia.com

Sunny Dhillon-Globe and Mail-October 29, 2012.

56. Correctional Service of Canada-csc-scc-.gc.ca

57. www.psac.ca

58. Keith Fraser-Colour TVs for Prisoners as Guards Fight Cutbacks-The Province-March 11, 1998.

59. Author unknown-Kent's New Warden Says She Focuses on Issues, Promotes Rehabilitation and Opposes Capital Punishment-Vancouver Sun-Date unknown.

60. John MacKay-Vancouver Sun-June 1997.

61. Neil MacLean-Campaign Brochure-2001.

    Neil MacLean-Newsletter, Pacific Region UCCO-SACC-CSN-2001.

62. Abbynews.com-New Role for former MP Randy White-August 22, 2012. Federal

63. Court-Verville v Correctional Service of Canada Kent-September 4, 2003.Robert

64. Freeman-Our Families Think It's Worth It-Chilliwack Progress-2000.

    Robert Freeman-Federal Prison Guards Fight for Right to Wear Body Armour-Chilliwack Progress-2000.

    Simone Blais-Bullet Proof Vests Reviewed-Chilliwack Times-May 20, 2000.

    James Kwentes-Chilliwack Progress-Guards Protest for the Right to Better Protection While on Duty-March 23, 2001.

65. Lisa Morry-Guards Fear for Safety Chilliwack Times-2000Neil MacLean-Regional President Newsletter-UCCO-SACCC-CSN-Winter 2001-email-gate.

    Property of American Express.

66. www.csc.scc.gc.ca

67. csc.gc.ca/harmreduction

68. Author Unknown-Kidnap Suspect Kills self Calgary Herald-1995.

    Wikipedia.org

    Public.journals.yorku.ca

    Unsolvedcanada.ca

69. Author anonymous Neeson Biel Shooting Film at Kent-Agassiz Harrison Observer-September 24, 2009.